We All Giggled

LIFE WRITING SERIES

In the **Life Writing Series,** Wilfrid Laurier University Press publishes life writing and new life-writing criticism and theory in order to promote autobiographical accounts, diaries, letters, and testimonials written and/or told by women and men whose political, literary, or philosophical purposes are central to their lives. The Series features accounts written in English, or translated into English from French or the languages of the First Nations, or any of the languages of immigration to Canada.

From its inception, **Life Writing** has aimed to foreground the stories of those who may never have imagined themselves as writers or as people with lives worthy of being (re)told. Its readership has expanded to include scholars, youth, and avid general readers both in Canada and abroad. The Series hopes to continue its work as a leading publisher of life writing of all kinds, as an imprint that aims for both broad representation and scholarly excellence, and as a tool for both historical and autobiographical research.

As its mandate stipulates, the Series privileges those individuals and communities whose stories may not, under normal circumstances, find a welcoming home with a publisher. **Life Writing** also publishes original theoretical investigations about life writing, as long as they are not limited to one author or text.

Series Editor
Marlene Kadar
Humanities Division, York University

Manuscripts to be sent to
Lisa Quinn, Acquisitions Editor
Wilfrid Laurier University Press
75 University Avenue West
Waterloo, Ontario, Canada N2L 3C5

Thomas O. Hueglin

We All Giggled

A Bourgeois Family Memoir

Wilfrid Laurier University Press

We acknowledge the support of the Canada Council for the Arts for our publishing program. We acknowledge the financial support of the Government of Canada through the Canada Book Fund for our publishing activities.

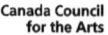  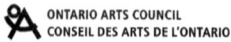

Library and Archives Canada Cataloguing in Publication

Hueglin, Thomas O. (Thomas Otto), 1946–
    We all giggled : a bourgeois family memoir / Thomas O. Hueglin.

(Life writing series)
Also issued in electronic format.
ISBN 978-1-55458-262-4 (paperback)

    1. Hueglin, Thomas O. (Thomas Otto), 1946– —Family. 2. Hueglin family.
3. Wachendorff family. 4. Germany—Biography. 5. College teachers—Canada—Biography.
I. Title. II. Series: Life writing series

DD247.H83A3 2011   378.71'092   C2010-903902-5

ISBN 978-1-55458-315-7 (PDF).— ISBN 978-1-55458-709-4 (EPUB)
Electronic format.

    1. Hueglin, Thomas O. (Thomas Otto), 1946– —Family. 2. Hueglin family.
3. Wachendorff family. 4. Germany—Biography. 5. College teachers—Canada—Biography.
I. Title. II. Series: Life writing series (Online)

DD247.H83A3 2011a   378.71'092   C2010-903903-3

Cover design by Sandra Friesen. Cover photos from the collection of Thomas Hueglin. Text design by Catharine Bonas-Taylor.

© 2011 Wilfrid Laurier University Press
Waterloo, Ontario, Canada
www.wlupress.wlu.ca

Every reasonable effort has been made to acquire permission for copyright material used in this text, and to acknowledge all such indebtedness accurately. Any errors and omissions called to the publisher's attention will be corrected in future printings.

No part of this publication may be reproduced, stored in a retrieval system or transmitted, in any form or by any means, without the prior written consent of the publisher or a licence from The Canadian Copyright Licensing Agency (Access Copyright). For an Access Copyright licence, visit www.accesscopyright.ca or call toll free to 1-800-893-5777.

The stories are for Hannah and Jacob
The book is for Gerda

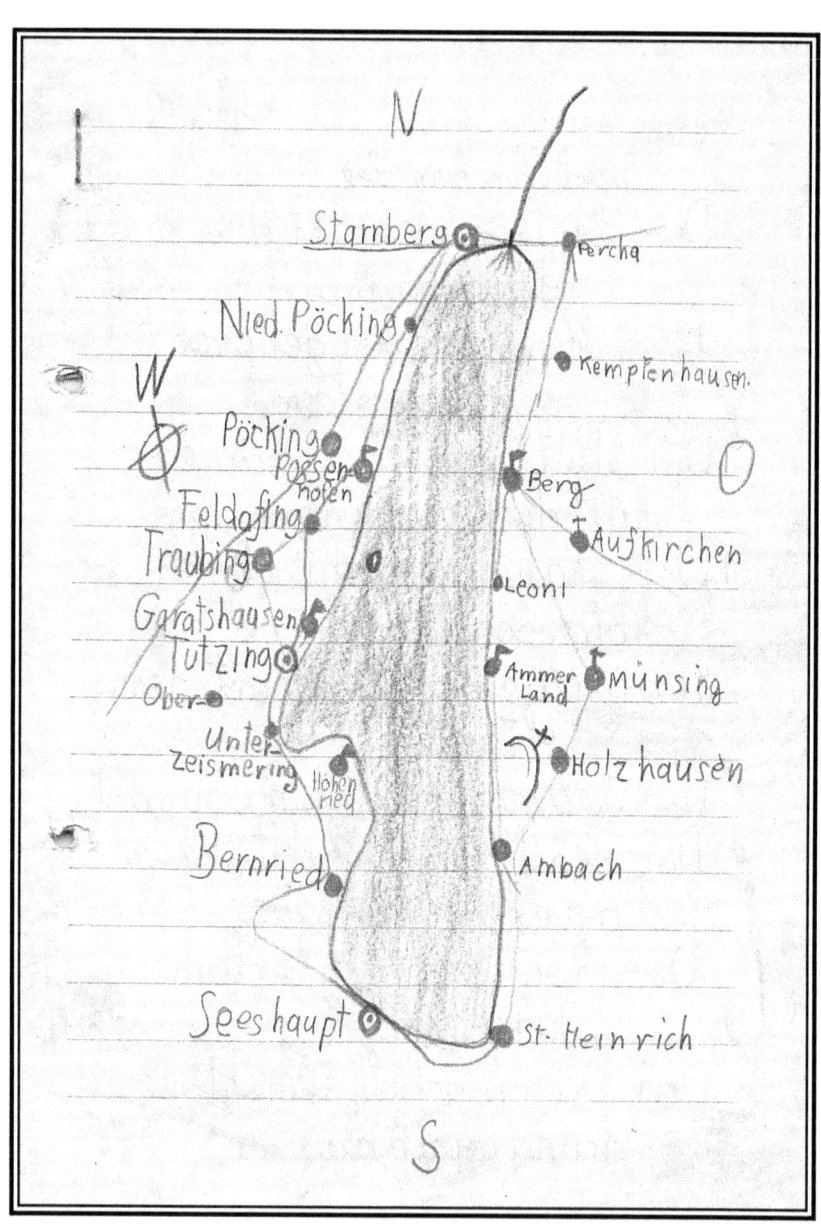

A map I drew of Lake Starnberg in grade 3 under the watchful eye of Herr Kopp.

Contents

Thanks *xi*
What This Is About *xiii*

PART I: THE HÜGLINS
  1. Tango *1*
  2. A nearly missed wedding *2*
  3. Madonnas and Buddhas *4*
  4. Diaspora *8*
  5. Les artistes *9*
  6. Nationalökonomie *13*
  7. Rhenish humour *16*
  8. Genealogy of men *18*
  9. (Some) artists again *19*
  10. The villa(s) *22*
  11. Christmas *30*
  12. Mucki *32*
  13. The Planter *34*
  14. Nemesis *35*
  15. Zauberberg *37*
  16. Varasdin on the Isar *41*
  17. Nüssli mit Likör *44*
  18. The surroundings *46*
  19. Kids *50*
  20. School *53*
  21. Cars *55*
  22. The Jewish question (I) *57*
  23. Black Forest *60*
  24. From music to medicine *63*
  25. War *67*

PART II: THE WACHENDORFFS
    26. A sombre beginning *71*
    27. A macabre anniversary *71*
    28. Back stairs *73*
    29. The photographer *75*
    30. The factory director *77*
    31. The gardener *81*
    32. Tyrant and charmer *84*
    33. Possible encounter *89*
    34. Another Chile connection *93*
    35. Hattenheim *94*
    36. The Rhine *98*
    37. Freie Heimat *103*
    38. Books and poems *104*
    39. The Jewish question (II) *110*
    40. Same subject continued *117*
    41. Postscript *119*
    42. In from the cold *120*
    43. Favourite aunt *122*
    44. Hans-Erich *126*
    45. Family reunions *130*
    46. Gamelan meets baroque *133*
    47. Reborn *134*
    48. Middle names *136*
    49. Middle ground *136*
    50. Skin of our teeth *137*
    51. War again *138*

PART III: RENATE AND HANS
    52. Presto agitato *141*
    53. Courtship *143*
    54. The crossing *143*
    55. Occupation *147*
    56. Wings *150*
    57. Degrees of separation *151*
    58. Presto agitato again *153*
    59. Interlude *158*

Part IV: Tutzing (1950s)
    60. Little house on the lake *161*
    61. On the town *163*
    62. Boys and girls *165*
    63. Catholics and Communists *166*
    64. The hotel *169*
    65. Erika *174*
    66. Piano lessons *177*
    67. Music, caviar, and space *181*
    68. Star-struck *186*
    69. Beaulieu-sur-Mer *188*
    70. Disaster *190*
    71. A few months later, back to the memoir *190*
    72. Geneva *193*
    73. On the radio *196*

Part V: Munich
    74. Esmeralda *199*
    75. The apartment *200*
    76. The doctor *202*
    77. The piano *207*
    78. Dallas *210*
    79. School again *214*
    80. The group *217*
    81. Girls *220*
    82. Ambach *224*

Thanks

I was surprised when everyone seemed to think that these stories should be published. The first one to suggest it was Brian Henderson, director of WLU Press, to whom I had mentioned only in passing that I had put together a kind of family memoir. Then Rob Kohlmeier, managing editor at WLU Press, very diligently and congenially reviewed the first draft and made a number of great suggestions for revision. I still could not quite believe my luck and therefore sent the manuscript to Alison Wearing, a former student, a good friend, and a successful author. It was her supportive enthusiasm that convinced me that, yes, perhaps this could be published after all.

But it probably wouldn't have all come together without Gerda, my aunt who is a vigorous ninety-one years old now and who still lives in the old house on the Rhine. According to her own count she read the manuscript no less than three times in its various stages. I made several trips back to Germany, and together we rummaged through piles of old photos, letters and diaries. As always, we also had endless conversations, while I was visiting as well as over the phone.

We had some disagreements over how this, that and the other really happened. I suppose that she would be mostly right at least with regard to those stories that were about her in the first place. Sometimes I relented but for my own sense of authenticity I mostly I kept to my own recollections, the way I had heard it first, mainly from my parents, and the way I had remembered it. Regarding one particular episode, Gerda exclaimed: "Well, I really don't' think that it could have happened this way!" And then she added: "But it's such a good story!" Here and there, I have simply acknowledged our disagreements in the book.

My daughter Hannah also read various portions of the manuscript, and she corrected a few details her daddy had gotten wrong. Although she grew up far away from me in Europe, Hannah has always been a regular participant in my Canadian life. When I finally became a Canadian citizen last year, she sent the following note, which was read to me during a surprise party organized by Sherry Howse, the indispensable human anchor of the political science department I belong to:

"You showed me moose, beavers and loons. You taught me the J-stroke and let me hold the steering-wheel while you cleaned your glasses—what were you thinking?! You have given me Canadian fiction to read, you've taught me about the history of that country, and through you I've learned about the multi-cultural and exciting place it can be. So—next time you drive down the strip in Grand Bend (towards a horizon that could be anywhere), in your Bavarian car, blasting British hits and wearing your Cuban hat, with a trunk full of Italian wine and Spanish cheese, and a Canadian steak to throw on the BBQ, I think that yeah, you'll fit right in … and I'll be happy to know that you're at home."

My son Jacob will read the book some time later. He is sixteen and mostly preoccupied with the unfolding of his own life. But when he sometimes puts his hand on my shoulder I know that he cares.

The last year has been very difficult for me. But I also found out how many true friends I have. Especially, I want to thank Sherry, Ay-ling, Gerry, Wendy, and Jerzy for seeing me through it.

What This Is About

The plan was simply to write down the old stories for my children, Hannah and Jacob. My father had been the storyteller in our family, and we had urged him many times to write it all down. But he was nearly incapable of writing. He said it hurt his thumb. From one of the very few trips he ever took without us, accompanying a group of film actors on a Mediterranean cruise as the invited ship's doctor, he wrote us a postcard, from Carthage, I think, one of the very few written documents he left behind. It read: "Warm greetings, Dr. Hans Hüglin." My mother fumed for weeks.

When he died, in 2002, not quite ten years after his wife, I was the only one who could remember most of the stories. Taking a hiatus from my usual academic productions, I sat down and began to write. I was astonished how it all began pouring out of me. During the process of putting memories into sentences, and of talking to other family members, especially my favourite aunt Gerda, I began to remember things that had been buried in my mind almost all my life. And when I looked at the finished draft, to my surprise there seemed to be more than just a compilation of family stories and anecdotes.

The contours of a bourgeois family memoir emerged, spanning several generations. My great-grandparents amassed considerable wealth during the so-called founder years in nineteenth-century Germany. My grandparents had to manoeuvre their families through war and Nazi dictatorship, losing most of the family fortune along the way. By the end of the Second World War, all that was left were a few houses, a considerable art collection, a much-admired flower garden, and the remnants of two businesses whose days were numbered. My parents' lives unfolded in the shadows of what had mostly become memories of lost glory.

While dramatic changes occurred from generation to generation, and often within generations, a common set of values and traditions never changed. Even now, living with my family in twenty-first-century Canada, there is still the same love for good food, wine (mostly red), music and art (in that order), family reunions, and the kind of impromptu reactions to people, places, and situations that often result in uncontrollable giggles.

Giggling is a quintessentially bourgeois form of expression. Socialists, reactionaries, utopians, ideologues, and other earnest folk don't giggle. Giggling serves many purposes. It conceals both embarrassment and aloofness. It can release tension or fear. It might be a simple statement of joy. It is a communal exercise. It is difficult to giggle alone, or in a large crowd. Mostly it happens between two people who know they are of one mind without saying so.

The stories in this book are all true. I am telling them as I remember them, or heard them, with the embellishments that came from those who told them to me. In that sense, the embellishments are true, too.

PART ONE

The Hüglins

1 | *Tango*

When I was very little I was woken up one night by strange shuffling noises coming from downstairs. My mother was alarmed, too. Together, we tiptoed to the railing of the big staircase and peeked down. There, illuminated only by the light coming from his open study door, was my grandfather, in his felt slippers, practising tango steps on the yellow marble tiles of the big entrance hall. The study light dimly cast his shadow on the opposite wall, grotesquely augmenting his motions. But I was not scared. I already knew that my grandfather was strange but harmless. My mother and I giggled, silently, of course, and went back to bed.

Ballroom dancing was his passion, and billiards. Almost all his life he danced and played in local tournaments, in Freiburg and in Munich. Only his blindness stopped him, and that was when he was in his seventies. He had a regular dancing partner, Frau Gruber, or *die Gruber* ("the Gruber"), as she was generally and somewhat disrespectfully referred to in the family. My grandmother did not like her, but she put up with her. *Die Gruber* simply allowed my grandfather to pursue this other life, in dance halls and smoky clubs, which he craved as an outlet and compensation for his dull life as a businessman—but of which his wife did not want any part.

That my grandfather was a businessman may come as a surprise. He also was sublimely inept at it. He had taken over from his father, the Kommerzienrat Otto Hüglin, a rather impressive array of hotels and spas that at some time or other included the Grand Hotel Bellevue in San Remo on the Italian Riviera, the health resort Bad Schinznach in Switzerland,

and two German jewels in the Black Forest: the hotel and spa in St. Blasien, and the famous Schlosshotel Bühler Höhe near Baden-Baden. When the Grand Duke and Duchess of Baden visited St. Blasien on 16 October 1908, my great-grandfather was given a pocket watch complete with commemorative inscription inside the golden lid. On the official photograph, taken at the hotel's grand entrance, he stays discreetly in the background.

And then there was the Sanatorium Ebenhausen near Munich, which had been bought by my grandfather in 1923 in order to enable Professor Ernst Edens, a cardiologist, to develop a new therapy for heart insufficiency based on an African herb named strophanthin. Edens moved on to the university in Düsseldorf after a few years and took his fame with him. The Hüglins remained stuck in Ebenhausen, a place they did not really care for, always regretting having left Freiburg and the Black Forest. By the end of the Second World War the sanatorium was all that was left. In 1947 my grandfather donated it to the Innere Mission, a Lutheran charity, and it became the Hüglinsche Stiftung (Hüglin Foundation). It was to be my grandfather's last business transaction, and his most colossally stupid one as well.

2 | *A nearly missed wedding*

I have no idea how or where this paternal grandfather of mine, Albert Hüglin, met my grandmother, Elisabet Hüglin, née Erbes (she was adamant about Elisabet without an h at the end). He was from Freiburg in the southwestern corner of Germany. She was from Neuwied, farther up in the Rhine Valley near Bonn. But I do know that he almost missed his wedding. It happened on the train ride from Freiburg to Neuwied. Somewhere along the ride, the train stopped and my grandfather's wedding party got off for refreshments. I don't know whether they had coffee or something more fortifying, but in any case the train left without them. An embarrassing apology had to be wired from the station to the prospective father-in-law. My grandmother would tell this story whenever she was annoyed with her husband's chronic absentmindedness.

The wedding still took place as scheduled, on 2 July 1914, a mere month before Germany declared war on Russia. The participants had no idea what the next four years would bring. The menu included Malossol caviar, clear turtle soup, filet of sole, veal roast Imperial style, lobster, roast duck with vegetables and compote, artichokes, an ice cream "wedding bomb," warm cheese pastry, fruit, and desert. The caviar and wedding bomb came with Pommery and the rest with a variety of German whites,

My grandparents Elisabet and Albert Hueglin leaving church on their wedding day, 2 July 1914.

except for the duck, which was accompanied by a 1904 Margeaux. Nobody in their right mind would have ruined a perfectly good meal with a German red back then. The orchestra played Wagner's "Entrance of the Guests to the Wartburg," Strauss's waltz from *Der Rosenkavalier*, a tango titled "Seduction," a serenade by Moskowski, and other pieces such as "Spring Is Here" and "Love Flowers Waltz."

3 | *Madonnas and Buddhas*

I also do not know why my grandmother fell for this strange man. For as long as I can remember, he spent his days in his huge dark study, which besides an enormous desk surrounded by cupboards full of file folders contained a grand piano and a large collection of madonna sculptures on wooden pedestals: Romanesque, Gothic, and baroque, carved of wood or stone. He had inherited most of the collection from his father and kept adding to it. My grandmother always told the story of how she had sent him to Vienna during the war in order to buy himself a coat, and how he had come back coatless, in the middle of winter, but with yet another madonna under his arm.

There was also a large collection of mostly dark sixteenth- and seventeenth-century paintings—madonnas again—and Dutch landscapes. Whenever he came home with another one and my grandmother wanted it hung in a particular place, she would point to the spot and say: "Albert, you can hang this picture wherever you want but not there." She was sure that this was precisely where he would hang it then.

And there was a large collection of Chinese and Japanese art: Tang figurines, Hiroshige and Utamaro prints, vases, and Buddhas—lots of them, in all shapes and sizes—as well as tapestries of Muslim warriors holding on to their fiery horses, all happily mingling with the madonnas in an innocent multicultural embrace. The Tang figurines, considered to be worth a fortune, were hidden in a huge old sacristy armoire and shown to us only on rare occasions. And we really discovered the prints only after my grandfather's death, because they were all hung in his bedroom, which we hardly ever entered and most certainly not in order to hang around and admire art.

In hindsight, it is quite curious how my grandfather filled the entire villa with art—and furniture!—that was mostly dark and gloomy, even while surrounding himself, in the privacy of his bedroom, with the extraordinary lightness of colour and design in Chinese and Japanese prints. It seems that he filled the villa with what bourgeois taste of the time demanded, while reserving for himself what his own sensibilities preferred.

As far back as I can remember also, my grandfather wore a cutaway and a white tie and he smoked forty Mercedes cigarettes a day, which came in sturdy little boxes that I used to play blocks with. I had hundreds. He also drove an obscure English car, a Riley, with the steering wheel on the right-hand side. And he drank beer out of champagne flutes only.

In his seventies, when he was diagnosed with glaucoma, he stopped smoking entirely from one day to the next. It did not help. And neither did his odyssey to eye specialists all over Europe. He was going blind. At some point I accompanied him on a final trip to a famous ophthalmology clinic in Salzburg. Everybody knew it would be in vain. As we left the house, my grandmother cried, standing on the marble tiles in the hallway where he had practised his tango steps so often. It was the only time I ever saw her cry.

The trip to Salzburg was one of only two times I spent an extended period of time with my grandfather. I am not sure that my father ever spent much more one-on-one quality time with him. He still belonged to that generation among whom—at least in affluent bourgeois families—children were brought up mainly by nannies and knew the cook better than their parents. There is a photo of my grandfather—in his cutaway, of course—looking down at his little son, my father, still a bit wobbly on his feet and dressed up for the occasion. The whole scene looks as if they were both surprised by the encounter.

Surprise encounter between father and son.

In Salzburg we took quarters in the best hotel, naturally—the Österreichischer Hof (now the Hotel Sacher Salzburg). The Hüglins have a habit of staying in the best hotels only. Until recently, that is: Canadian professors' salaries do not really permit a continuation of that habit. I do not remember much about that trip. I had to accompany my grandfather to the eye clinic every day, and we also went for walks along the promenade between the hotel and the river. I remember being surprised how frail he was. I had to help him dress and undress in his room. It was the first time I ever saw an old person close up. In the evenings I was supposed to study for an upcoming chemistry exam. Instead, I sneaked out of the hotel after my grandfather had gone to bed (we had separate rooms) and explored Salzburg by night. Up to that point I had never been on my own in a different city. (The exam would be a disaster.)

I remember every moment about the other time with my grandfather. This was when he died. During one of his last excursions with Frau Gruber, to Garmisch, where he thought the Alpine air would do him good, and where Frau Gruber no longer was his dancing partner but his travel companion and aide, he suffered a debilitating stroke. He was delivered to the local hospital and never regained consciousness. I was a student at the university in Munich at the time. One summer Sunday, my father told me to take my brother and drive out to Garmisch so that we could see him one last time.

He was lying in his hospital bed in a white nightgown, his eyes open but without motion or any sign of recognition. He had white stubble over his cheeks (I had never seen him unshaven) and his mouth was open. He was breathing, but with obvious difficulty, each breath making a rattling sound. My brother Michi was so terrified he could hardly look at him. I don't know whether I tried to talk to him. Over the course of perhaps half an hour, a nurse came in once or twice and wiped his mouth out with a wet cloth. The breathing then sounded a bit calmer for a while. At some point I held his hand and felt his pulse. And then I felt how that pulse became weaker and weaker until it finally stopped. I had been holding my grandfather's hand when he died. I went out into the corridor and told a nurse that I thought my grandfather was dead. She came and, after a brief examination, confirmed the obvious. She told us to wait and left. My brother had at that point dived behind the footboard of the bed. A few minutes later, a woman appeared who obviously was not a nurse, who spoke with a far too loud voice, gave us her condolences and (I think it was her) closed my grandfather's eyes. She then proceeded to announce, very loudly again, and with an artificial cheerfulness, that *der Herr Doktor Hüglin* now would have to be dressed and shaved. She also took a small linen towel and tied it around my grandfather's jaw and head so that his mouth would be closed when rigor mortis set in.

I thought for sure that this must be Frau Gruber. Politely, I stepped forward and told her that I did not wish my grandfather to be either dressed or shaved. With all the determination I could muster, I explained to her that my grandfather had gone down fighting, in his nightgown, and with his stubble, that this should be respected, and that he should be buried as he had died. The woman relented. When she briefly left the room, I quickly gathered and hid in my pocket his family ring and the golden pocket watch he had always worn. I was sure that Frau Gruber would otherwise take them.

We finally left and drove back to Munich. I gave the ring and the watch to my father, who delivered them to my grandmother. As it turned out, the woman was not *die Gruber*. She had left after my grandfather suffered the stroke, and she had been replaced by Schwester Maxa (Nurse Maxa), who really was not so much a nurse (the title came from her days at the sanatorium) as she was my grandfather's administrative assistant and bookkeeper. She continued to work for my father in that function, and I am convinced that this contributed to the fact that nobody in our family ever knew for sure how much money we actually had. But Maxa's loyalty and honesty were entirely beyond reproach. She would never have taken anything from my grandfather (and neither would have Frau Gruber, really). The following Christmas we were able to laugh about my confusion at the time, and my grandmother gave me the gold pocket watch. It is a Patek Philippe. According to the combined invoice/warranty still neatly folded up in the red leather case the watch came in it was watch No. 159,779 made by the company.

A few years later, after my grandmother died as well, my parents moved into the villa, not the old one in Ebenhausen but a new one, bungalow-style, which my grandfather had built shortly before going blind, in Solln, a posh suburb of Munich, and thus closer to taxis, hospitals, and theatres. My parents also inherited the art collection and the furniture around which the new villa had been designed.

Thinking that he had a fortune to protect, my father had an alarm system installed, and every door and window of the villa was equipped with a security lock. He also insisted that every door inside the house be locked at night—to slow down the robbers, as he put it. He once even locked my mother into the bathroom, turned on the alarm, and left. He had this security mania from his mother. After her death we found hundreds of keys in her desk, all labelled in ink with her delicate handwriting. But since the ink had faded, we had no idea what all those keys had been for.

The robbers never came. They were probably scared off by the countless false alarms my father caused by unlocking and wandering through the rooms at night when he could not sleep. The art collection turned out to be not nearly as valuable as we had been led to believe. When my brother and sister and I inherited it, the plan was to sell most of it at auction. A lovely lady came from Christie's and calmly informed us that the value of the Tang figurines and Buddhas in particular was a fraction of what we thought it should be and of what it had been only a few decades earlier, when China imposed the death penalty on anyone caught exporting its art illegally. Now, it seems, tourists can go there and dig up their own Tang figurines. The lovely lady mainly had eyes for the villa itself, by the way, and she bought it from us a few years later.

We did not sell the Tang figurines and Buddhas in the end. I have a lovely Tang dancer on one of the bookshelves in my Canadian study now, and there are Buddhas all over the place. There is a spice Buddha on a shelf in the kitchen, surrounded by coriander, turmeric, and cayenne, and there is an olive-oil Buddha next to the stainless-steel container holding the Tuscan olive oil in the pantry. Julia thinks that when we go camping next time, we should take a camping Buddha.

4 | *Diaspora*

Where did he come from, this old-fashioned and stubborn gentleman, with his perfect manners and his passion for tango, madonnas, and cars with teak trim? His father, the Kommerzienrat Otto Hüglin, had been the son of a wine farmer, Georg Jakob Hüglin, from Königschaffhausen in the Kaiserstuhl. Blessed by a warm sun, the Kaiserstuhl rises as an almost circular hill in the south German Rhine Valley and produces some of Germany's best—if harmless—white wines. As the story goes, and as it has been told many times with few variations, there were three brothers. One stayed and continued growing wine. Another emigrated to America. The third, my great-grandfather, moved across the Rhine to Freiburg and became a businessman. *Kommerzienrat* was an honorary title given to successful businessmen under the old Imperial regime and bestowed on him, complete with a parchment with embossed seal and signature, by Friedrich, Grand Duke of Baden, on 21 December 1912.

A few years ago I was contacted by a Joe Hueglin, a retired marine in New York, who had found me on the Internet and wanted to know whether we were related. I told him the story of the three brothers, and he said he had never heard it but that he had a box of his parents' letters and documents in the attic and would look through them. A few days later he sent me another e-mail saying he had found postcards from Königschaffhausen, dated 1903.

Around the same time, and also owing to the genealogical reach of the Internet, I met Janet Hueglin in Toronto. By then I had been living in Canada for almost twenty years, teaching political science at Wilfrid Laurier University in Kitchener-Waterloo. I had remarried, and with my wife, Julia Roberts, had a son, born in 1994, whom we named Jacob. I knew that Jacob was a name that ran in the Hüglin family, but I had no idea there had been another Jacob Hueglin living in Kitchener—or, rather, Berlin, as it was called at the time. He was Janet's great-great-great-great-grandfather, and he also was from Königschaffhausen. In old Berlin, Ontario, he had kept a tavern at Cedar and King. One sunny Sunday afternoon, we found his grave in the old cemetery. He had died in 1857.

5 | *Les artistes*

As a young man, the future Kommerzienrat Otto Hüglin regularly travelled to Geneva, Switzerland, on business and regularly took his lodgings in a small pension run by a Madame Elisa Baud and her daughter Jeanne. Over time, Otto and Jeanne took a liking to each other. They married on 4 January 1882, in Freiburg. Presumably, the wedding took place in Freiburg rather than Geneva because Madame Baud did not have the means to make the wedding arrangements of the sort that the Hüglins naturally would expect. She had left her husband, Jean Marc Baud (my great-great-grandfather), which was why she had to support herself and her children by so mundane an activity as running a pension.

Jean Marc Baud was a well-known *emailleur* who specialized in broaches. He had at one point been invited to Paris by none other than the Emperor Napoleon III, who was an admirer of his art. According to family anecdote, he refused to sell to the emperor a single piece. The reason: Jean Marc was a radical republican who some years after that visit to Paris fired shots at the governor of Geneva because he disagreed with his France-friendly politics. It most likely was a symbolic act rather than a serious attempt at assassination, because he missed by a wide margin. But it got him a few years in Geneva's old town jail. His cell, however, with a window overlooking the lake, was converted to an art studio, and his food was brought daily from one of Geneva's better restaurants. The only serious consequence was that his wife left him.

Elisa Baud came from a family of musicians and organ builders. Her grandfather (my great-great-great-great-grandfather) was Aloys Mooser, who built the world-renowned organ of St. Nicholas Cathedral in Fribourg en Suisse. It was one of the largest instruments of its kind at the time, with four manuals and sixty-one stops. Franz Liszt came to play it, and so did Felix Mendelssohn and Louis Spohr.

Elisa's father Joseph Mooser also was an organ builder as well as a virtuoso of the instrument. He moved to Geneva when he became the principal organist of St. Pierre Cathedral. Duplicitous family history: Elisa's mother also separated from her husband. According to her grandson, the music critic Aloys Mooser, she did so because of her husband's "detestable character." In her salon, on Cour St. Pierre right next to the cathedal, Elisa's mother entertained many artists of the day. Among them was Franz Liszt again, who lived in Geneva in 1835–36, during his scandalous escape from Paris with Madame d'Agoult. Liszt took to practising the piano in the salon because of its acoustics, which he found superior to those in his own quarters. Little Elisa had one of her first piano lessons on his knee.

In the first draft of this family memoir, following my father's tales, I had written that it was Jeanne, Elisa's daughter and my great-grandmother, who had sat on Liszt's knee for her first piano lesson. Since Jeanne had not even been born during Liszt's 1835–36 sojourn in Geneva, I had assumed that the famous composer had returned to the city later, during the 1860s. He would already have been a priest by then. But he would not have been averse to having a pretty and talented young girl sitting on his knee.

However, my father most likely got it wrong. And this I didn't find out until I revised the manuscript, in April 2008, and searched the Internet for my great-grand-uncle, the music critic Aloys Mooser. To my surprise, I discovered that his much neglected memoirs had been translated from French into English and had been published, only a few months earlier, as *The Russian Life of R.-Aloys Mooser, Music Critic to the Tsars*. Even more surprisingly, the book's editor, Mary Woodside, was a musicologist at the University of Guelph, only a few miles from my home in Canada. Soon I held a copy of great-grand-uncle Aloys's book in my hands.

This great-granduncle Aloys Mooser had honed his skills as a music critic in St. Petersburg, where he also studied counterpoint with Mily Balakirev and played Wagner scores on two pianos with the piano teacher to the Imperial Family. On one occasion, he turned the pages when Alexander Siloti and Igor Stravinsky played, for the first time, and in the presence of Nikolai Rimski-Korsakov, Stravinsky's *Scherzo fantastique*, in a four-hand piano version. It was also then that he began his long and close acquaintance with Sergei Diaghilev and the Ballets Russes.

After his return to Geneva, Aloys became that city's foremost music critic, a leading scholar and expert of contemporary Russian music, and a close friend of Arturo Toscanini. During a family visit to Geneva in 1959, he boasted, according to my father, that Toscanini never released a recording before he, Aloys, had heard and approved it.

His closest friend by far for many years was Ernest Ansermet, the principal conductor of the Ballets Russes since 1916, and the founder of the Orchestre de la Suisse Romande in 1918. But the two had bitter disagreements, with Aloys publicly accusing Ernest of being a conservative who neglected to conduct contemporary music. This was an old theme for Aloys, who already in St. Petersburg had championed the New Russian School of Balakirev and his circle over the "facile pathos" of Tchaikovsky and Rachmaninov. As his daughter-in-law told me later, Aloys refused to even talk to Ansermet during their last years, and only when the conductor lay on his death bed in February 1969 did the stubborn music critic hurry to the hospital to make up with his old friend. Aloys himself died a few months later. The Geneva newspapers ran a half-page headline in deep black: "Mooser est mort."

Mary Woodside, who unearthed the manuscript in the Bibliothèque de Genève, speculates that it probably remained neglected for so long because Aloys was not much liked in Geneva. His concert reviews were feared. Allegedly, he once wrote one containing only two sentences: "Madame so-and-so gave a recital last night. One wonders why." His criticism was relentless indeed. In his memoirs he recounts a six-day mountain hike with another friend, the composer Ernest Bloch. They slept under starry skies and sang Beethoven's *Pastoral* Symphony from a pocket score. Bloch was so elated by the experience that he exclaimed: "Ah, it's beautiful, it's beautiful. One day I'll write a symphony about it." Aloys remarks that he impatiently awaited the arrival of this work for more than a quarter of a century—but then continues: "It turned out to be, alas, the Symphony Helvetica."

Aloys did not talk to his son for forty years (and did not ever make up) because he disapproved of his profession. "Five generations of Moosers have been musicians," he hollered, "and my own son is a radio technician." I met great-grand-uncle Aloys during that family visit to Geneva in

1959. He lived with his wife in an Old Town apartment, three storeys up and right near where Jean Marc's prison cell had been. The Romanian pianist Dinu Lipatti, also a close friend, had lived on the same floor next door until his premature death. His widow dropped in for a cup of tea while we were visiting. On the wall of the staircase leading up to the Moosers' apartment was a little framed note: "Please keep quiet so that my friend Aloys can work"—handwritten and signed by Arturo Toscanini. The title page of *La Patrie Suisse*, 13 July 1946, shows Mooser and Toscanini arm in arm at the opening of the Lucerne Music Festival.

When we visited uncle Aloys and his wife, he was eighty-three years old. He was nicknamed "the Pope" by his family, probably as much for his patriarchal demeanour as for the black skullcap he habitually wore. From the intense conversation carried on in French between him and my father, the rest of us—my mother, my brother, and I—got only a synopsis later. It seems that my father, also on the conservative side of musical taste, was appalled that Aloys's latest contemporary music prodigy was Luigi Nono, who was about to become one of twentieth century's most important composers. Although he probably did not really know any of Nono's music, my father would have objected on two principles: Nono followed in the serial footsteps of the Second Viennese School (and had even married a daughter of Arnold Schoenberg), and he was an avowed Italian communist and political activist.

Uncle Aloys also must have been able to speak German, because I remember that he told us, over tea and cake, a funny story about my grandfather Albert. They were cousins, one generation removed but only seven years apart in age. They had been mountain hiking, they had gotten drunk, and when they returned to their hotel they pissed into some of the boots left outside the doors for cleaning. I found this hard to believe, since I knew my grandfather only as this serious and withdrawn cutaway-clad penguin. But I am sure it is true. Aloys mentions drinking a few times in his memoirs, and mountain hiking—even serious rock climbing—obviously was one of his passions. So it would have been natural to take the younger cousin on a tour. My grandfather and Ernest Bloch were not the only ones sharing mountaintops with Aloys. According to his memoirs, he also first met Arturo Toscanini high up in the mountains, in the Torino hut between France and Italy, where he and his fellow climbers, ascending from Chamonix in France, had taken refuge during a spell of bad weather and were joined by a group of climbers that included the Italian maestro.

This is the family the Hüglins became related to when my great-grandfather Otto married Jeanne. She was an accomplished pianist who collected a handful of prizes and medals from the Geneva Conservatory even though she most likely never sat on Franz Liszt's knee. My father, however, most certainly received his first piano lessons on *her* knee. When he talked about his grandmother, he always mentioned that the two pieces she played most often were Beethoven's *Appassionata* Sonata and Liszt's *Harmonies du Soir*. Of the latter, Liszt himself once remarked that it was one of his favourite compositions.

Jeanne died in 1947 in Ebenhausen. I had been born the previous year, so she saw me as a baby. She was buried in neighbouring Zell, not far from the sanatorium. Until recently there still was a grave with an overgrown stone bearing the inscription "Jeanne Hüglin, née Baud, 1859–1947, from Geneva." When the grave was dissolved because no one would look after it any longer, I had the stone rescued. It now sits abandoned on a concrete fence post in my sister's yard in southern Bavaria. It is my fancy to have it shipped to Canada one day and find a new home for it on the shores of Lake Huron.

Jeanne's brother Maurice Baud became a painter who specialized in wood engravings. One of his most accomplished *gravures-sur-bois* is an astonishingly refined portrait of Beethoven, which he made after years of studying the composer's life from letters, biographies, and known portraits. Only two prints were taken from the block. One hangs in the Geneva Museum of Art and History. I grew up with the other one, which now hangs above the piano in our Canadian kitchen. I also have, in my study, an oil painting of Maurice as a thirteen-year-old boy. He looks grown-up and pensive, as if anticipating that life will require courage. It is signed "*à mon brave Maurice, 1879, A. Baud Bovy*." Auguste Baud Bovy was a cousin of Maurice and one of the leading nineteenth-century Swiss painters.

6 | *Nationalökonomie*

My grandfather did not inherit the artistic talents of the Bauds or the Moosers. But he was well educated and obviously loved music and the visual arts. One of his friends in Freiburg and St. Blasien was the legendary Polish pianist Josef Hofmann, whom my father heard play the silky Blüthner grand piano in his parents' salon. Hofmann had become a sensation after giving his debut recital at New York's Metropolitan Opera in 1887 at the age of eleven, before he went on to study with Moskowski and Anton Rubinstein at the St. Petersburg Conservatory, and long before Rachmaninov dedicated his Third Piano Concerto to him. Surprisingly, the great virtuoso also played tennis. A postcard he wrote to "dear Albert" from Baku on the Caspian Sea expresses his hope to be back in St. Blasien soon. It is signed "your old tennis comrade Josef."

But as the son of the Kommerzienrat, Albert had to study economics, of course, or what was then called *Nationalökonomie* (national economy). He studied in Munich with Lujo Brentano, which was a suprising choice. Brentano was one of the most progressive economists Germany would ever produce, a social reformer who even served, ever so briefly, as Minister of Trade in Kurt Eisner's revolutionary government, which had overthrown the Bavarian monarchy in November 1918. Brentano's interventionist theories profoundly shaped an entire generation of economists, some of whom would eventually craft the West German welfare state after the Second World War.

Before all that, my grandfather in 1906 received his Ph.D. under the tutelage and obvious influence of Brentano. His dissertation was published under the title *The Collective Agreement between Employers and Employees*. His main argument was that such agreements, still in their infancy and of uncertain legal status at the time, were there to stay and—since they could be made to serve the overall objective of social peace—ought to be provided with binding legal status and regulated by the state. Otherwise, he wrote, employers would honour such agreements only if and as long as they were faced with a realistic possibility of strike. One can find in this dissertation a number of passages that seem to go well beyond the common sense of "enlightened reactionaries"—as Karl Polanyi would later call those who saw proactive social policy as the best means to ensure their own privileges and fortunes. Thus my grandfather wrote:

- that it is wrong to treat workers legally in the same way as entrepreneurs, given that workers are expected to sell their labour as a free commodity in the marketplace;
- that it is wrong because workers cannot manipulate the price of labour as freely as entrepreneurs can manipulate the price of any other commodity; *and*
- that entrepreneurs can achieve such manipulation by thinning out supply, whereas workers have to sell at any price in order not to starve.

To rectify this situation was a matter of simple human decency. Decency or *Anständigkeit* was one of my grandfather's favourite words. And he practised it, most notably in the treatment of his own employees at the sanatorium. Every year at Christmas, for instance, before our own festivities commenced, we all had to troop through the snow from the villa to the sanatorium, where laundry baskets full of presents waited to be distributed among these employees, together with their holiday bonuses. There was a decorated tree, and there was singing, with my father usually at the piano. These employees remained loyal to my grandfather, both during the Nazi years, when he was picked up several times by the Gestapo because of his refusal to collaborate actively in the local Nazi organizations, and at the end of the war, when the Americans temporarily suspended him as director of the sanatorium because the same people in the village who had first denounced him for not being a Nazi now denounced him for having been one.

It was probably his upper-class arrogance that prevented him from finding Nazism attractive. Nazis simply were not *anständig*. But the same arrogance, never towards those working for him but regularly towards those in a position of power above him, also did not endear him to local mayors, bureaucrats, and other persons of public authority. Although respected, the Hüglins were not exactly popular in Ebenhausen.

My grandfather was twenty-three when he published his dissertation, which received favourable reviews in all leading newspapers. It was also read by Hugo Stinnes, one of the most influential German industrialists and the owner of a large shipping line. As a child, I still saw the big "H. Stinnes" steamers going up and down the Rhine when I visited my other grandparents, in Hattenheim, a small wine village in the Rheingau between Wiesbaden and Rüdesheim. Stinnes was a member of the Reichstag in the early years of the Weimar Republic, and though staunchly conservative, he was the German industry's spokesperson in its dealings with trade unions. In these capacities, he contributed to laying the foundations for what would become, after the Second World War, Germany's neo-corporatist system of industrial relations. Because of his political influence and enormous wealth, *Time* magazine put a picture of Stinnes on its 17 March 1923 cover with the caption: "The new emperor of Germany."

Stinnes had read my grandfather's dissertation much earlier—presumably in 1906, when it appeared—and it is not far-fetched to assume that it helped shape his views about the importance of an organized and legally grounded relationship between employers and employees. In any case, he must have been impressed enough with what he had read to invite my grandfather to become his private secretary for a year. Of course, there was no payment. But every Friday, at dinner, my grandfather found a gold coin under his napkin.

That year in the Stinnes household was followed by a year of apprenticeship at the Deutsche Bank in Berlin. Both years provided valuable practical experience for someone who aspired to a career as an economics professor. However, that career was not to be. After his father suffered an early and debilitating stroke in 1910, Albert had to rush home and join the family business.

In his own business dealings, the academic-turned-entrepreneur often was his own worst enemy. Everything he knew better, and everything he had to do himself. During one of the first cold winters after the Second World War, when coal was scarce, he sent a three-page single-spaced letter to the stoker of the sanatorium's heating furnace with instructions on how to shovel the coal into the furnace more efficiently. When my mother later told me this, she giggled and added that she could well imagine what the stoker had done with the paper—which was itself a scarce commodity at the time, perforated or otherwise.

My grandfather also insisted on writing himself the contract that donated the sanatorium to the Innere Mission. One of its crucial clauses was that my father would have the right to remain at the sanatorium as physician for life. The Innere Mission never intended to honour this agreement, and after ten years of court wrangling, my father, at the age of forty-two, had to leave and start a new career. When the final verdict came down, the judge said that everyone in the courtroom understood full well how the contract had been meant but that unfortunately my grandfather's formulations were not legally precise enough.

The reason for all this was not that the Innere Mission disliked my father or did not appreciate his contributions to the well-being of the sanatorium that was now in their hands. They simply saw the stipulation of his life tenure at the sanatorium as a real-estate liability that they did not want to put up with. As it turns out, they would soon transform the sanatorium into an old-age home, and they could not have done this—or at least not so easily—with my father still there. My grandfather's miscalculation was that as a church organization, the Innere Mission would adhere to more ethical standards of conduct than other business organizations. Had he studied church history instead of national economics, he might have known better.

7 | *Rhenish humour*

My paternal grandmother, Elisabet Hüglin née Erbes, had a wicked sense of humour. After all, she was from the heart of German Carnival country on the Rhine, where you either appreciate that sort of humour or find it merciless. I must have been nine or ten when she told me that in her opinion I was becoming somewhat overweight. My pride wounded, I shot back that my weight was so-and-so-many pounds only. Her dry reply: "That must be because your head weighs so little." Naturally, I was off to my room sobbing and slamming the door.

She had a dog, a Scottish terrier named Teddy. And in her kitchen she had a set of brass scales complete with an assortment of weights stored in a felt-lined wooden box. I loved to visit her in the kitchen, and I longed to play with those weights, which were off limits. She had Teddy trained to bark at me every time my fingers came too close to the weights.

As a young woman, she had been taken on an extended tour of Europe. She seems to have travelled mainly by steamer. She took tiny black-and-white photographs, probably with the same camera she still had when she took pictures of my brother and me in Ebenhausen and of her dog Teddy. She kept a travel diary that recorded her active social life—for example, that she had dinner at the captain's table. In England she purchased Shakespeare's works, in English, in a one-volume miniature edition. Her trunks probably were already full to the brim. Elisabet had a real talent for illustrative drawings, often with a cartoonish bent. A series of coloured drawings shows her and two other young women on a shopping spree, almost collapsing under packages and then chatting away in a restaurant or café, with the packages surrounding them almost like a fortress.

Like her husband Albert, my grandmother was of rather slight build and always remained slim. She played tennis and won club championships repeatedly. A 1923 photo shows her reaching over her head for a serve in a long white skirt, blouse, and tie. For reasons unknown to me, she began losing her hair rather early, and I only know her wearing a wig. But she was proud of her figure. Sometime during the 1960s, when she was already in her seventies, she reported that a couple of young men had followed her whistling at the Munich railway station. When she turned around, the young men fled. "From behind they thought I was a young girl," she gushed, and her eyes sparkled as if she still was.

Probably shortly after she got married, a large portrait was painted of her. It is a fabulous period piece of the early 1900s, all pale greys and blues (or greens: like her, I am nearly green-blue colourblind and can't ever tell). As long as my grandparents lived, no longer in Ebenhausen but rather in the new villa in Solln, that portrait filled almost the entire wall behind the grand piano in the salon. One day, she took my mother aside and said: "When you move in here, you can of course rearrange the house any way you want. But this picture," and she pointed to her portrait behind the piano, "stays where it is." And there it stayed indeed, for as long as my parents lived. Now it is hanging on my brother's staircase wall and thus not in a place as dignified as before. But that was the only place where it would fit after the villa in Solln was sold.

8 | *Genealogy of men*

I know much less about this grandmother and her family. The stories were all about the Hüglins and their illustrious ancestors. My father very much admired his piano-playing grandmother, of course, but what really interested him were the famous painters and organ builders, not their wives and wherever they came from. Genealogy is a form of inquiry that mainly follows the male family name. Perhaps, however, there is reason for this besides patriarchal chauvinism.

Among my father's papers, I found his so-called *Ahnenpass*, or passport of ancestors, a sort of schematized family-tree document that the Nazis required every German to have, with notarized entries for all family members five generations back. The purpose was of course to investigate whether there was Jewish blood running in anybody's veins. Typical for the bureaucratic totalitarianism of the Nazis, the names to be recorded were numbered, from one to sixty-three: number one for the bearer of the document, and then two parents, four grandparents, eight great-grandparents, sixteen great-great-grandparents, and thirty-two great-great-great-grandparents.

Every entry then proceeded in the same schematic way. Entry number six, for example, Robert Heinrich Erbes, was recorded as "father of number three," my grandmother Elisabet. Probably because the Second World War intervened, and my father was shipped off to Russia, he had his *Ahnenpaß* completed only to number fifteen, Johanna Sophie Wilhelmine Henn, mother of number seven, Sophie Wilhelmine Wagner, in turn mother of number three again. But already there were seven family names: Hüglin, Erbes, Baud, Wagner, Arnold, Hermann, and Henn, not to speak of Mooser, Bare, Welker, Hossler, Henninger, Repingnon, Groff, Pfordt, and Völker, the maiden names of those wives whose family names would appear in their own right only one previous generation further back. And this is only my father's side of the family.

It was certainly easier, then, to simply concentrate on the Hüglins. One of those, the oldest on record, was the Ritter (Knight) Hüglin von Schönegg, who during the 1360s co-financed the rebuilding of the St. Leonhard Church in Basle, which had collapsed after an earthquake.

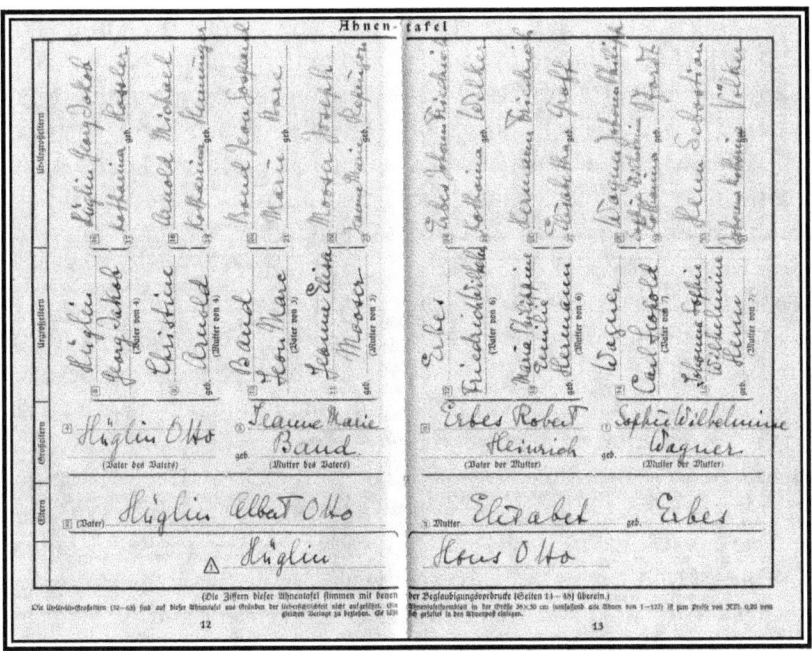

Pages from my father's Ahnenpass, *as required by the Nazis.*

A small sandstone sculpture in the church shows him lying in full armour on top of his grave, although he was probably buried elsewhere, in Spoleto, where he served in the Papal Guard and was later appointed Marshal of the Duchy of Spoleto. Another was Jakob Hüglin, who served as notary on behalf of the local authorities at the Council of Basle in 1438–39. And then there was Johann Hüglin, a Protestant minister who was burned at the stake in 1527 because of his involvement in the peasant wars. In a small town at the end of Lake Constance in southwestern Germany, there still is a Hüglinstrasse (Hüglin Street).

9 | *(Some) artists again*

Whether the Erbes clan had equally interesting ancestry I don't know. They most likely did, but nobody ever talked about them. My grandmother's father, Robert Erbes, was a businessman in Neuwied and with his wife, Sophie Erbes, née Wagner, raised three children, Friedrich, Helene, and Elisabet. There is an elaborately handwritten family tree of the Wagners all the way back to the Thirty Years War, but it records only names and does not say anything else.

While Elisabet's brother Friedrich became a civil servant in Berlin, her sister Helene turned to painting and pottery in a serious way. She married Wilhelm ("Olof") Herberholz, also a painter and a professor at the Fine Arts Academy in Düsseldorf. One of his master pupils was Otto Dix. Whether Helene was a member of that academy, again I don't know. But she did wonderful paintings, one of them an Art Nouveau-ish self-portrait that also hangs in our Canadian kitchen today. When they married, Helene and Olof had their wedding rings made up as earrings—they did not want to lose them in the clay they moulded and turned.

It is a shame that the Hüglins did not pay more attention to the Erbes side of the family. As I found out going through my father's estate, they were a much livelier bunch than the Hüglins. Robert gave his wife Sophie a wonderful sterling-silver coffee set complete with tray. The engraving on the lid of the coffee pot says: "Robert Erbes to his dear wife Sophie, Christmas 1886." And on the occasion of their twenty-fifth wedding anniversary, 18 July 1901, she gave him, or he gave her, a crystal decanter with an Art Nouveau silver lid, one of the most beautiful pieces now in our possession (but not in the kitchen). And as far as Helene and Olof in Düsseldorf are concerned, there are photos of a grand motor yacht in the Rhine harbour and of wild costume parties on it.

One can see the bohemian lifestyle in the paintings of Otto Dix, of course. Dix was a Social Democrat whose seminal works of German Expressionism were later banned as *entartet* (degenerate) by the Nazis. His gruesome 1923 painting *The Trench*, an antiwar manifesto comparable to Picasso's *Guernica*, and depicting Dix's own experience as a soldier during the First World War, caused such a furor that the Wallraf-Richartz Museum in Cologne hid it behind a curtain until the mayor of Cologne at the time, Konrad Adenauer, had the purchase cancelled and forced the museum director to resign. In 1937 *The Trench* was shown at the Nazi exhibition of "degenerate art" in Munich before it was eventually burned.

Dix painted *The Trench* and other antiwar works during the two years he was the master pupil of Wilhelm Herberholz, with whom he mainly seems to have studied watercolour and etching. In my Canadian study I have now hanging an etched portrait of my twelve-year-old father signed "W. Herberholz 1927." Underneath is written: "Joyous greetings Christmas 1927, Helene and Olof." Like Otto Dix earlier, Uncle Olof in 1938 lost his position as professor of fine arts when the Gestapo arrested him. (He survived the war and got his job back.)

My family never talked about any of this. The male Hüglins were a rather conservative lot, and they were probably embarrassed by what they must have heard or read about the Düsseldorf "scene." Though not at all religious, my grandfather collected Renaissance and baroque madonnas, not German Expressionists. And though most certainly not a Nazi, he shared with them a petty bourgeois predilection for wholesome rather than problematic art. My father inherited this predilection. He loved the positivist bourgeois triumphalism in Richard Strauss's tone poems, and he hated the febrile gloom of Gustav Mahler's symphonies. In hindsight, I can only imagine with deepest sympathy how my grandmother Elisabet's joie de vivre must have been stifled in that family.

As a child in Ebenhausen, I met aunt Helene and uncle Olof only once or twice when they came visiting for Christmas. Olof was the first person ever to give me money as a Christmas gift. But Friedrich—"uncle Friedel" as we called him—came regularly because he liked taking his summer vacations near his sister in Bavaria. He was a nice uncle with a wonderful sense of humour, and he always brought presents and took me out for hot chocolate and cake. That usually happened at a *Gasthaus* in a neighbouring village, after a healthy hike of an hour or so through Bavarian fields surrounded by vistas of the distant Alps he loved so much. Teasingly, and also because he was very short-sighted, he would point to the cows in the fields and ask me whether they were mountain goats.

Uncle Friedel had a gentle soul and was not terribly life-savvy. He once told me how his sisters had always teased him, and how they had escaped him on at least one occasion when he was sent along with them as chaperon during a shopping trip to Berlin. He smoked, not much, but whenever he did, he lit his cigarette very ceremoniously with a simple brass lighter he carried in one of the pockets of his waistcoat. My father inherited that lighter and used it in a very similar way: the cigarette between the lips, the lighter held in one hand, the lever pressed down with the thumb of the other. This lighter, too, is now part of our Canadian kitchen, where its exclusive and daily duty is to light the tea warmer for the morning tea.

Friedel was a *Staatsfinanzrat*, a high-ranking position in the German finance department. He held that post all the way from the last years of the Weimar Republic through the Nazi years and into the first decades of the Federal Republic—an uninterrupted and politically unblemished career, hardly typical for those troubled times. He always lived in Berlin, but he regularly spent time in Hindelang in the Swabian Allgäu. He had an ex-wife there with whom he had remained friends and whom he visited. I cannot recall any more details about this rather peculiar arrangement.

Those two had a son, Wolf Eicke (presumably, he had taken his mother's name), who had become some sort of businessman in London.

In 1964–65, while still a high school student, I was taking language courses in London and visited Wolf twice in his little Kensington apartment. That apartment was yet another peculiar arrangement: it actually belonged to a rich American who came to England for only two months of the year and let Wolf live there the rest of the year. During those two months, Wolf had to move out. Usually he went to visit his mother in Hindelang.

Wolf himself was rather peculiar. Impeccably dressed as almost the caricature of a City businessman, he spoke English fluently but with a terrible German accent (especially when he said "frrrightfully nice," which was his standard response to almost everything and anything). He sipped sherry in the afternoon and always carried an umbrella. Dinner invitations meant arrays of delicate little sandwiches brought over from some nearby restaurant and thimble-sized glasses of claret.

On Easter Sunday 1965, he took me to the opening of the polo season at Smith's Lawn near Windsor Castle, where we both were almost run over by Prince Philip. My left leg and Philip's horse made the front-page picture of the newspapers when the prince, attempting to score, could not stop his horse in time and rode into the spectators. According to the press, Philip had a most "unsportsmanlike" tendency to play too aggressively.

Wolf was a lifelong bachelor but apparently not by choice. On one occasion I brought along an English girlfriend, Angela, to one of the sandwich dinners. After I headed back to the continent, he pursued her with annoying telephone calls. We were teenagers, and he must have been in his fifties then. That was the last I heard of Wolf—in Angela's letters complaining about him.

10 | *The villa(s)*

My grandfather bought the huge house in Ebenhausen together with the sanatorium in 1923. My grandmother did not like it. "I have to live in a house where the only balcony faces north," she used to complain. She had her own little entrance hall, sitting/bedroom, a large bathroom, and the balcony (actually a stone terrace) upstairs. Her realm was separated from the rest of the house by a door made of frosted glass that partitioned the second-floor hallway. Even her husband's bedroom was outside that glass door.

My parents, my brother, and I occupied the rest of the second floor: three rooms, with a toilet and sink across the hall. There was no kitchen because, among my grandfather's weird stipulations in the donation

The villa in Ebenhausen.

contract with the Innere Mission, lunch—the main meal of the day—was to be brought over from the sanatorium kitchen. For making supper, my mother had a little stove in the combined sitting/dining room. My brother and I shared a room across the hallway. That room had a sink built into a wall cabinet and underneath that sink my brother Michi and I played our favourite game, which we called *Papierfabrik* (paper factory). We collected old newspapers and spent hours kneeling in front of a large box underneath that sink, shredding the paper with our hands into ever smaller bits. Games were simple back then. Fantasy was at a premium.

From the combined sitting/dining room a doorway led into my parents' bedroom. In that doorway my parents had a swing mounted. I once fell out of it, the first traumatic experience I can remember. Swinging away, I could watch my mother preparing supper or hear my father on the phone, usually talking to Schwester Maxa (Nurse Maxa) at the sanatorium, who even then talked very loudly. My mother and I would giggle at each other because we could hear her through the phone from across the room while my father held the receiver far from his ear.

The headboards of the two beds in my parents' bedroom were pushed against a door connecting to my grandfather's bedroom. That door was insulated by mattresses stuffed into the frame and covered with an old rug. No wonder, then, that both their first two children were conceived elsewhere. I "happened" a couple of months before their October 1945 wedding, when my father visited his bride in Hattenheim, the little village on the Rhine where she had grown up. My brother Michael may owe his existence to a weekend visit there as well, three years later. My mother and I moved back to her parents' house in Hattenheim for a year while my father completed his medical training as an intern in nearby Göttingen. When my sister Andrea was added to the family, ten years after my brother, we finally acquired our own little house, in Tutzing on Lake Starnberg.

As a child, I loved my parents' stuffy bedroom in Ebenhausen. Once, I was allowed to sleep in my father's bed for a week. This was when my parents went on a trip to Venice with my mother's parents and we were looked after by Anneliese, their housekeeper from Hattenheim. Anneliese gave us cornflakes with hot instead of cold milk in the morning. I remember how gross it was to see the skin of the boiled milk stretch from flake to flake. Anneliese came with us when the composer Charly Kalman drove us around in his Cadillac, and she forbade us to constantly press the buttons of the car's electric windows because she was afraid we might break something. But I was allowed to sleep in my father's bed for the week, next to the little bedside table with the brass handles on the drawer and the door, and to listen to the little radio on top of it. That bedside table is now next to my bed in Canada.

There are other memories from that bedroom. When I was sick, I would be propped up in my mother's bed. On one occasion I received a series of daily penicillin shots administered to my increasingly sore bum. My father meant to alternate sides but once forgot, and the second shot on the same side was particularly painful. Once, on another occasion, he already had the needle in my bum when he realized that he had forgotten one of the medicines he was going to administer. So he pulled the syringe from the needle which stayed stuck in my bum, told me to lie still, ran over to the sanatorium, returned ten minutes later with another syringe, put it back on the needle, and finished the job. In hindsight this makes for a good story, but at the time I was greatly offended.

The Ebenhausen living arrangements had been made in 1945, of course, when my parents got married, when refugees from the east occupied the third floor of the house as ordered by the authorities, and when even the Hüglins did not have a lot of cash. There is a story that my parents had to pawn their wedding rings in order to buy me a crib, but I have not been able to verify that. Later, when the refugees moved out, my mother got her own kitchen, and a dining room, upstairs on that third floor.

But there never was much privacy, since moving from one room to the next meant crossing the hallway that my grandparents used as well.

One of my most vivid memories as a child is lying in bed and hearing my grandparents coming up the stairs and going to their respective bedrooms: first my grandmother, fast and with hard heels, *tack-tack-tack-tack*, followed by a loud clank when she smashed the glass door behind her; then, later and much more slowly, my grandfather in his felt slippers, *shuffle-shuffle-shuffle*, and a low clonk when he shut his door, which was made of heavy dark wood.

The villa was enormous, with some fifteen or sixteen rooms, a huge attic, and a cavernous basement. In the basement there was a bar complete with a billiard table, which I was not allowed to enter. The rest of the basement could be reached only from the back of the house, where the doors were always locked, or from my grandmother's kitchen. All of which meant that we children had no unsupervised access. In fact, I have no idea what was down there, and I can remember going there only once, with my parents and grandparents and a contractor who explained that all the basement walls would have to be dug up and aired in order to get rid of some nasty wall fungus.

The attic was forbidden, too, but I could sneak up there unseen and by myself. I did so quite often. It was a huge, dusty space with all kinds of suitcases, boxes, and old furniture covered by sheets of white linen. As I poked through the boxes, I found some of my father's old toys, a railway set, and a steam engine. When I confessed the trespassing and discovery, though, I was told that I was too young to play with either. I never did, and I have no idea what happened to all that stuff.

There was a small basement apartment at the side of the house. It consisted mainly of one poorly lit basement room and a small toilet on the stairs halfway up to my grandmother's kitchen. The occupants were a mother and her two small sons. She was a refugee from eastern Silesia and spoke a terrible dialect that I could not understand. She must have been a widow, because she always wore black and a headscarf. The two sons were Hansi and Seppl. Hansi was about my age, Seppl a few years older. Hansi was physically handicapped from polio. He had a piece of rubber hose attached to the wall, with the help of which he had to do exercises to strengthen his arm.

I sometimes played with Hansi. The living quarters for these three people were shameful, no better than a dark hole in the ground, as I remember. But I think that my grandparents paid for Hansi's rehabilitation therapies, and everyone was very nice and friendly to them. All the other spare rooms in the house were occupied by refugees as well. These moved out after a few years (and hence my mother got a kitchen of her own), but Hansi, his mother, and his brother stayed on. They were still there when we moved away in 1955.

My grandmother's realm was her huge kitchen with its long working counter in the middle, long before kitchen islands became fashionable, and at least three times larger than any of those. I am not sure what my grandmother did all day in that kitchen, since the main meal was brought over from the sanatorium. I can only remember her standing at that large working counter occupied with one of her games of solitaire. She knew many rather complicated ones, and she would cry out with exasperation when one of them did not come out (they usually did).

Only now, as I am writing this down, does it strike me like lightning: my grandmother spent so much time in her kitchen because she did not have a living room, at least not one at her disposal. What was meant to be the living room had been turned into my grandfather's study, and it was off limits at all hours while he was sitting there at his desk brooding over documents. This was why the study was not called a study but the salon: there was in fact a set of beautiful if uncomfortable antique settees and chairs, Empire style, grouped around a black-marble tea table. But it was usually covered with piles of file folders. Only on special days such as Christmas or birthdays were the chairs and table cleared for afternoon tea or coffee.

My grandmother's kitchen had an adjacent pantry. Among many other things (I suppose), she kept cookies there. She liked plain sugar cookies. So did I. When I was older, I sometimes sneaked in there by myself, in the evening, after the glass door upstairs had been slammed shut.

But the culinary treat my grandmother was famous for was the *Omamakuchen* (grandma's cake). This was a plain cake mainly consisting of eggs, flour, and sugar that she baked in her little black stand-alone oven. She had to bake one of these for everyone's birthday every year. When the grandparents moved to the smaller villa in Solln, the little black stand-alone oven went with them and was installed in a spare room in the basement. My grandmother continued to bake *Omamakuchen* in it. She insisted that the oven upstairs in the new kitchen wouldn't do it as well.

When my grandmother died, my mother continued the tradition, and she continued to use the little black oven in the basement. One of the last *Omamakuchen* she baked for me arrived in the mail, in 1984, care of *Herrn Professor Dr. Thomas Hüglin* in the Political Studies Department of Queen's University in Kingston, Ontario. She had sent it for my birthday. I found it in my departmental mailbox. But she had not wrapped the package very well. My colleagues teased me that there was a trickle of crumbs all the way from the mail room to the department office. And indeed, the cake had almost entirely crumbled into small pieces. Over the next few days I ate from it in my office, with a spoon.

My sister baked the very last *Omamakuchen* I ever had in Solln. It was for Jacob's first birthday, which we celebrated with my father. My mother had died two years earlier. Julia, Jacob, and I had flown across the Atlantic so that my father could meet his grandson. Jacob was a good traveller as a baby. We had our seats in the front row of the economy class, and there was a little crib that one could attach to the wall that divided us from the business-class section. Jacob slept peacefully through almost the entire flight. I think that Julia baked a few *Omamakuchen* later on, in Canada, and as far as I can remember they were just as good. But somehow it wasn't the same. Eventually we lost the recipe. I have no idea what happened to the little black oven.

My smoking-penguin grandfather usually hid behind the heavily carved baroque wooden door of his study-salon. (The door would move with him to the new villa in Solln.) He would come out to see us, but we were never allowed to go inside to see him except when we had one of those rare afternoon teas or my father played the Blüthner grand piano for us and we had to sit still.

Outside the study door, in the marble hallway of tango-steps fame, there was one of the most noteworthy items in the villa: the Welte Mignon. The Hüglins were from Freiburg, and it was in Freiburg that the Welte Mignon Company had invented a player piano that not only reproduced faithfully the respective pianist's every subtlety and touch but also and mysteriously moved the keys. It did so by means of paper rolls, which were inserted into the piano's built-in mechanism case and whose millions of punched holes activated the keyboard pneumatically.

The grandparents had an upright piano that happened to fit perfectly into a niche left by the ascending staircase. For a few short years they had the rolls made by just about everybody who, before the invention of the phonograph, came to Freiburg to make recordings: d'Albert, Rachmaninov, Teresa Careño, Edvard Grieg, the young Wilhelm Backhaus, and so on. There were some sixty rolls. Much later, we would play them in Solln on a Welte Mignon grand piano my father had inherited from his Aunt Greta Hüglin in Freiburg. Of course, there was also the Blüthner in the new and smaller salon. My mother had not been very enthusiastic to begin with when she had to move into that villa overstuffed with antiques and other Hüglin memorabilia. But she was particularly miffed now that she also had to put up with two grand pianos in her living room.

I happened to come by the day the Welte Mignon grand piano arrived from Freiburg. I found my mother in tears. The two big black instruments almost filled the entire salon. She had them placed as is common on concert stages, with the keyboards at opposite ends so that the two players could face each other. This way, however, they could not be pushed to the wall, because room had to be left for the player seated with his back to the wall and looking into the room. Thus, they were standing practically in the middle of my mother's living room.

We resolved the situation by turning one of the pianos around. That way, both their sound boards could be pushed right to the wall, and the two keyboards, now parallel to one another, could form a clean line. The two pianos now occupied only about one-quarter of the salon, and they did not stick across doorways. My mother was gratefully relieved. I actually thought that the two grand pianos gave the otherwise stuffy salon some badly needed (albeit unconventional) appeal and character.

Back in Ebenhausen, we lived fairly separate lives. We remained upstairs and the grandparents (except for the bedrooms) lived downstairs. The grandparents rarely emerged from behind the doors of their respective realms—my grandmother's kitchen and my grandfather's study-salon. Quite often there was little direct interaction for entire days or even weeks.

When my mother went out shopping with us, or for a walk, we usually stopped in my grandmother's kitchen to say hello, and sometimes my grandfather emerged from his study for a moment. Since we had only the little toilet and sink across the hall, we also were given baths, once a week, in my grandmother's tub behind the glass door. And we came to play on her stone terrace in the sun (although it faced northeast, there was sun on that terrace sometimes).

But most of our encounters were in passing, on the staircase, in the upstairs corridor, or in the entrance hall. Only on occasion was there a more purposeful gathering—when we asked to hear the Welte Mignon player piano, for example. There was a white porcelain bust on top of it that my grandmother used to stretch her hats on after she had washed them. There also was a little suspended bronze gong with a leather-covered beater that was used to summon the family for particular occasions.

I also remember an impromptu nocturnal gathering, when a bat had found its way into the house and helplessly fluttered back and forth in the upstairs corridor. Everybody came out of their rooms, yelling and pointing at the ceiling. My grandmother donned a scarf so that the creature would not get into her wig. My father had a broom with which he tried to chase the bat out through an open window. I do not know any more how the adventure ended. Probably someone finally had the good sense to switch off the lights so that the poor animal could find its own way out.

There were several reasons why my grandparents moved from the large villa in Ebenhausen to the smaller one my grandfather had built in Solln. This happened after we had already left Ebenhausen. One reason was that they resented the regular bell ringing emanating from the Lutheran church across the street. Naturally, the property my grandfather had bought in Solln was directly across from a Catholic church, which made for more bells and many more ringings. Another reason was that my grandmother wanted to move closer to the city so that she could attend plays and concerts on her own. Naturally, my grandfather built the new house a twenty-minute walk from the nearest subway. My grandmother came to rely on taxis. And finally, my grandfather knew by then that he would be blind within a few years and wanted to move from a large three-storey villa to a smaller bungalow-type home. The new villa was completed just in time. My grandfather memorized everything about and in it just before he lost sight of it all. Thus he was able to move around in it at ease, and he knew precisely where he had put every single painting or statue.

There was an architect, of course, but he had to comply with every last one of my grandfather's specifications. He either was a bad architect, or he did not care, or the commission drove him to the brink of insanity. Because the new villa's stately front had to face the square in front of the church, it was positioned so that the bathroom faced south, not the living room. Once again, my grandmother had to cope with a terrace that had only limited sun exposure. And because there had to be an imposing driveway, the house had been placed in the middle of the property, leaving only a rather narrow stretch of garden on the other side. So that nothing would interfere with the stately front, a stand-alone single-car garage was built on the side. It was so narrow that only the door on the driver's side could be opened once the car was in it. Naturally also, there had to be an imposing cast-iron gate. It turned out to be so heavy that it was impossible to open and close from the house by remote control.

Besides the art collection, the madonnas, Buddhas, and Tang figurines, and the furniture and paintings, there were a number of antique doors that made the move from Ebenhausen to Solln, complete with their frames. And because some of the paintings had to hang above the doorways as they had in Ebenhausen, the ceilings had to be the same height again, twelve feet or more. Salon and study were separated at last. The salon held the entire set of elegant but uncomfortable Empire furniture as well as the grand piano (and as it turns out, it would later accommodate *two* grand pianos). My grandmother could finally have her afternoon teas regardless of what her husband happened to be doing.

My grandfather's study was even larger than the salon, with dark wood panelling and some twenty or so madonna and Buddha statues, the humongous sacristy armoire holding the Chinese collection, and my grandfather's huge Renaissance desk (which turned out to be a fake). When my parents moved into the villa, that study became the television room.

The kitchen was probably the most impractical one anybody ever had to cope with—a passageway, really, with no less than five doors leading from it: to the entrance hall, to the dining room, to the little office where my grandfather kept his piles of papers, to the pantry that doubled as a broom cupboard, and to the basement. In between, along the few free walls remaining, there was an odd assortment of furniture that had made it to Solln from the Ebenhausen kitchen, as well as a new stove that was far from top quality. No wonder my grandmother continued to bake her *Omamakuchen* in her old black oven in the basement.

Yet somehow, despite all the impracticalities, the new villa turned out to be an impressive ensemble of architectural space and art, almost a kind of *Gesamtkunstwerk*. The large rooms facing the garden were all interconnected with double doors. When they were all open, the impression was of spacious bourgeois grandeur. The artwork was matched by the high ceilings and the large windows with their round arches. There were mirrors and chandeliers of Bohemian crystal. There was even an entrance hall with a broad stairway leading upstairs. The entrance hall was not as large as the one in Ebenhausen, of course, and the stairway only led to the attic. And there was the terrace with its blue-and-white awning that could be rolled out during the few hours of hot Bavarian afternoon sun. We had a few grand parties in that house.

11 | *Christmas*

In Ebenhausen, the most important family gathering was Christmas. The little bronze gong on the player piano in the entrance hall would summon us down to the candlelit tree, gifts, and dinner. My grandmother played old 78s on an even older gramophone that had to be cranked by hand. She always played Christmas hymns sung by the Regensburger Domspatzen, a famous German children's choir, and after some insistence on the part of the rest of the family, one or two numbers by the Comedian Harmonists, with "Ich wollt ich wär ein Huhn" (I wish I was a chicken) the all-time favourite, and perhaps even one of her cherished Caruso recordings.

The nicest times I remember in that old villa were the four weeks of Advent before Christmas. There was an Advent wreath, of course, with one more candle lit every week, and there was an Advent calendar with windows to open every morning. (We only had one, and window-opening rights alternated between my brother and me. There were fights over who would be allowed to open the big window on Christmas Eve, usually a double gate with a picture of the Holy Family in the Bethlehem stable behind it.) On dark afternoons during those Advent weeks, my mother would light the correct number of candles on the wreath. Then we would sit around the table, sing Christmas songs, and make Christmas presents. I remember making little wooden figurines for a crèche with a fretsaw. My mother helped paint them. There would be hot chocolate and Christmas cookies or gingerbread.

One of those days was Saint Nikolaus. Before going to bed on the evening of 5 December, we would find in front of our bed, or in the hallway, little coloured paper plates, lit by a single candle in the centre and full of cookies, candies, and a chocolate Nikolaus. The idea was that Nikolaus would bring sweets if the children had been good and a bundle of brushwood for spanking if the children had been bad. Sometimes there was a bundle of brushwood, for good educational measure, with chocolates dangling from it as a redeeming feature. Of course, we always got sweets.

One year, my brother and I got into a fight after we had already had our Nikolaus plates. Angrily, my mother exclaimed that she wished Nikolaus would come back to give us a good spanking. At that very moment the doorbell rang, and there in front of the house stood none other than Nikolaus with his helper Ruprecht. It was the custom in Germany, then, for people to dress up as Saint Nikolaus and Ruprecht, going from door to door, visiting children and giving them sweets.

My mother was as surprised as we were shocked. Nikolaus asked us whether we had been good. We were so scared that neither one of us was able to say a word. Unaware of the situation they had unwittingly become part of, Nikolaus and Ruprecht were very nice to us and left us with more cookies and candy. They had no idea what a devastating impact their appearance had made on us. We behaved like angels for quite some time.

My mother rather hated Christmas in Ebenhausen. We had our own little tree with candles and ornaments in our upstairs living room, and we got presents from our parents, but the *real* gifts (because more expensive and therefore more impressive) came afterwards, downstairs, from the grandparents, under a much bigger tree. So my brother and I hardly looked at our tree, the presents, and the efforts my parents had made upstairs. Instead, we kept asking when we would finally be allowed to go downstairs. My mother sometimes cried.

Christmas was not the only occasion when she cried. My grandmother, her mother-in-law, did not treat her very kindly, at least in the beginning—typical "mother thinks that daughter-in-law is not good enough for her darling son" stuff, but aggravated by the fact that they all had to live under one roof in a house that did not allow for much privacy.

12 | *Mucki*

My grandmother also thought that her daughter Mucki was so much better than her daughter-in-law. That's right, my father had a (younger) sister. It is easy to forget that, because Mucki would not play a big role in our lives. Her real name was Ruth. She was my godmother. She was also a spoiled brat. When my mother played with us in one of the few rooms we had, my grandmother would sometimes come running up the stairs, yelling at her not to make so much noise because Mucki was taking her afternoon nap.

Mucki worked as a physiotherapist at the sanatorium. Sometime during the early 1950s, one of her patients at the sanatorium was the wife of a wealthy Chilean avocado planter who was in the final stages of cancer. She asked Mucki to accompany her back to Chile because she did not want to die abroad. As my mother told me much later, Mucki asked her, some time before the departure, what kind of papers she might need in case she wanted to get married in Chile. My mother's suspicious conclusion was that Mucki planned on replacing the wife of the wealthy planter even before the poor woman was quite dead.

And so it happened. Mucki became pregnant almost immediately. The planter married her. It turned out later that he had faked the marriage contract and that Mucki, after he threw her out, had no legal recourse to any part of the estate. As he told it to the family, he had thrown her out because she had tried to incite his staff and even his grown sons against him. She had also refused to perform any of the duties required of the wife of a Chilean landowner in a traditional South American society, such as appearing at his side at social events. Instead, as in Ebenhausen, she had mostly taken to her room and her bed.

And the reason in turn for *that* was that Mucki was an alcoholic—and probably had been, so my father suspected, from the moment her parents gave her her first glass of wine as a teenager. She returned to Germany with her son Andreas, who suffered from a mild mental handicap. He probably suffered from what would be known much later as fetal alcohol syndrome. Andreas ended up in various homes; his mother took quarters in a small apartment that my grandfather (her father) bought for her near the new villa in Solln.

I do not know whether she ever visited her parents. She certainly was never part of the annual Christmas and birthday gatherings in Solln. But after my grandparents died and my parents moved into the Solln villa, Mucki began to appear for occasional brief visits. She was usually drunk. On one occasion it was my sad task to escort her out of the house when she threw a tantrum and began to scratch the paintings on the walls with her fingernails. I still remember well how shocked I was when I edged her towards the door and realized that she weighed almost nothing. Shortly afterwards, she died. One morning the neighbours saw black clouds of smoke coming out from her upper-floor apartment window. She did not just drink in bed, she also smoked there.

By that time she had long been declared incompetent and had a legal guardian, a lawyer, who took my father to court over the inheritance. My grandfather's will had stipulated, quite stupidly again, but with the intention of keeping the estate together, that my father was his sole heir. This meant that Mucki was by inheritance law entitled to twenty-five percent of the overall value. The guardian-lawyer launched litigation long before my father even had a chance to determine what twenty-five percent would amount to. The lawyer was acting under the pretence of serving his ward's interests, but of course, his fee was to be a percentage of the amount he won for her.

As a consequence, lawyers, accountants, as well as property and art assessors descended on us like vultures. The court proceedings would drag on for a decade. Since Mucki was dead by then, her share went to Andreas, who was also represented by a legal guardian, which drew out the affair even longer. But Andreas received what was to be his—mainly the house still owned by the Hüglins in Freiburg and a cash payment. For this, my father had to sell some of the more valuable antiques and some pieces of land. This was only fair, of course, but the way it came about turned my father's life into hell for a significant number of years. In many ways, he never recovered fully.

13 | *The Planter*

I liked the avocado planter. His name was Roger Magdahl. He was German, from Hamburg, and he had run away from home at the age of fourteen. Working as a deckhand on various ships, he had ended up in Chile. There he had started his avocado groves and eventually acquired huge amounts of land. Avocados were called "paltas," by the indigenous people of Chile, he told us, in 1955, when he came with half a dozen of them carefully packed in a metal briefcase. He let us try one of them. It was a taste so different from anything I knew that I have never forgotten. He was on his way to Spain, where he would be establishing the first commercial avocado grove in Europe, near Almuñecar in southern Spain. He later complained that producing them there was too expensive, due to huge irrigation costs. Spaniards, it seemed, did not immediately take to the strange new produce. At the time, his only hope was to find a niche market among rich Americans in Madrid and perhaps a few other cities. Today of course, the whole world eats avocados. According to the Internet, they are still grown commercially in Spain, the acreage there having grown from the original 7 to some 25,000.

The Magdahls visited Ebenhausen a few times during the years that Roger stuck it out with Mucki. At least initially, he had every intention of doing so. He liked being part of our family. He entertained us with his stories. He bought me my first bicycle and went on rides with me through Ebenhausen. Later he bought me my first plane ticket when he heard that I was going by train to visit my relatives in Geneva. "One does not take trains any more," he declared. "One flies." This was in 1962, when we lived in Munich.

That flight to Geneva on Easter 1962 firmly established my fear of flying. It has never left me (my palms are getting wet as I write this down), even though by now I have been to all five continents several times over and spent countless hours in the air. That first flight was in an old DC3 two-engine prop machine. From Munich to Geneva is only some 500 kilometres, but there was a stopover in Basle. The plane remained in the clouds almost the entire time. Due to a strong wind, seat belts had to stay on all the way. At some point after the takeoff in Basle, I actually fell asleep, dizzy from the constant turbulence.

When I awoke, I was hanging slouched forward in my seat belt. The plane was descending steeply and the engine noise seemed alarmingly loud. Just as I looked out the window the clouds parted and I saw that we were headed straight towards a black sea of water covered with huge whitecaps. I thought we were doomed. But just before I panicked, a strip of asphalt miraculously appeared below. The runway of Geneva's airport begins right at the edge of Lake Geneva. Once safely landed, of course, I was greatly admired by my cousins, Elisabeth and Denise, the daughters of Alexandre Mooser, the radio technician, and his wife Olly. Although they lived next to that runway, my Swiss cousins had never been on an airplane.

Roger the planter had come by himself this time, from his avocado business in Spain. He had driven from Madrid to Munich. He had used up two brand-new Citroën limousines along the way, totalling one somewhere on the Côte d'Azur and simply buying another. During his visit to Munich, he intended to buy camera equipment for a film he wanted to make about avocados in Chile. I accompanied him to the largest downtown camera store. He had all the various best models shown to him. When the salesperson asked him which one he might take, his reply was to pack up all of them. And out of his pocket came a huge wad of bills, from which he peeled off only a tiny portion to pay cash for it all.

My mother's favourite story was a good one, too. He took her downtown shopping in his second Citroën. After he had gone through several red lights at high speed, my mother saw a policeman pick up the phone to alert a colleague at the next intersection. But, according to my mother again, Roger drove so fast that they had already passed that next intersection—through red lights again. She saw the policeman there put down his phone and run after them.

After Mucki returned to Germany, we never saw Roger again. According to the Internet, the Magdahls still own and operate a huge avocado and fruit-exporting firm in Chile. I sent them an e-mail but did not get a response. Perhaps they fear I might make some sort of claim, or they fear that any news from the Hüglins must be bad news, or Roger's grandchildren simply no longer know who the Hüglins were.

14 | *Nemesis*

Everything revolved around the sanatorium. My father was one of the physicians there. Not the chief physician, though: according to the donation contract, this position was reserved for someone appointed by the Innere Mission. As it transpired later, from documents and letters among the papers we found on the estate, my grandfather did not think his son suitable for such a position. He probably was right. The post of chief physician or chief of staff required considerable administrative skills, which no one in the Hüglin family had ever possessed, not my grandfather, not my father, and certainly not me.

As appointed by the Innere Mission, the chief physicians came and went. During most of the time I can remember, the position was held by a Dr. Stark. There was always tension if not outright warfare between Stark and my father. The main reason was jealousy: my father attracted most of the high-profile patients. Another reason was that most of the employees of the sanatorium remained loyal to the Hüglins, who had always treated them decently (*anständig*) and with respect. So whenever there was a conflict, they sided with my father and probably even disobeyed Stark's instructions.

A final reason was that Stark was outright indecent (*unanständig*). He tried to badmouth my father behind his back, with my father's patients as well as with the Innere Mission. His machinations clearly contributed to my father's final and forced exit from the sanatorium. In the meantime, Stark was a lousy administrator himself. In fact, that role was mostly played by his wife, with whom he had almost as many fights as with my father. Mrs. Stark came from a wealthy background, and when the two of them had one of their public showdowns, she would routinely end the argument by yelling at him: "It's my money."

The Starks also had a son, Franzl, my age, who randomly bullied me all through the first three years of public school. He also played nasty tricks on me. Once, he drowned an entire litter of young kittens in a barrel behind the sanatorium and went around telling everybody *I* had done it. On that occasion, when I complained tearfully to my mother, she made me phone and tell Franzl's father myself—which I did, sitting on my father's bed, next to that bedside table that besides the little radio also kept the telephone. I cannot remember what Dr. Stark's response to my sullenly forwarded complaints was. But I'm sure there were no serious repercussions for dear Franzl.

Franzl would wait for me after school and kick me or prevent me from mounting my bike. Being a wimp, I never really fought back. Only on one of the last occasions, shortly before we moved away, did I kick him in the shin, more accidentally than bravely, with my hard boot. To my great surprise, he ran away screaming. I later bragged to my little brother how I had mercilessly beaten him and left him unconscious in a patch of nettles—but nothing could have been further from the truth.

Long after we had left Ebenhausen, we read in the newspapers that Dr. Stark had murdered his wife and then faked a suicide attempt in his car, where he was found unconscious. Franzl by then had been placed a boarding school for the educationally challenged, on an island in the middle of a Bavarian lake, the Chiemsee. Dr. Stark ended up in jail.

15 | *Zauberberg*

My father went to work in the sanatorium every day, on foot, through the park. The walk took less than five minutes. He came back for lunch, usually arriving at the same time as the food, which was fetched by my grandmother's part-time housekeeper. It came in two sets of stacked aluminum containers, one for the grandparents and one for us: soup, meat, vegetables, potatoes or rice, salad, dessert. Like in a hotel. My mother really learned how to cook only after we left Ebenhausen.

I have very few memories of actually visiting the sanatorium. I remember the Christmas celebrations mainly because I was so impressed by the laundry baskets full of presents. I remember a piano recital by the German pianist and Beethoven specialist Wilhelm Kempff. My father had organized in the sanatorium the first series of concerts in the region after the war. Kempff lived nearby. I remember thinking it strange that Kempff wore sandals with his suit. Also, that my mother thought he played everything too loud. The sandals were in part a reflection of his anthroposophical philosophy, a kind of back-to-nature philosophy complete with sauerkraut and barefoot walks in the early-morning dew.

That philosophy went back to Rudolf Steiner, who had also given the world the Waldorf school system. Kempff had first encountered it in the Bavarian Alps at Schloss Elmau, a hotel and spa founded by Johannes Müller, another disciple of anthroposophy, whose ingenious idea—apart from the anthroposophical rituals—it was to invite artists for a free stay in return for some concerts. After each concert, the artists and the other guests would have dinner together before retreating to their comfortable but rather bare rooms. My mother insisted that on one of her visits to the Elmau, she had heard doors opening and closing all through the night and that partner swapping obviously was part of the program.

Years later, in the 1970s, while my first wife Suzanne Bradbury was a master student of Kempff's, we attended one of his recitals at Elmau. After the concert, Kempff was surrounded by a flock of adoring elderly ladies (Kempff himself was in his early eighties by then), and we heard one of them say to him, in a polite tone, but not without some indignation, and staring at his feet: "But maestro, you are not wearing *them!*" She meant the sandals. Kempff had long since switched back to patent-leather shoes.

The Zauberberg Sanatorium in winter.

I vaguely remember my father's office and consulting room at the sanatorium. There was a sofa and chairs upholstered in a blue and white zebra pattern; there was a desk with lots of files and papers; there was a window overlooking the entrance and parking area. As a physician in a hospital-like sanatorium, he went to see his patients rather than them coming to him. The most prominent among them was Margarete Hauptmann, widow of the playwright and Nobel laureate Gerhard Hauptmann. His compassionate drama about the 1844 uprising of the Silesian weavers had so impressed even the Soviets that when the Red Army swept through eastern Germany in the spring of 1945, instead of ransacking Hauptmann's Agnetendorf estate in the hills of Upper Silesia, the commanding general, Georgi Konstantinovich Zhukov, politely asked to be received for tea and conversation.

Margarete Hauptmann lived out the remaining years of her life in a suite of rooms in the east wing of the sanatorium. There is a photograph of her sitting on her bed, elegantly smoking a cigarette, her snow-white hair cut page-boy style, and my father beside her. Because of her white hair and pale complexion, my mother and her sister Gerda called her "the negative"—giggling, of course. I was probably taken along to visit her once or twice, but I do not know any more whether I remember her from those visits or from the photos and my father's stories. She died at the sanatorium in 1957.

Probably through her, my father met other visiting luminaries of literature and theatre, who then became his patients as well. One was Carl Zuckmayer, in trouble during the Nazi years for his 1931 play *Der Hauptmann von Köpenick*, which had so memorably mocked the empty and empty-headed authority of military uniforms. Another was the actor Gustav Gründgens, son-in-law of Thomas Mann and immortalized—albeit not in a flattering way—as the Nazi careerist in *Mephisto*, Klaus Mann's controversial 1936 novel about a pact with the devil. (Decades later, in 1981, it was made into an award-winning movie of the same title.) While the Manns were in exile during the Nazi years, Gründgens had remained in Germany, where he continued to perform his trademark role—Mephisto in Goethe's *Faust*.

Gustav Gründgens had come to Ebenhausen to kick his morphine addiction. As he told my father he had acquired it just before performing his trademark role at the Royal Theatre in Stockholm. The Swedish king was attending that night, and Gründgens had come down with the flu. The king's personal physician suggested a morphine shot to get him through the evening. That one shot had led to a lifelong addiction. When my father told the story, he would add, "Just like Mucki," for whom one glass of wine had been enough to make her an alcoholic.

I vividly remember overhearing wild stories of two nurses holding down the actor during his worst bouts of withdrawal while my father slapped his face with wet towels. Bewildered, I asked my mother how my father could slap someone in the face. She explained to me that this was a kind of therapeutic slapping that was not meant to hurt. As a five or six year old at the time, I never quite got it.

Another story I did not quite get had to do with a magician by the name of Kalanag, who stayed at the sanatorium while performing at the Deutsche Theater in Munich. We got tickets to see him with his wife, who performed as his assistant. He made cars disappear. His trademark trick was pouring out a jug of water—"water from India," he would announce. Over the course of the evening, he would repeatedly empty the jug, and each time water would come out of it, again and again, without ever being refilled.

What impressed me much more, though, was the story I overheard my father telling my mother. When the Kalanags returned to the sanatorium from a performance, he said, they were so tired they had to climb the stairs on hands and knees. Mistaking this figure of speech for a literal description, I imagined for a long time how the magician in his white dinner jacket, and his wife in her glittering outfit, would slowly crawl up the staircase.

Another celebrity patient was the Crown Princess Cecilie, the widow of Crown Prince Wilhelm, son of the last German emperor, Wilhelm II. I was at some point introduced to her, on one of her walks in the environs of the sanatorium. As usual, she was on the arm of Otto Groha, officially her chauffeur but in reality a close friend and possibly lover during her last, lonely years. I remember her as tall and thin, wearing an elegant white winter coat and enormous strands of pearls around her neck. Groha got into trouble after her death, in 1954, when it transpired that the princess had left him some of her jewellery, worth millions. The Hohenzollern family accused him of being a cheap (and of course common-born) fortune hunter. The courts eventually took the jewels away from him.

My mother always contended that Groha's feelings for the princess were genuine and that the princess really had meant to leave him the jewellery. The princess, my mother insisted, was generous and did not really care about possessions. Indeed, on one occasion the princess had carelessly slipped from one of her fingers a ring with an enormous stone—I have forgotten what kind of stone, but probably worth more than what my father made in a year—and offered it to my mother as a gift. She was so shocked that she politely declined, whereupon the princess just as carelessly slipped the ring back on her finger.

Also among the patients were Wolfgang and Ellen Wagner. Wolfgang, a grandson of Richard Wagner, suffered from physical as well as psychological exhaustion. The Bayreuth Festival was to reopen in 1951, in the same theatre, the Bayreuther Festspielhaus, that his grandfather had built in 1876. Since the end of the war, it had been occupied by American soldiers. The Wagners had had to fend off lingering hostilities associated with Richard Wagner's unabashed anti-Semitism and with Bayreuth's close association with Hitler during the Nazi period. Throughout the 1950s, Wolfgang Wagner not only invited my parents to attend the festival's general rehearsals but also provided tickets for some of the performances.

Bayreuth became a regular point of reference in our lives. Every year, our parents disappeared for a week or two and we were left in the care of someone else, our visiting grandmother from Hattenheim (the one in Ebenhausen never looked after us), or, also from Hattenheim, a temporarily dispatched housekeeper. One year, none of this worked out, and we were placed in a *Kinderheim* (children's home)—an unforgettable experience, our first exposure to the world outside our sheltered life in the villa. We met other children, children for whom the *Kinderheim* was permanent home; we slept in bunks; and we spied on the girls in the washroom.

My mother had been brought up in the rather unglamorous surroundings of Hattenheim, so for her Bayreuth was a revelation. She wore gowns to match her husband's tuxedo; she mingled with celebrities from politics, opera, and film; she was blown away, not necessarily by Wagner's music itself, but—just as the composer had intended—by her absorption into a *Gesamtkunstwerk*, a total artistic design, which included not only what were (at the time) the world's most avant-garde stage designs but also the daily pilgrimage of the world's music lovers from the Bayreuth hotels up to the "Green Hill" with its wooden festival theatre, a shrine more than a mere opera house, the beer tents surrounding it, and the trumpet players summoning the operagoers for the beginning of each act.

My mother told me all this in such great detail that the entire scene almost felt familiar when I visited Bayreuth myself, only once, for a performance of *Parsifal*, with my father. This must have been during the early 1960s. My sister still was a baby, and my mother could not go. *Parsifal* is Wagner's last and most problematic opera. It is also very long. The conductor, Hans Knappertsbusch, in one of his last Bayreuth performances, made it even longer by choosing very slow tempi. I was a teenager. I fell asleep during the second act.

My mother also told me how they usually ended up, after the performance, in Die Eule (The Owl), a popular artists' restaurant in Bayreuth at the time, with the Wagners and some of the musicians and singers. One year my parents came home with a stray black cat they had found sitting between the restaurant's swing doors. They named him Georgie, after the tenor George London, who had sung the title role in the *Der Fliegende Holländer* and who was enjoying his beer alongside the Wagners and my parents that evening.

16 | *Varasdin on the Isar*

And then there were the Kalmans. Emmerich (Imre) Kalman was a Hungarian composer two of whose fellow students at the Liszt Academy in Budapest had been Béla Bartók and Zoltán Kodály. However, Kalman had taken to writing operettas, which were far more profitable, such as the *Csardasfürstin*, which premiered in 1915 in Vienna, then in 1917 in New York as *Riviera Girl*, and finally in 1921 in London as *The Gipsy Princess*. Kalman's wife Vera was a Russian emigrée and an aspiring young actress when the already famous composer spotted her in a Viennese café, fell in love with her, and married her. Kalman, who was Jewish, had escaped to

California and New York during the Nazi years, but he returned to Europe after the war and settled in Paris.

The Kalmans stayed at the sanatorium in 1953. When they departed, we all lined up in front of their huge black Cadillac, complete with chauffeur, to say goodbye—father, mother, I, and my little brother. The composer placed his hand on my head and mumbled that I looked like a girl, or too bad I wasn't a girl, or something like that. It was extremely embarrassing. Shortly after this departure, my father was summoned to the Kalmans' apartment at 26 avenue Georges Mandel in Paris to continue his treatment of the composer's failing heart. My father told us that on the first morning, when the chambermaid woke him with breakfast, the coffee and croissants came on a silver tray that had "Sanatorium Ebenhausen" clearly embossed underneath. There was not much my father could do. Kalman died of a stroke later that year.

Kalman invited my parents to join him and his wife in their private box when one of his operettas was performed in Munich's Gärtnerplatztheater. It probably was *Gräfin Maritza*, with its memorable tunes "Komm Zigan" (Come, Gipsy) and "Komm mit nach Varasdin" (Come with Me to Varasdin), which my parents whistled and sang for years afterwards. It is easier to whistle Kalman than Wagner. At the sanatorium, Kalman probably worked on his last operetta, *Arizona Lady*, which would have to be completed by his son Charly and which premiered posthumously in Berne in 1954.

Charly came to the sanatorium after his father's death, in the summer and fall of 1954. He befriended my father for reasons he inscribed in my parents' guest book on 21 August 1954: "My dear friend Hans! It has been only a year, but seems as if we have known each other for a long time. We had so many wonderful times as well as memorable and moving moments. Hoping that we shall forever remain united in our great love for music, I extend this handshake to you and your dear wife Renate. In old friendship, Charly." Above this entry, Charly scribbled a few bars from the opening line of "Times Square" (Tempo di Blues), generally considered one of his best compositions.

It was Charly who drove my brother and me around in his huge Cadillac convertible. In Ebenhausen in the 1950s, that was a huge thrill. We desperately hoped that some of our friends would see us driving by. My brother invited Charly to his fifth birthday party, and Charly, then in his mid-twenties, did indeed come, and sat on a chair on the front lawn, eating cake with all the children. Then he pulled out a little composition he had written for my brother, "Un-Deux-Trois," which he played for us on the Blüthner in my grandfather's study-salon. Unfortunately, we have lost the single sheet of music with the dedication.

We also lost contact with Charly. Only when I searched the Internet while writing down these stories did I learn that he still is active and well. In 1992, he wrote the music for Tankred Dorst and Peter Zadek's production of *Der Blaue Engel* (The Blue Angel) with Ute Lemper in Berlin. In 2007, a premiere of his musical *Novecento—Die Legende eines Ozeanpianisten* (Legend of an Ocean Pianist) at the Gärtnerplatztheater in Munich was trashed for its mediocre production but not for the quality of Charly's music.

After Emmerich's death, Vera Kalman remained a faithful patient and friend for many years. I don't think she actually needed any particular treatment. She mainly liked to stay in large, luxurious hotels, and at least in the early years the sanatorium could compete with the best of them. She wrote letters to my father, sometimes addressed to "my wonderful friend and doctor" and signed "many dear greetings, your Vera Kalman." The letters invariably were written on the stationery of some grand hotel: the Ascott in Zurich, the Gehrhus in Berlin-Grunewald, the Park Residence in Zurich again, the Frankfurter Hof in Frankfurt, the Windsor in Berlin-Charlottenburg, the Bristol in Vienna, and La Pace in Montecatini.

Most of these letters were no longer addressed to the sanatorium, though. In fact, Vera Kalman was done with the sanatorium even before my father was. In a letter from Paris dated 4 July 1954, she informed him that she would not be returning to the sanatorium and that she had explained the reasons in a separate letter to Dr. Stark and his wife, copy enclosed. This typed letter ended with a handwritten note: "The cheque will be sent July 8th directly from New York."

In that enclosed copy, she complained that the food was dreadful ("third-rate meat at top restaurant prices") and that Mrs. Stark was never available when she wanted to complain to her. She also mentioned that she had heard that my father might have to leave the sanatorium. She pointed out that this would be a shame because it was only because of him that she and others had come to Ebenhausen in the first place.

She kept her word. After being ejected from the sanatorium, my father opened a private clinic in the Hotel Kaiserin Elisabeth in Feldafing on Lake Starnberg. In her very next letter, Vera Kalman announced her imminent arrival in Feldafing, in a handwritten letter dated 14 September 1955. When she arrived, she told the hotel page to get the luggage from the trunk of her Cadillac. The poor lad, noticing that she had left the key in the ignition, couldn't resist starting the engine of what was to him and at that time a very impressive and exotic automobile. It also was an automatic, and not knowing how to drive one, he crashed it into a concrete pillar. Somehow, the hotel managed to have the Cadillac repaired without Vera Kalman ever finding out. She kept coming back. Her youngest daughter Yvonne got married in Feldafing. I held her six poodles in front of the Town Hall entrance while the civil ceremony was performed.

Then, in a letter dated 1 June 1958, she wrote that she had heard that my father had "opened another sanatorium," and that she would like to come "next week." She added: "Where is it?" That new "sanatorium" probably was my father's private practice in Munich, which he opened after his partnership with the hotel in Feldafing did not work out. I don't think Vera Kalman ever showed up at this new practice. For a while longer, her letters kept coming, asking my father to make reservations for her in various Munich hotels. On occasion, she would also commandeer him for other kinds of services. He gladly obliged, because it always meant meeting interesting people, and dinners with caviar and champagne. So it passed that she asked him to drive her to Vienna, this time in a brand-new Chrysler. This was the first time my father had ever handled power steering. "Two hundred kilometres per hour on the Autobahn with one finger," he proudly reported.

I know most of the sanatorium stories only from my father's tales, of course—except when they happened right in front of my eyes. Such was the case, for instance, when Vera Kalman decided that she and her daughter had to learn how to ride a bicycle. Two shining bikes were acquired, matching outfits were donned, and a bespectacled colleague of my father's, Dr. Baumüller, was commandeered as instructor. Looking out the villa's window, my mother and I watched Vera and Yvonne wobble down the street and, at increasing speed, head directly for the ditch in front of our house, with Dr. Baumüller desperately trying (and failing) to catch them. I am not sure but I think that was the end of bicycle lessons.

17 | *Nüssli mit Likör*

My father's tales included stories about patients who did not stay in the sanatorium. One of them was the German film actor O.W. Fischer, who lived in a neighbouring village. Fischer was one of the highest-paid actors in post-war Germany, but he never made it to Hollywood, as some German actors were by then doing—Horst Buchholz (The Magnificent Seven), for example. The closest Fischer came to international stardom was with the 1958 movie *Helden* (Heroes), a romantic comedy set during a nineteenth-century war between Serbia and Bulgaria in which he starred as the Swiss mercenary Hauptmann (Captain) Bluntschli. That film was nominated for a Best Foreign Film Oscar. It costarred Liselotte Pulver (unforgettable in Billy Wilder's *One, Two Three* [1961]). What I remember most clearly about *that* movie is how the homesick Swiss captain always munches on Swiss-chocolate pralines and then exclaims: *"Nüssli mit Likör!"* (nuts with liqueur). That was also the last line of the film. The captain (Fischer) finally gets to kiss his bride (Pulver), with whom he has already shared his chocolates. Separating his lips from hers, he once more sighs, this time doubly delighted: *"Nüssli mit Likör!"*

One evening, my father was called to O.W. Fischer's house "on an urgent matter." Upon arrival, the actor insisted that my father give him an injection of this, that, or the other, even though it seemed obvious that there was really nothing wrong with him. But my father obliged, probably with one of those intravenous vitamin C shots he often administered to patients suffering from fatigue or the flu. Afterwards, Fischer laughed and revealed that he had only wanted to study my father's movements because he was playing a physician in a new film and there was a scene to be filmed the next day in which he had to make such an injection.

There is a kind of postscript to this episode. In most of his films at the time, O.W. Fischer's leading lady was Ruth Leuwerik, who also starred in corny lapses of good taste such as *Die Trapp-Familie* (the German original of what would become in English the equally corny *The Sound of Music*). Decades later, Ruth Leuwerik became one of my father's patients as well, during the time of her brief marriage to the baritone Dietrich Fischer-Dieskau, also a patient. Sometimes my father had to visit her on the set, and on one occasion she talked him into a brief walk-on part, riding down an elevator with her. The scene had to be shot several times because my father was so nervous that he kept pressing the wrong button. Leuwerik had a nice photo taken of the two of them, by the set photographer.

I once met Ruth Leuwerik, under peculiar circumstances. My father had this nasty habit of combining house calls to various patients with family excursions. We sometimes spent hours waiting in the car and in front of some gate to some estate or villa, while my father did whatever he did when he made these house calls—mostly talk, I suspect. In this particular instance, however, he had picked me up from hospital where I had had a minor operation on one of my toes. On the way home, he said he would "just ever so briefly" stop at the house of Leuwerik to give her an injection. Because I was supposed to keep my bandaged foot resting high, he brought me into her house with him. So I was greeted by the famous and elegant actress while I was sitting in her living room with my bandaged foot oozing on one of her sofa cushions lying on her coffee table. She seemed unfazed and was very nice to me. I was maybe thirteen then.

I also met Fischer-Dieskau a number of times, again in uncommon circumstances. By then I was living in a spare room in my father's Munich practice, across the hallway from our apartment. The practice was small and had only the consulting room and one waiting room. My father preferred making house calls to having patients come to him. This obviously also suited his many celebrity patients from film and opera. So on the few occasions that they did show up at the little practice, my father spared them from waiting with others in the common room by putting them in my room instead. Sometimes, therefore, when I came home from school, I found FiDi, as Fischer-Dieskau was known among friends, lying on my bed waiting for his injection. He once helped me out with some math homework.

18 | *The surroundings*

In front of the villa in Ebenhausen, there were meadows divided by several driveways, in between large, mature trees. Opposite the main entrance was a thicket of lilac bushes. As children, we loved playing in that thicket. It was our fortress. A few steps framed by stone walls led to the entrance. Here, family members gathered for photos and for the first warm sun in the spring. It was always cold in the villa. Here, we also picked up milk and fresh *Semmeln* (rolls), which were delivered every morning by the baker on his motorbike, which had a sidecar.

The meadow in front of the villa served all kinds of purposes. Birthday parties were held there, such as the one for my brother when Charly Kalman came. Under one of the trees we built nests of moss, where the Easter Bunny then laid its eggs. One year, I built mine so large that the always educational Easter Bunny reduced its size. There was a folding metal table with chairs for lunches and teas. When the grass was high, before it was cut, we could play hide-and-seek in it. All the meadows around the villa were full of flowers. There were lots of them especially in the spring: yellow cowslips and blue forget-me-nots. The meadow was good for napping. There are photos of my mother looking down at my crib under a lilac bush, and similar photos of the same scene with my brother. There are some photos of me resting hollow-eyed in a kind of deck chair when I had whooping cough. I was a good boy. According to my father, I got up from the table and apologized when I had a coughing attack.

Sometimes there were unexpected visitors—cows, which on their way back to the stable of a neighbouring farm would take a shortcut through the park. One day my mother, who sometimes put me out on the grass in a playpen during warm summer afternoons, looked out the window and saw the playpen surrounded by an entire herd of curious cows staring down at me. Apparently, I was delighted by the entertainment. Later, my brother would be placed in that playpen with me. He would watch me, smiling angelically, while I built a nice castle or tower from the wooden building blocks I had. Then, just before it was finished, he would smash it. The solitary paradise of the first-born had ended.

A path went through the park from the villa to the sanatorium, past an area of groomed gardens and lawns where the patients could wander about. This was the path my father took when he went to work; it was also the path our lunch took when it was delivered from the sanatorium kitchen. We were not really supposed to go over there, all the way to the sanatorium, but we often did nevertheless. It was tempting. The path ended at the sanatorium's parking lot, and there were cars—mostly big and expensive ones, such as Mercedes limousines and what we called American street cruisers: Cadillacs, Buicks, and Chryslers.

The entire back of the park, all the way from below the villa to the sanatorium's service buildings, consisted of mixed-growth forest interspersed with a meadows. For a little boy, this was true wilderness. A neighbouring farmer would come with his tractor to cut the grass on those meadows. Sometimes I was allowed to ride on the tractor with him. On one such occasion, he had behind the tractor a giant rake, which he raised and lowered in order to arrange the hay in neat rows across the meadow. Once, the branch of a tree swept me off the tractor and under the rake, and one of the rake's teeth pierced my Bavarian leather shorts, *Lederhosn*, and went right into my thigh. For some weird reason I was much more scared about my father's reaction than I seemed hurt by the wound. All afternoon, I kept worrying about what my father would say when he came home. Of course, when he came he was not angry with me at all, and my mother had already repaired the hole in the *Lederhosn*.

Villa, park, and sanatorium were all at the top of a hill carved by the glaciers of the last ice age. North of it, behind the villa, the landscape descended gently into a valley of fields and farmyards. The next village, Hohenschäftlarn, was about one kilometre away, straddling another hill. In front of the villa, the hill descended more sharply: past the Lutheran church and a few houses; down the Zechberg road, which was short but so steep that cars often got stuck in the winter; and into the village of Ebenhausen with its shops and railway station.

The most important of Ebenhausen's businesses was the Kaufhaus Ittlinger on the main street. This was a general store my mother sometimes sent me to, a ten-minute walk and back from the villa. I liked those assignments because Frau Ittlinger regularly gave me candy, which she called bonbons but mispronounced as *bons-bons*. Ever since, my brother and I have called candy *bons-bons*. Sometimes I diverted ten pfennings from my mother's purse and bought a piece of chocolate with coconut filling. Frau Ittlinger never told on me, or at least my mother never said anything.

Almost next to the Ittlinger store was the Hossfeld dentistry. Günther Hossfeld was one of my father's best friends, and I spent a lot of time in his practice because I had horrible teeth. I think I was *born* with cavities. When I had an appointment, I was simply sent down the hill by myself, though sometimes uncle Günther, as we called him (in German, children used to call all grown-ups other than their parents uncle and aunt), drove me back up the hill after a particularly painful treatment. Drills were slow and rackety back then, and a good dose of laughing gas, that pre-needle form of anaesthesia, was employed only for serious matters such as the extraction of a tooth. Laughing gas did not work as desired on all patients. Uncle Günther told me, in true dentist's fashion when my mouth was wide open and I could respond only with inarticulate grunts, that my grandfather, fully unconscious under the influence of laughing gas, had once gotten up from the chair and walked out of the house. Uncle Günther would laugh whenever I was told to rinse out my mouth in between drilling or filling sessions and I spat the water emphatically all over the floor. "Just like his father," he said to his assistant.

Uncle Günther remained the family dentist long after we had moved away from Ebenhausen. During the early 1960s in Munich, I fell from my bike and knocked out half of one of my front teeth when my mother sent me to fetch some expandable curtain rails and I somehow managed to jam them into the spokes of my bike's front wheel. Uncle Günther fixed the tooth with a "jacket crown." While my mouth was wide open again, he said, "Hmmn, Thomas" (he started every sentence with "Hmmn"), "if you are lucky this crown will last you ten years." It lasted forty-five. It became discoloured over time, though.

That is not where the tooth story ends. In 1987, meanwhile divorced from Suzanne and living in Canada, I had come back to Munich for a visit with my seven-year-old daughter Hannah. I waited for her at the subway station near her mother's apartment, where she emerged returning from school. Years later, she told me that when she saw me, she hesitated for a moment, not entirely sure whether it was really me. She was very young, it was a surprise visit, and we had not seen each other for a year. But when I smiled at her and she saw the tooth, she knew it was her daddy.

It was when she told me this that I made an appointment with my new Canadian dentist and had the crown re-enamelled. It was a quick fix that would get me through another decade or so. In fact, the entire contraption broke apart only a few weeks ago and the tooth finally had to be pulled out. As I write this, I am sitting at my desk with a gaping hole in my mouth, waiting for a bridge to be mounted over it.

A third and more appealing reason to descend to Ebenhausen was the garage of Georg Spickeneder, called Spicki, on the other side of the railway, near the Gasthaus Post, where Goethe had his horses changed on his way to Italy. Spicki was the local car mechanic. His shop was a dark, greasy cavern full of old motorbikes and cars. I loved hanging around there while my father discussed oil changes or whether his car was still worth repairing. Later Spicki ran a far more mundane gas station opposite the railway station.

My father, Spickeneder, Hossfeld, and a number of others were all part of the local *Schützenverein* (target shooting club), which held its monthly meetings at the Gasthaus Post. They ate, drank beer, and shot with air rifles at a piece of cardboard with black and white rings on it. Once a year, they shot at a round piece of wood, *Schützenscheibe*, usually with a boar or some other wild animal painted on it. The winner that evening was to be the annual *Schützenkönig* (shooting king), and it was he who had to provide the *Schützenscheibe* for next year's championship competition. They had to shoot through an opening in the wall because the main room of the inn was too short and the shooting distance would not have been long enough otherwise.

My father never quite lost contact with his shooting comrades after we left Ebenhausen. Much later, after my parents moved into the Solln villa, he resumed his membership. Solln was on the southern outskirts of Munich, only a fifteen-minute drive from Ebenhausen. At some point during the 1970s, my father became the shooting king.

By then, as I found out later, one of his younger shooting comrades was Dieter Neumann, one of my former classmates at high school in Munich. Dieter was one of my more unusual friends. His parents had escaped from East Germany and found a new home in Ebenhausen. His father worked for the West German secret service. When he first arrived, Dieter was an average high school student like most of us. But he excelled in the gym, where he dazzled us with his routines, at the parallel bars in particular. Communist school curricula apparently took the old adage of a keen mind in a healthy body more seriously that was the case in the capitalist West. Dieter later had an affair with the wife of the local baker, married her, and stayed in Ebenhausen.

19 | Kids

At the far end of the hill, to the west beyond the sanatorium, was another little village, Zell. It actually was part of Ebenhausen, but it was at the top of the sanatorium hill rather than down in the valley, and it had its own little church, with the graveyard in which my great-grandmother Jeanne Baud was buried. In one of the little farmhouses there lived the Pröbster family. I say *little* farmhouse because when I visited the Pröbsters, coming from the villa, everything seemed incredibly small and narrow. The elder daughter, Lieselotte Pröbster, about eighteen or so at the time, came to us a couple of times a week to clean house. During the summer months, I sometimes got up early in the morning and hid in the high grass in front of the villa, jumping up and trying to scare her when she came walking through the park. She had a younger sister, Hannelore Pröbster, who was only a few years older than me—which, however, makes a lot of difference when you're only eight. Hannelore stopped me once in front of the sanatorium and demanded to see my penis. I obliged, but was miffed when she told me that mine didn't look like a mushroom, as was the case with the other (and older) boys. I had no idea what she was talking about.

At the near end of the hill, eastward across from the road leading to Hohenschäftlarn, my grandfather owned an old abandoned *Kiesgrube* (gravel pit). It was surrounded by a fence, but somehow some of the older kids and I managed to get in there. During one illicit visit, I stepped on a piece of broken glass that cut my main vein above the ankle. One of the older kids carried me back to the house, with me screaming and leaving a trail of blood along the way. It turned out to be much less harmful than it looked. The *Kiesgrube* was secured with a new padlock, though.

Beyond the *Kiesgrube*, another five minutes or so through a little forest, was the main road linking Hohenschäftlarn and Ebenhausen. There was a little shop there, too, where my mother sometimes sent me to buy stuff. On one occasion, she did not have small change and gave me a hundred-mark bill—an enormous amount of money at the time. When I arrived at the shop, I had lost the money. I had not stopped anywhere, I had not lingered, I had not met anyone. I could not remember doing anything but proceeding to the shop directly through the forest, with the money safely tucked in my pocket. But it was gone. Nobody ever said anything.

Next to the shop, directly descending from the edge of the road, was a steep hill where my schoolmates and I went skiing. After a time, we were skilled enough to continue doing slalom through the trees at the bottom of the hill. I once had my parents come out to admire me. I had first learned skiing on the more gently sloping meadow in front of the sanatorium, and my first solo outing had been a disaster. Falling again and again into the deep snow, I yelled out in anguish, only to hear someone mockingly yell back at me from the bottom of the hill. I worked myself into a virtual little temper tantrum as whoever this annoying person was yelled back up at me whatever I yelled down. Foaming at the mouth, I finally stormed home and demanded that my mother come and see who this terrible person was. She came and burst into laughter when she realized that I had fallen victim to an echo. All hurt pride, I did not think it was funny at all.

Two older children in our neighbourhood were the twin brothers of a tennis friend of my father's, Herr Janke, who also was his accountant and remained so for as long as they both lived, way up into their eighties. These twins were nicknamed *die Totenköpfe* (skull heads) for their shorn angular heads, and they were a bit of a menace. Once they chased the much older and taller Sommerfeld boy all across the meadow in front of the sanatorium, threatening him with some thorny branches. I was very impressed. All the neighbourhood kids usually gathered in front of the church. I remember how one day the Sommerfeld boy brought along a girl from Italy who was visiting on an exchange program. She had shiny black hair and shining black eyes, and everybody was in love with her. She had a rather un-German temperament, which earned her the nickname *wilde Furie Bestie* (wild furious beast), which was some concoction of German and Italian.

That church I just mentioned was the Lutheran one across the street from the villa. My grandparents objected not only to the bell ringing but also to a recently built annex that blocked their view. According to my grandfather, it had not been built the way he had been shown on the plan that he had been asked to approve. As usual, he probably had misunderstood the drawing or misread the fine print. This was also the church where my father had been playing the organ on Sundays since he was a teenager. He still did when I was little, but he would leave during the sermon, smoking a cigarette outside instead of listening. "I have already heard it all," he would tell us. Sometimes he would return late for the next round of hymns and the pastor would glare at him angrily across the nave. Playing with his back to the nave and altar, my father caught those glares in the little mirror mounted on the organ that allowed him to follow the proceedings behind him.

We hardly ever went to church, and when we did, it was for the music. My father loved all the great church chorales and often thundered them at home on the piano. On Sundays, my treat as a small child was sitting on the windowsill and watching the people walk to church. Not that there were many of them. My mother once asked me: "Are they streaming into church already?" According to cherished family anecdote, my answer was a long silence followed by the excited exclamation: "Oh, yes, there streams another one." Church attendance was already low, and particularly so in a Lutheran church in rural Catholic Bavaria. I liked looking out the window. There was no television yet. One evening, I watched the full moon in a cloudy sky, and my mother heard my solemn commentary: "And now it is diving into the cloud waves."

I had few friends in Ebenhausen. The earliest playmates I can recall were the Schejas, a boy (Peter?) and a girl from a Swedish family that visited relatives in Ebenhausen for a few summers. Peter Scheja, I think, was present when I fell out of the swing. Then there was Michael Stengel, the son of the Lutheran pastor. The Stengels lived in a brand-new house in Hohenschäftlarn, next to the aforementioned ski hill. Even at my tender age, and knowing only the old villa, I thought it was a house strangely void of character. Another friend was, yes, I have to admit it, Franzl Stark. Our relationship was not always hostile.

There also was Thomas Mayer, the son of Otto and Erika Mayer, probably my parents' closest friends in Ebenhausen. But the Mayers moved soon to Munich, and we saw them only during occasional visits. I didn't like Thomas Mayer much. He played chess and, at least according to his father, he was a genius at everything he tried. Otto Mayer was an architect. He later received the commission to rebuild the bombed-out historical centre of Würzburg, including the baroque castle and the cathedral. He received a papal medal for his work on the cathedral, even though it stirred up quite a controversy at the time because he replaced destroyed parts with modern architecture instead of reconstructing them.

He also was a gifted painter. There was a row of old portraits of church dignitaries in the cathedral, and one of them had been destroyed. He painted a copy and inserted his own face into it. The paintings were hanging in a dark corner of the cathedral, and the artistic prank probably was never discovered. A shameless if harmless flirt, Otto Mayer got on most women's nerves. His wife rolled her eyes but put up with it. Thomas Mayer became a professor of literature, but his career turned out to be less stellar that his father had predicted. There were moments when I could not quite suppress thoughts of malicious pleasure over that.

Finally, there was Axel Baumüller, the son of my father's bespectacled colleague and cycling instructor, and a few years older than I. Axel had a pocketknife and taught me how to carve my name into the bark of the big red beech tree at the end of the sanatorium park. Axel's mother once invited me to eat battered and deep-fried elder bush blossoms, which I thought were wonderful. Somehow my parents weren't impressed when I told them. I never had them again, but I can still remember the taste.

It was a class thing. Most of my schoolmates were the children of farmers, and I had little or no contact with them. Because I was a good student, they teased me as a teacher's pet. There was only one whom I sometimes played with—he must have been some sort of outsider himself. His name was Jackl, but commonly called by the unflattering nickname Jackl-Dackl–Hutzifackl. Jackl never came to our house, but I went a few times to his, a large farmhouse in the middle of Hohenschäftlarn.

20 | *School*

I entered public school in Hohenschäftlarn in September 1952. I had new clothes and the traditional big bag of sweets. I had a leather satchel on my back with a little wet sponge hanging outside on a string. This was for wiping clean the slate board I was carrying and on which I would now learn to write. The first three words I wrote were *Otto und Dora* (Otto and Dora). My mother walked me to school that first day. It was a long walk for a six-year-old, about half an hour. We had to go down the hill behind the villa, across the open fields and then up to the school on a narrow pathway with stairs.

After that first day, I had to walk on my own, but my mother would usually see me off at the top of the hill behind the villa and then wait for me there when I came back. She could see me coming across the fields for a good fifteen minutes and often had to admonish me, when I finally arrived, that I shouldn't saunter so much. After a few years I had a bicycle. But since I could not ride it up the pathway steps, and was not allowed to use the main street, I had to leave it at the local bakery at the bottom of the hill and walk the rest of the way.

That bakery was the same one that delivered milk and *Semmeln* to us every morning. It also sold homemade ice cream. At some point, the homemade ice cream was replaced with commercially produced and packaged ice-cream cones. This was progress, like canned peaches instead of fresh ones. Once when I bought one of those ice-cream cones, the wife of the baker gave me a lengthy speech why it was not nearly as good as her homemade ice cream. "Full of potato starch," she explained. Why she bothered to explain this to a seven- or eight-year-old I have no idea.

The school was at the highest point of Hohenschäftlarn. It was clearly visible across the valley with its rounded gable and next to the Catholic church. The school had only two rooms—one for grades one and two, the other for grades three and four. And there were only two teachers, a young dark-haired woman named Hanne Jenac for grades one and two, and an older women for grades three and four whose name was Frau Eggerdinger.

I immediately fell in love with Hanne Jenac, and I was heartbroken when she beat me with the school rod in front of the class, on the insides of my dutifully outstretched hands, three times, not really hard, in grade two, because during class I had got in a fight with my neighbour over who had the better fountain pen. The Bavarian word for this kind of corporal punishment—still allowed back then—was *Tatzn* (literally "paws"). That day, when I went home, my mother was not waiting for me at the top of the hill. She was late getting back from some errands in the village. My grandmother told me so when I arrived at the villa. I was so upset that I immediately ran off to find my mother. I burst into the farmhouse where she still was, chatting with another woman. They both looked at me, and my mother said: What is it with you? How was school? You haven't received a beating today, have you? My red face told the story, and everybody laughed—except me, that is.

Everybody hated the other teacher, Frau Eggerdinger. I dreaded the day I would have to enter grade three. Every morning at the beginning of class, Frau Eggerdinger would check whether we had clean handkerchiefs. There were no disposable tissues back then. My brother and I had a little game we played in bed before falling asleep. We imagined that all the people we knew came walking past our house and that we threw stuff out of the chimney for them: good stuff for the people we liked, bad stuff for the people we did not like. Frau Eggerdinger always got dirty handkerchiefs.

However, I was the best student in her class, so she liked me, which is why I got the reputation as a teacher's pet. We moved away from Ebenhausen halfway through grade three. At the end of my last day in the Hohenschäftlarn school, Frau Eggerdinger took me aside and told me that I did not have to be afraid of going to a new and unknown school even if it *was* in a bigger town. I should hold my head high and make my old school and teacher proud. Then she hugged me. I was so embarrassed, both because of the hug and because I realized only then how nice she really was.

For an overprotected middle-class brat, going to a rural school in 1950s Bavaria was an eye-opener. The curriculum focused very much on peasant life. We learned about the seasons and sang: *Im März en der Bauer die Rösslein einspannt* (In March the farmer puts the horses before the plough). We read a story about a farming family that impressed me to no end. At dinner, the mother comes with a big pot of boiled potatoes, which she empties out on the rough surface of the wooden table—no tablecloth, no bone china, no silverware or crystal, no meat or dessert. In the corner, the old grandmother says: "So long as we have enough of these, and milk, nothing is lacking." I ran home that day asking my parents whether people could really live that way.

21 | *Cars*

The first car I can remember was a tiny red Fiat Topolino station wagon that belonged to the sanatorium. My father first had only a motorbike. Before my brother was born, the three of us—father and mother, with me squeezed between them—would go for the occasional ride to Percha, on Lake Starnberg, about half an hour away. In Neufahrn, a village along the way, there was a shortcut, an old pathway that cars could not take because a wooden post had been planted in the middle of the road. Once, my parents got into an argument and my father circled that post several times before, to my great relief, it was decided to go on after all.

I'm told that at the public beach in Percha, I often played with a little girl named Sylvia, who was the daughter of Vera Brühne and the actor Hans Cossy. Brühne was later convicted of murder in one of Germany's most sensational postwar criminal trials. She spent seventeen years in prison (1962–79) and always maintained her innocence. Probably because Brühne had been such a harmless and pleasant beach companion, my mother always insisted that "she hadn't done it."

After the motorbike came a DKW, a product of the Auto Union company, today better known as Audi. It had a stinky two-stroke engine that required oil to be poured directly into the tank along with the gas. "*Benzin-Benzol Gemisch*," I can still hear my father requesting at the gas station. The DKW did not have electric signal lights. You had to turn a knob on the dashboard; depending on which way you had turned it, a little red arrow would pop up either on the left or right side in between the car's side windows. The manual shift was known as "revolver stick" because it was actually a handle sticking out of the dashboard that you had to hold like a revolver in order to shift gears, by pulling, pushing, and turning it. It was in this DKW that my father fell asleep and drove into the ditch when he returned from Munich after having his wisdom teeth pulled. He was full of drugs and, as a physician, should have known better.

After that came a mustard-coloured and egg-shaped 1948 Ford Taunus, which was so embarrassing to be seen in that I bragged to my friends that it had some secret racing engine built into it. (The Starks, of course, had a Mercedes.) The Ford was followed by a silver Tatra, a Czech contraption that produced amazing amounts of smoke and noise. I was late for school one day because of that car. On one particularly bad winter day, my father said he would drive me. I was in grade two. The Tatra first wouldn't start, of course. When it finally did, we slowly manoeuvred down the hill behind the villa—a hill called Toter Hengst (dead stallion), for some unknown reason. At that time, in the early 1950s, that stretch of road was still cleared by a wooden plough pulled by two horses. As my father tried to drive up the hill leading to the school at the other end of the valley, in Hohenschäftlarn, the Tatra hit an ice patch and spun right into a stone wall.

When I told my teacher these reasons for being late, she asked: "Is that car really so bad?" I was devastated. She was Hanne Jenac, of course, and she had now discovered some other Hüglin imperfection. On the whole, I preferred walking to school on bad winter days, because sometimes the wind was so strong and the snowdrifts were so high that I turned around—or rather, let myself be compelled sideways—to the house of Frau Bauer, the wife of the local building contractor Michi Bauer, who lived along the way. She would give me hot chocolate, listen to my tales, and drive me back home.

The Tatra was the last of the used cars that Spicki had to maintain for us. It was replaced by a brand-new Opel Rekord (a GM car built in Germany), the first of several to follow before my father switched to a series of Fiats. It was a convertible, and in it we made our first trip to Lake Garda in upper Italy. That large lake is surrounded by the Alps at its narrow northern end but then widens into the plain of the Po valley. I will never forget the first scent of southern warmth after we had stopped, on the eastern shore, somewhere between the towns of Riva and Malcesine, and for the first time my father took the car's roof down (and even though our parents made us wear ridiculous nylon caps to protect our tender scalps from the wind blowing in the back of the car).

I fell for Italy and the south, immediately and irrevocably, just like Goethe had when he rhymed: *Kennst Du das Land wo die Zitronen blühen ...* (Do you know the land where lemons blossom ...). The trip lasted only a few days and took us to a grand old hotel (my father stayed only in grand old hotels) in Sirmione at the southern end of the lake. The only other memory I have from that trip is of the gigantic poached salmon trout from the lake that was rolled around on a trolley, feeding the entire dining room. Overfishing was still an unknown concept and reality.

22 | *The Jewish question (I)*

Apparently, I liked car excursions more and at an earlier age than most children. I once drove with my daughter Hannah all the way down the American west coast from Portland, Oregon, to San Diego on the Mexican border, and all she remembered later was a traffic accident in Hollywood. And my son Jacob now is invariably texting on his cellphone during car rides, rarely ever looking out of the window.

But while I enjoyed our family excursions, I was also perfectly happy at home in Ebenhausen. Besides the local thrills already mentioned, there was a movie theatre. It had been opened after the war by a Frau van Laak in the annex of the local inn, the Gasthaus Post. I saw my first movie ever in that theatre: the coronation of Queen Elizabeth II in 1954. The only other movie I remember was *Flicka*, the story of a young boy and his wild horse. While walking back up to the villa afterwards with other kids and a few grown-ups, I remarked repeatedly that the fifty pfennigs for the movie really had been worth it. The 2006 remake most definitely isn't.

I cannot remember which movie we saw on one other occasion much later. Because Dieter Neumann still lived in Ebenhausen, my friends and I still went to see movies in the old theatre during our last high school years in Munich, when some of us already had a driver's licence. It was there on a November night in 1963, coming out of the theatre, that somebody said: "Kennedy has been shot." We thought it was a joke until we saw the newspaper headlines on the way to school the next morning.

Frau van Laak was Jewish. I don't know how many Jews there had been in Ebenhausen before the war and the Holocaust. After the war it seems that Frau van Laak and her son were the only ones. She was always especially nice to me, and I heard some story that my grandfather had helped her out with accommodations somewhere on the sanatorium grounds when she was forced out of her own home. This might have been after her husband, a non-Jewish army officer, perished in the war and could no longer protect her—but I don't know that for sure. The Hüglins were *anständig,* but they did not talk about these things.

As I mentioned before, the Hüglins were not Nazis. What luckily protected them from falling for the abominable mixture of racism and parochial nationalism was not conscientious objection, however. It was the cosmopolitan family background and the arrogance of the better educated. But neither my grandfather nor my father were able to avoid entirely the embrace with the totalitarian powers of evil. By the time the nightmarish war was over, they both had joined the Nazi Party.

I do not know why and how my grandfather acquired that membership. In the case of my father, it happened towards the end of the war. He had come home from the Russian Front on a brief furlough, and because he had participated as a field physician in several battles against the rapidly advancing Russians, he found at home a letter stating that in light of his bravery he was being offered honourable admittance to the party. He did not give it much thought but obviously found it unwise to decline. A few days later he was back in Russia.

Years later, he told us that on his way back to the Russian Front the train had stopped in Warsaw, and there he had seen groups of undernourished people in striped prisoners' clothing being herded onto cattle cars. His first thought had been that these must be convicts of some sort. His second thought had been that their fate would probably be better than his own on the Russian Front. Of course, the Hüglins, like everyone else, were aware of the Nazis' brutal anti-Jewish policies, and possibly even of the deportations. But they had no idea about mass exterminations in concentration camps.

After the war, my father like everyone else had had to fill out the questionnaire that was part of the Americans' de-Nazification program. For being a party member he was classified as a *Mitläufer* (passive collaborator) and fined 5,000 marks. For my grandfather, de-Nazification did not come so easily. He had been the sanatorium's director, and soon after the Nazis had come to power, the sanatorium's brochure included a stamp that read: "Non-Aryans of German citizenship cannot be admitted."

I am certain that this was my grandfather's own deliberate formulation. Had the stamp been provided by the Nazis, it probably would have read: "will not be admitted." The "cannot be admitted" was meant to signal that such refusal was as decreed by the Nazis and was not part of the sanatorium's own policy or philosophy. Nevertheless, my grandfather was denounced as a Nazi. He was also suspended as managing director of the sanatorium by the Americans, and he was placed on trial to decide whether he was guilty of Nazi crimes.

The trial took place in the fall of 1946, more than a year after the war. A lot had happened in the meantime. Right after the war, while my grandfather was still in charge, thirty-seven survivors of the Dachau concentration camp were sent to the sanatorium for recuperation. Most of them were Hungarian Jews. Five of them wrote a letter to my grandfather, dated 27 August 1945, in which they thanked him for having done everything possible to allow them "to forget the cruel times of the past and regain their health." Another letter, dated 2 October 1945, was signed by "Dr. Robert Schneider, Vienna I, Elisabeth Street 8, Dachau KZ (concentration camp) number 138359." In this letter, Dr. Schneider identified himself as the "spokesperson" of the Dachau group and once again thanked both my grandfather and my father for the care they had received.

Apparently it was the American military government that had ordered the group to be placed in the sanatorium's care in the first place, for a period of five weeks, from 19 June to 23 July 1945. After that, the Americans had intended to transfer them to the hospital at Föhrenwald, a camp for displaced persons in nearby Wolfratshausen. The group had then approached my grandfather and asked whether they could stay at the sanatorium for the entire period of their recuperation. My grandfather agreed to this and arranged the required permissions from the American military government for the entire group to stay on for another eleven weeks, "first class and entirely at the expense of the sanatorium," as the letter states.

One can only wonder why these concentration camp survivors bothered to be so grateful for something that my grandfather more or less had to do on American orders in the first place. They probably sensed and were relieved that they were dealing with someone who was *anständig*. But it surely would not have been lost on them that a trial for Nazi crimes against my grandfather was imminent and that a nice letter from a large number of Dachau survivors would be helpful. Judging from the tone of the letters, it seems quite plausible that my grandfather had asked the survivors to write them on his behalf.

The court judgment came down on 1 October 1946. It is worth quoting at some length. I am translating and summarizing from a transcript made by my grandfather's lawyer, a Dr. Rothmüller:

> Dr. [Albert] Hüglin has clearly resisted participating in Nazi politics wherever this was possible without risking the entire loss of his possessions. In particular, he never tried to exercise any [pro-Nazi] political influence upon his employees. Moreover, he did not distinguish between

non-Jewish and Jewish patients. He allowed Jewish patients to come to the Sanatorium at a time when this was extremely dangerous because the Sanatorium was at the same time frequented by high-ranking Nazi officials. The Nazi party membership of both father and son was not based on a free decision and clearly was not motivated by any kind of interest in the party. Therefore, Dr. Hüglin is hereby declared politically innocent.

When I read those letters written by Dr. Schneider and his group, I stumbled across a passage in which they also apologized for the "extra work and the disturbances" caused by the extended sojourn of the group. I then remembered that my mother had told me how these survivors had already begun during their sojourn at the sanatorium to rebuild their lives and businesses, and that they had for this purpose regularly commuted between Ebenhausen and Munich on the local train, sometimes arriving late at night back at the sanatorium, where they were supposed to rest and regain their strength. Stricter regulations at the Föhrenwald camp probably would not have permitted that. That's why they asked my grandfather whether they could remain at the sanatorium.

These activities also produced the first postwar Jewish joke. The train between Ebenhausen and Munich is called the Isartalbahn (Isar Valley train). When it transpired that Dachau survivors were regularly commuting on it, the locals dubbed it *Israeltalbahn*.

23 | Black Forest

My father, Hans Hüglin, was born in Freiburg on 24 July 1915, during the opening phase of the First World War. For the Hüglins, this war probably had few immediate life-changing effects. Life went on as normal, whether at the house of my father's grandparents in Freiburg, at his parents' house in St. Blasien, or in Höchenschwandt where the family had a summer house, on the southern edge of the Schwarzwald (Black Forest) hills and with the entire range of Swiss mountain peaks in full view across the Rhine Valley to the south. There was one change, though: my grandfather was appointed captain of a cavalry unit that had as its objective border defence against foreign infiltration and subversion. The border, however, was the Swiss border between Basle and Constance, a rather harmless assignment. There are lovely photos of my grandfather in uniform admiringly if somewhat awkwardly looking down at his baby son.

I never saw the house in Freiburg, and St. Blasien was abandoned by the Hüglins when they moved to Ebenhausen in 1924. But with our six-year-old son Jacob, Julia and I did a trip to the Schwarzwald in 2000. We visited Königschaffhausen, where we still found some Hüglins (one was the cook in the restaurant where we ate), and we had fabulous *Rehrücken Baden-Baden* (rack of venison, Baden-Baden style) in the best restaurant in Höchensschwandt. It was served in two consecutive portions with a different array of side dishes each time. The excellent old-fashioned waiter also took extra time to consult with our son about his menu choices.

It was exactly the kind of setting my father liked (and had spent most of his money taking his wife and children a million times). When we returned to Munich we told him everything; but at that point, a few years after the death of my mother, he had already begun to lose interest in life. We never found the house in Höchenschwandt. I had been there only once before, as a child. But the view of the Swiss Alps was still there, though it was by now almost overwhelmed by the constant traffic of aircraft descending to Zurich's airport. We stayed overnight in a little apartment. For our son, the main thrill of the entire trip, apart from the restaurant meals (which he enjoys as much as his grandfather did), was that the television set happened to be in *his* bedroom, not ours. Together lying on his bed, we watched some of the swimming competitions at the Sydney Olympic Games.

According to my mother, when my father was a child in St. Blasien, he was woken up each morning by a maid who asked him whether he preferred scrambled eggs or roasted pigeon for breakfast. My father never confirmed this story, though. He *did* confirm that whenever he caught a little cold, he would be wrapped in blankets and driven through the Black Forest in a carriage drawn by two horses (sometimes he said six). And once, when the coughing became more insistent, his grandmother, the piano-playing Jeanne Baud, would take him to the Swiss Alpine resort of Gstaad for a month, so that he could breathe what was then still clean mountain air. She also bought him a goat so that he could have his own goat's milk every day.

As mentioned before, my grandparents moved away from the Black Forest in 1924, when my grandfather bought the sanatorium at Ebenhausen. It was a traumatic move for the Hüglins. My father was nine years old. The Black Forest would always remain the landscape love of his life. The Hüglins thought that the Bavarians were crude compared to the much more refined Alemanic tribes inhabiting that southerly triangle stretching from the Black Forest in Germany to the southern Alsace across the Rhine in France, and to the northernmost cantons of Switzerland: the Thurgau and the Aargau. They also thought that the Bavarian landscape with its pointed mountain peeks was rather vulgar compared to the softly rolling hills of the Black Forest, not to speak of the harsher climate and of Bavarian Catholicism.

Hitler, my father insisted, could have arisen only from the beer halls of Munich, never from the wine taverns of Baden. Whenever my father drank beer—which he did, in great quantities and with much pleasure—he never failed to mention that he did so only because his kidneys needed a thorough rinsing. The Freiburgers, because of their self-professed reservations about official Nazidom, were so sure they would be spared the ordeal of an Allied bombardment of the city that they routinely ignored air-raid alarms. When that bombardment came, on the night of 27 November 1944, most of them were above ground in their houses, and the results were accordingly disastrous.

I have no idea whether the people of Baden really were more reluctant Nazis than other Germans. Freiburg University, after all, was the first one in Germany to officially endorse the Nazis, right at the beginning, in 1933, under the leadership of the new rector, Martin Heidegger. But then again, the great philosopher was not from Baden: he was a Swabian. In German folklore, Swabians are often portrayed as both daring and foolish. Heidegger actually went to Berlin, where he unsuccessfully tried to tell the Nazis how to govern Germany according to his own ideas of fate, folk, and fear. After his return, he met a philosopher colleague in Freiburg's market square who greeted him, in allusion to Plato's ill-fated trip to the dictator Dionysos in Sicily: "Ah, Heidegger, back from Syracuse?"

The Black Forest is in the historical region of Baden. It was still a grand duchy when my father was born, and it continued to be so for a few years more, until the end of the First World War. After the Second World War, Baden was amalgamated with Swabian Württemberg into the *Land* (province) of Baden-Württemberg. The Swabian Stuttgart became the new provincial capital. Not much love was lost between the two parts. My father always told the anecdote of a Latin teacher in Stuttgart who reminded his class of a student who had consistently made the same grammatical mistake in his Latin sentence constructions. "Do you know what happened to him?" the teacher would ask his class. Then came the answer: "He died over there, in Baden." Apart from being daring and foolish, the Swabians also have a reputation as the Scots of Germany, thrifty if not outright miserly. By comparison, the Badeners think of themselves as more open-minded and generous. How often did I hear my father exclaim, at the beginning of a meal with or without friends, the old saying from Baden: "Eat, eat, what we put on the table, we consider to be gone already."

On my father's seventy-fifth birthday, my mother organized a family excursion from Munich to Freiburg. That was in 1990, and I flew back from Canada for the occasion. The trip by car takes the better part of a day, at least if you take it slowly, which we did, for my mother had also organized a nice family picnic on the banks of the Neckar, still on the Swabian side. We then drove through the heart of the Black Forest and into Freiburg, where we stayed in the Gasthaus Traube on the market square right next to the cathedral. Having miraculously escaped the Allied bombardment almost unscathed, that cathedral is one of the gems of German Gothic. Naturally, the entire excursion was organized around food and music. The Traube is known for its exceptional regional cuisine, including the famous *Spätzle* noodles, and through one of my own musical connections in Munich, I had managed to organize a private organ recital in the cathedral. It ended with Charles Widor's thundering Toccata.

There was another family gathering at the Traube three years later, when the urn with my mother's ashes was placed in the Hüglin family grave. I wasn't there: I had flown to Munich earlier, right after she died, to be with my father, brother, and sister, and this time I had to teach. But I phoned the Traube from Canada and spoke to my father, who yelled through the entire dining room that his son from Canada was on the phone and then burst into tears. Also absent from that gathering were my mother's two sisters, who both had the flu and were too ill to attend. The older sister, Gerda, my favourite aunt, later stopped in Freiburg (on a train journey back from Italy), a single red rose in hand, meant for her sister's grave. But she could not find it in the large cemetery. Finally, with a grand gesture, she tossed the rose into a pond lined with willow trees and left, all in pouring rain, grave unseen. She giggled, because she knew her sister would have appreciated the moment.

24 | *From music to medicine*

After the move from Freiburg, my father's life in Ebenhausen continued with the usual ease and comfort. Before he started taking the train to attend high school in Munich, he was educated privately in the neighbouring village of Icking, under the tutelage of a certain Baron von Such-or-Other, whose name has escaped me though it would be mentioned every time we drove through Icking later on. When he was sixteen, my father was allowed to pick up his girlfriend, Marianne, for tea, in his father's red six-cylinder Lancia convertible. He was regularly taken to all the important musical events in Munich, especially the philharmonic concerts conducted by Wilhelm Furtwängler in the old Odeon concert hall (later destroyed by the war) and several premieres of new operas by Richard Strauss.

My father played the piano, and he played it quite well. He had good teachers, not least among them his own grandmother Jeanne Baud. His teacher in Munich was Professor August Schmidt-Lindner, a pianist, musical pedagogue, and scholar of considerable reputation. He also may have studied with the conductor Siegmund von Hausegger, a friend of the family who was president of the music academy in Munich and who had made the first phonographic recording of Bruckner's Ninth Symphony.

My father claimed that had it not been for music, he would have failed to graduate from high school, the Theresiengymnasium in Munich. Apparently he had bombed in the final exam in Greek. But the school administration implored the Greek teacher to let him slip through with a pass in order not to jeopardize the graduation ceremony, where he was scheduled to play Mozart's D-minor Concerto, K. 466, with the school orchestra.

After graduating from the *Gymnasium* in 1935, my father, like all other boys and girls during the Nazi era, had to do six months of *Arbeitsdienst* (work service). In his case it meant that he was dropped at an upper-Bavarian creek near the Benediktbeuern monastery, just about the same time that Carl Orff was composing his *Carmina Burana* based on the medieval peasant songs that had been found at that monastery. In the creek, my father had to cut stone steps into the riverbed. As was pointed out to us many times, one can still see those stone steps from a nearby road bridge.

Then came military service. According to various photos and his own tales, my father enjoyed military service. After cutting those steps in the river, he was in excellent physical shape, and after years of high school it felt good, at least for a while, to be ordered around without having to think at all. I know the feeling, having done military service myself, albeit after the war and under altogether more harmless circumstances.

As with almost all life circumstances, one blissfully remembers only the good moments afterwards. My father's favourite moment had to do with music, of course. The already legendary pianist Elly Ney came to give one of her support-the-troops concerts for the officer corps. She came with some other musicians for an evening of chamber music and needed a page turner. Knowing my father's musical talents, the commanding officer of his unit told him to get up onstage and help out. Fifty years later, when he told this story, he would still marvel at the feeling of being up there, in his recruit's uniform, with the musicians, and in front of all the military brass.

Because of her omnipresence on Germany's concert stages during the Nazi period, because of her unconcealed if totally naive admiration for Hitler, and because she was quite old even then, Elly Ney had been nicknamed *Reichsklaviergrossmutter* (official piano grandmother of the Reich). This was one way of poking fun at the regime that even the Nazis could not suppress. But all this notwithstanding, Elly Ney was one of the twentieth century's important pianists. Some of her recordings still available are vivid testimony to her interpretative as well as her pianistic skills. She lived in Tutzing on the shores of Lake Starnberg, in an apartment attached to a large textile factory. My father had already been introduced to her. During the 1930s, when he was a serious piano student, he was allowed a few times to sit on the steps leading up to her music studio in that apartment and listen to her practising.

He finally entered university in 1937 or 1938. I don't think he ever wanted to be a professional musician. Because of his fabulously steady hands he had the idea of becoming an eye surgeon. But because of the sanatorium, he had to settle for internal medicine and cardiology. He began his medical studies in Munich, and he did fail one of the preliminary exams in chemistry. His chemistry teacher was Nobel laureate Heinrich Wieland. Wieland's daughter Eva was part of a small circle of friends to which my father belonged. There also was the future Nobel laureate Feodor (Fitzi) Lynen, who was Wieland's assistant and had just married Eva, and there was my father's girlfriend Ilse. During the oral exam, Wieland asked a few questions, then told my father he'd have to do it again in the fall, paused, looked at his pocket watch, and added: "Dinner at seven?"

Ilse probably was my father's first serious relationship. It was she who rented a room where she kept my father cramming for the repeat exam (its window in downtown Munich was pointed out to us whenever we drove by, which was often), and it was with Ilse that he eloped to Graz (in southern Austria), where they both would continue their medical studies. There was some story as to why my father and Ilse did not stay together in the end, but I have forgotten. Probably it was simply the war. My father was shipped out to the Russian Front immediately after he had completed his qualifications in 1942; Ilse stayed on and married a rich nobleman from Graz. She became a successful physician and lived in a castle. Decades later, my parents visited them.

While in Graz, my father befriended Karl Fischer, the artistic director and principal conductor of the opera there. Opera would remain one of his principal passions. Fischer remained a lifelong friend. He later became conductor at the opera in Mannheim, and my parents went there from Munich for not a few memorable premieres. The opera in Graz was an important springboard for aspiring young singers at the time, often the first step to the Vienna State Opera or even the Metropolitan Opera in New York.

One of these singers was Ljuba Welitsch, the sensational Bulgarian soprano who was about to take the world by storm. My father had first heard her at the opera in the neighbouring Croatian city of Zagreb and had recommended her to his friend Fischer. After three seasons in Graz, Welitsch would quickly conquer the operatic stages of Dresden, Munich, Vienna, London, and finally New York. Her 1949 performance of Richard Strauss's *Salome* at the Met would drive scalper ticket prices to an unprecedented one hundred dollars. The studio recording of that performance, under the baton of Fritz Reiner, is the stuff of legend.

Strauss had written *Salome* in 1905 based on Oscar Wilde's play. It created a scandal. Premieres in Vienna and London were cancelled or delayed. When Strauss conducted the premiere in Berlin, the German emperor, Wilhelm II—Queen Victoria's grandson and a known prude—summoned him after the performance and told him that this opera would hardly add to the composer's reputation. "I just bought a house in Garmisch from the proceeds so far, Your Majesty," was Strauss's calm reply.

The plot combines biblical material with eroticism and murder. Salome's amorous advances are spurned by the imprisoned prophet Jochanaan (John the Baptist), who refuses to kiss her. Meanwhile her lecherous stepfather Herod begs Salome to perform the Dance of the Seven Veils for him. She can have anything she wants in return, he declares, even if it is half his kingdom. After the dance, lying naked in front of her stepfather, Salome demands Jochanaan's head as her reward. Herod is horrified, but acquiesces and has Jochanaan killed. The severed head is brought to Salome on a platter. Salome kisses Jochanaan's lips and sings, during the opera's climactic moments: "Ich habe Deinen Mund geküsst, Jochanaan. Es war ein bitterer Geschmck auf Deinen Lippen" (I kissed your mouth, Jochanaan. There was a bitter taste on your lips).

When Ljuba Welitsch sang those lines, the mad sensuality in her voice was unmatched, and as my father never tired to point out, one could also hear her Eastern European accent, which added to the immediacy of her delivery. That was a polite way of saying that Welitsch had a certain vulgarity about her. As noted in the text accompanying the CD release of her Columbia recording in 1996, she referred to herself as "a sexy Bulgarian."

I am not sure how well my father got to know Welitsch. His girlfriend Ilse probably had him well under control at the time. But they obviously had become friends. At one point my father arranged an audition for her with some famous visiting conductor he knew, presumably from Munich. During the audition, my father waited nervously in a nearby café. Finally she came storming through the door, yelling across the café: "It all went well even though I just got my period."

One conductor whom my father befriended was Oswald Kabasta, who was appointed conductor of the Munich Philharmonic in 1938. Kabasta was a highly gifted musician who has only recently been rediscovered, from recovered live radio recordings, as a phenomenal interpreter of Bruckner symphonies in particular. But he was also an enthusiastic supporter of the Nazi movement who signed his letters "Heil Hitler." Like so many artists, he was captivated by Hitler's declared ambition to elevate German culture to new heights; but like so many artists again, he chose to remain ignorant about politics and about what was really going on in the Reich. His letters to my father on the Russian Front indicate a warm and genuine friendship. In 1946, when the Allies decreed that he would no longer be permitted to conduct, Kabasta committed suicide at the age of fifty-one. He pushed his grand piano from the balcony of his apartment and jumped after it.

25 | *War*

As a physician, my father automatically was ranked as an army officer, and as such he was entitled to wear a pistol on his belt. He spent the better part of two years in Russia without ever firing a shot. As a physician, he also had to be right behind the battle lines so that he could gather and tend to the wounded. This meant that as long as the German troops still were moving forward, or at least holding their positions, his life as a field physician was relatively safe, because he operated behind the lines and could on occasion even retreat to the hinterland.

As head of a field hospital, my father had a corporal to serve as his batman. He also had a little horse and cart. With the help of these, he sometimes returned to the base to "organize" additional supplies. The brass back there tended to keep scarce supplies for themselves instead of sending them on to where they were needed most. My father and the corporal would simply raid the base canteen and load up the cart. From that time stems my father's lifelong passion for canned peaches. Nobody dared to interfere or complain. On occasion, my father would also put the horse to recreational use. He had a pair of skis and would let the horse pull him across the fields on sunny winter days.

The field hospital my father ran essentially consisted of two tents. One was the surgery, where he learned quickly that under the circumstances, the best method for saving lives was a procedure he had never performed in medical school: amputation. The other tent was a makeshift sauna where soldiers were deloused. I read a very similar account of this by another field physician, the writer and philosopher Peter Bamm, who among other things wrote a wonderful biography of Alexander the Great. It seems that all field hospitals were standard issue and that my father's therefore did not differ much from any other.

There was another medical activity for which he was unprepared. As the Germans advanced, they encountered towns and villages that were inhabited only by women and children. Just as (increasingly so) in Germany, all the men had been conscripted into the army. As a consequence, there was no longer any kind of medical support. More than once, then, my father helped Russian women who were giving birth. These women were grateful and gave him little gifts. One of these, a small religious icon made of brass, now graces a display case in my Canadian study.

My father became friends with the corporal, a wine grower from the Moselle who, like all seasoned corporals, held his protecting arm over his greenhorn officer. He, too, survived the war. My parents later visited him and his family at the Moselle, and there was a return visit by them to Munich. A big, jovial man with a great sense of humour, this wine-grower-turned-corporal saved my father's life and sanity in more than one sense.

Life at the front changed drastically for my father when the Soviets launched their great counteroffensive and the Germans were driven back across the Russian and Ukrainian steppes. My father still had to position himself just behind the lines, which now meant that he often did not know whether the tanks rolling over his trench were German or Russian. More than once, his makeshift field hospital was overrun by the Russians, and the first thing the Russians always did was look for the German physician. One time, my father was being led away at gunpoint behind the Russian lines when a sudden German counterattack saved him at the last moment. Another time, it was the rifle of his trusty corporal that saved him from a forced change of sides.

Then there were those cold winter nights. During the retreat, there was no time for a sauna, of course. One morning, he saw his little horse standing there, frozen solid. When my father touched it, it fell over, stiff as a wooden toy. More lives were lost to freezing than to fighting during those nights of minus-forty degrees Celsius and worse. For the rest of his life, my father insisted that his impaired kidney function had to do with the freezing cold he had endured in Russia. Hence the need to drink beer.

His involvement in Hitler's war ended abruptly when he was struck by grenade shrapnel at Kowel on the Ukrainian–Polish border. The Soviets had besieged the Germans there for much of March and April 1944. The encirclement was eventually broken by German tank reinforcements, but very few inside the pocket survived the ordeal. Even though he was seriously wounded—or rather, *because* he was—my father was among the lucky ones. One of his superior officers said, in effect: "Our doctor has already survived three Russian infantry attacks—he deserves to survive this one." (Indeed, my father by then had been awarded some sort of medal for bravery, which in his case simply meant doing what he was supposed to do as a field physician.) He was put on one of the last planes leaving the encircled pocket—one of the legendary Fieseler Fi 156 Storch single-engine ambulance planes—and flown out of the inferno.

He ended up in an army hospital at Brest-Litovsk, where his condition worsened—he was now critically ill with pleurisy. Delirious with high fever, he persuaded someone to put him on a homeward-bound train. He spent almost a week crouched over in various cattle cars, and he could never remember how exactly he got home. But somehow he did, and his father's professorial physicians, at the sanatorium and elsewhere, were able to bring him back to life and to have him assessed—even after his health was restored almost to normal—as no longer fit for combat.

Instead, he was sent to join a group of other physicians who had been retired from frontline duty on similar grounds, in a small village on the Rhine. The task of this group, at the so-called Heeresentlassungsstelle (army decommission office), was to make exactly these kinds of assessments: whether the soldiers appearing before them after recovering from their wounds were fit enough to return to the front. In performance of this task, these doctors occupied the main dining room of a small inn. Their shared subversive goal was to declare as many soldiers as possible unfit for combat, but they had to do so without arousing suspicions higher up. The name of the inn was Der Krug (The Jug), which served local wine with half-decent food. To my father, joining this group was like returning to civilization, if not paradise.

The only thing lacking in paradise was a piano. Up the cobbled street, there was a large house—a baroque palace, almost—trimmed with the red sandstone still so common in the area. *They* must have a piano, my father thought, so one day during the summer (or fall) of 1944, he walked up the three shallow sandstone steps and rang the bell at 33 Hauptstrasse, Hattenheim on the Rhine. The name on the brass plate on the massive wooden door was Wachendorff.

The woman who opened the door was my other grandmother. She stared at the thin, hollow-eyed soldier in his worn uniform, my father, whom she would later call "the little doctor," and thought he would likely ruin the piano with some rough banging on the keys. But she let him in, and when he started playing—a simple piece by Johann Sebastian Bach—she said to him: "Sie sind ja ein Mensch!" (You are a human being after all).

PART TWO

The Wachendorffs

26 | *A sombre beginning*

There was neither caviar nor music at the wedding of my other (maternal) grandparents. Money was not the issue. The wedding took place on 19 October 1918 in the northern German university town of Rostock. The groom, my grandfather, Alfred (Fred) Wachendorff, was still recovering from the loss of a leg during the opening days of the First World War. Indeed, the wedding had had to be postponed for a number of days due to another fever attack arising from the sepsis that was raging through his body at a time when penicillin and antibiotics were both still unknown. Only his parents and two sisters had made the trip from the family home in Wiesbaden. The bride, my grandmother, Helene (Lene) Martius, had already lost two brothers during that terrible war. A third brother, Heinrich, the oldest and her favourite, was not in attendance because he was serving as a field surgeon somewhere at the edge of the collapsing empire. There were sombre speeches about happiness and a better future. No official photos were taken. After a few honeymoon days in the Bavarian Alps, the couple settled into their large new house in Hattenheim on the Rhine.

27 | *A macabre anniversary*

In the late 1960s, I had to do military service in Germany, and for the last six months out of two mind-numbing years of boredom (lucky, though: no war!), I was stationed in Mainz, the old episcopal city with the huge cathedral, also on the Rhine and only half an hour upstream from my grandparents' place in Hattenheim. I got my own room there and spent

The "unofficial" wedding photo: my grandparents Alfred and Helene Wachendorff in 1918.

most weekends with them. During one of those weekends, my grandfather mentioned that it had been fifty years since he had had to learn to walk with an artificial limb. Jokingly, I suggested that we should celebrate the anniversary by having black salsify and dark beer for dinner. I did not manage to procure the black salsify, a common root vegetable at the time, delicious if properly peeled and cooked in a white sauce, but nearly inedible if poorly peeled so that hard wooden fibres remain. But I did get a few bottles of dark beer, we raised our glasses, and I offered a little toast in celebration of "fifty years on one leg." My grandfather was half flattered and half embarrassed.

When it happened, on 17 December 1914, somewhere in Poland, nobody would have bet even a penny on such an anniversary ever taking place. Grenade shrapnel shattered his left foot. His batman—my grandfather was a cavalry officer—dragged him back to the nearest field hospital in a wooden handcart. It took them three days to get there, resting in unheated churches along the way. By the time they reached the hospital, sepsis had set in, and the leg had to be amputated below the knee. The general blood poisoning caused abscesses on his body, weakened his heart, and kept him in a dangerously high fever. A large abscess on his side probably was cut open too late and caused permanent stiffness of the hip, a mobility handicap that would prove worse than the lost leg itself.

The parents received the news on Christmas Day 1914. A telegram of 18 January 1915 suggested that the situation was hopeless. That same evening, my great-grandfather Hermann Wachendorff boarded the night train to Berlin en route to Poland in hope of still seeing his son alive. He was accompanied by his daughter Erna. The idea was that Erna would care for her brother. Like most young women of society during the war, she had been trained as a nurse.

They made it, travelling the last eight hours in the back of a military vehicle. Fred was alive. While great-grandfather Hermann eventually had to return to his business in Wiesbaden, Erna remained with Fred until it was possible to transport him to a regular hospital in Berlin two months later. There he was reunited with his mother, Hedwig Wachendorff, my great-grandmother. She took over his care from Erna, who was on the brink of exhaustion. His body was still ravaged by periodical bouts of fever, but things were generally looking up now. There even was time to go to the opera. Hedwig, an enthusiastic Wagnerian, managed to hear two of the master's works conducted by none other than Richard Strauss: *Parsifal* and *Die Meistersinger*.

Two months later again, in May 1915, Fred finally made it back to Wiesbaden. He had still to take quarters in a local hospital, but he was beginning to move around in a wheelchair. Apparently a steady stream of young ladies of Wiesbaden society offered to look after him. But the stump of his leg would not heal, and a year later, in June 1916, another operation became necessary, during which the bone was shortened by another centimetre. Finally, everything healed and it became possible for him to wear an artificial limb. The family decided to take a summer vacation, on the shores of the Baltic Sea.

28 | *Back stairs*

Rooms with balconies overlooking the beach were taken in the Hotel Kaiserhof, in Binz, on the Baltic island of Rügen. Grandfather Alfred could no longer run around with the other young people at the spa, but he could swim. Before his wounding, he had been quite the athlete, active in mountain climbing, rowing, and all kinds of racquet sports. Now swimming became his only remaining sporting passion. To reach the water, he did what I saw him doing as a little boy during summer vacations on upper-Bavarian lakes: he unstrapped his artificial leg, rapidly hopped all along the pier on his one good leg, and then, without slowing down, dived headfirst into the water.

It was on that Baltic beach that the Wachendorffs met the Martius family. Thriftier than the Wachendorffs, they had rented a small summer house nearby. Their hometown of Rostock was only a few hours away. It seems that the two mothers befriended each other first: Martha Martius, who had already lost two sons to the war, and Hedwig Wachendorff, who had miraculously kept hers. The Martiuses had come with two children: thirty-one-year-old gynecologist Heinrich, on leave from duty as a front-line field surgeon, and Lene, their youngest daughter. According to a diary entry, her future mother-in-law thought she was seventeen. Actually she was turning nineteen that year. In the variety of photos taken that summer, she invariably looks more like fifteen. She was very pretty and very blond. Also training as a nurse, she befriended Erna, who had come along with the Wachendorff parents and her invalid brother. When the families went for excursions along the coast, or walks in the endless oak forests that began behind the beach, Erna usually stayed back with poor Alfred, and Lene opted to stay with Erna. Or so the parents thought. At the end of August, they all said their goodbyes to one another and departed to their respective hometowns.

The year 1917 came and went. The war raged on. Great-grandmother Hedwig wrote in her diary: "Still no peace bells, on the contrary. Irresponsibly, the beleaguered peoples of Europe beat up on one another more mercilessly than ever before." She also noted that there was no butter any more, that the potatoes were for the most part rotten, and that, even though hardly known previously, beets had become the main source of nutrition: "They taste absolutely disgusting." But life went on. The highlight of the year was Erna's wedding to Theo Hengstenberg, a navy captain and commander of a torpedo boat in the North Sea.

There was a second summer visit to the Baltic Sea. When the train pulled up in Greifswald, one of the main stops along the way, Lene Martius suddenly appeared on the platform. She was at the time completing her nursing degree in Greifswald, and she was meeting up with her parents, who were coming from Rostock. It was not a coincidence. Fred had known all along that the Martius family would be spending the summer in Binz again, and it was he who had talked his parents into going again as well. His mother Hedwig remained clueless. Her diary entry from that summer reads: "It was touching how the little Martius girl looked after Alfred. She is used to nursing after all. I did not sense any danger, as everywhere in Wiesbaden, where all kinds of pretend-nurses beleaguered him and I trembled."

In February 1918, Alfred travelled to a friend's wedding in Brandenburg and then on to Berlin, ostensibly for further consultations with the surgeon who had treated him four years earlier. After a few days, the surprised parents back in Wiesbaden received a long letter from Greifswald in which their son announced his engagement to Lene Martius. "Strangely, I had no idea," mother Hedwig wrote in her diary.

Before the sombre October wedding later that year, Lene came to Wiesbaden for a few weeks, to become more thoroughly acquainted with the family of her future in-laws. A telegram from Rostock announced that she would be arriving on the second Thursday in March. This was most inconvenient, because on Thursdays, Hedwig held her musical afternoons, which consisted mainly of playing Wagner opera transcriptions for four-hand piano (sometimes also eight-hand piano). Hedwig had no intention of cancelling her main weekly entertainment just because her son's bride was showing up. So a telegram was dispatched to Rostock asking that Lene arrive a day later. Unperturbed, father Martius cabled back that the ticket had been bought and that Lene would arrive in Wiesbaden on Thursday as scheduled.

And so it happened: Alfred went to the railway station all by himself to pick up Lene. And while the rest of the family was safely locked in the salon listening to the weekly piano thunder, Alfred quietly manoeuvred his bride up to his room by the back stairs, and there, way up in the turret, they had a precious and unsupervised afternoon to themselves. As Gerda tells it, their eyes got shiny whenever they mentioned that afternoon later on.

29 | *The photographer*

In at least one way, my grandfather Alfred Wachendorff in Hattenheim was a repetition of my other grandfather Albert Hüglin in Ebenhausen: he too had been forced by his father to run a family business for which he had little interest and limited talent. After the war destroyed his athletic career, his lifelong passions became gardening and photography. By the end of his life, he had accumulated thousands of slides, mostly of his own gardens and of Tuscany, his favourite photographic destination. I have inherited from him my own passion and (limited) talent for photography (and for Tuscany). The gardening part I gladly left to Julia.

I often think of him, and of how difficult it must have been for an increasingly heavy man with a serious mobility handicap, a wooden leg and a stiff hip, to take those thousands of photos. There were no zoom lenses at the time, and there was no digital editing. His shots had to be perfect the first time around. He had to physically move himself to the right spot for the right angle, he had to frame the picture using only his camera, and the lighting had to be perfect as well. He could not click away at dozens of pictures, hoping that at least one would turn out the way he hoped. And then he had to turn his images into slides. A lasting image I have is of him is sitting at his desk at home and framing those slides, one at a time, and ordering them into wooden cases from which he would assemble various slide shows. As children, well before he had a television set (and had the slides made by a photo lab), we loved his slide shows.

He drove his family mad because getting one picture right often took close to half an hour. Everyone else had to assist him: carrying his gear, passing it to him, smiling at the camera when he decided in the middle of a shot to take one of his innumerable family photos instead, and otherwise standing around idly. During my student years, when I had lots of free time on my hands, I sometimes assisted him. I drove him in his car, at home in the grandparents' beloved Rheingau; in Bavaria, when they visited us; and on occasion even in upper Italy, where I would meet them during their regular vacations on the shores of Lake Garda. On one occasion I shlepped his tripod through an upper-Bavarian baroque church for nearly two hours as the setting sun cast its evening rays through the stained-glass windows, bathing altars, balconies, and golden cherubs in ever-changing flashes of light.

The grandparents took their first extended trip to Italy in 1935. Their oldest daughter, Gerda (my favourite aunt), was not quite sixteen then. On one of the first evenings of their trip, still somewhere in Germany, they phoned Gerda to inquire how things were going with the parents away for the first time (the children had not been left alone, of course—there always was a cook and housekeeper). Gerda reported that she was anxious about her parents' absence and could not sleep at night. She was told to go to her father's bedside table and take one of his small white sleeping pills before going to bed in the evening. Gerda slept wonderfully for the remainder of her parents' absence, even though the pills she had been told to take were garlic pills.

My grandparents regularly travelled to Italy all the way into their eighties. On the way south, they usually stopped for a few days to visit us in Bavaria. They both drove. My grandmother even had her own car, an Adler convertible in which she drove us around, long hair flying. My grandfather's car was always the latest Mercedes-Benz. Before the age of automatic transmissions, it had to be fitted with a manual gas pedal attached to the steering wheel so that he could use his good (right) leg for the clutch and brake. Until the 1950s, the front doors of Mercedes cars opened towards the front, which allowed my grandfather to manoeuvre his body backward into the driver's seat. After that, safety regulations required that all car doors open towards the rear, and his had to be rebuilt (which required special permission) so that it would continue to open towards the front. Still later, when I drove him, Mercedes cars had become so large that he could manage to get into the right-hand seat even though the door there had not been changed.

My grandmother had stopped driving by then, and when my grandfather became too old to drive long distances himself, they had themselves driven to wherever their destination was by the factory chauffeur, Herr Pörner, whom they then sent back home by train, and whom they also summoned again at the end of their vacation to drive them home. This way they remained mobile into their seventies and even eighties. By the end of their lives, they had explored almost all of upper Italy, the lakes, Venice, the Riviera, Tuscany, and Umbria, many times over. Somehow, however, they never continued on to Rome. Since by then Rome had become one of my favourite cities, I tried to talk my grandfather into one last photographic excursion to the Eternal City.

I told him that he could fly, that I would pick him up at the airport in his own car, and that I would carry his equipment for as long as he wanted or needed. But by then he had gotten too old and did not dare take me up on this last offer of a photo safari. So he never saw Rome. His wife, my grandmother, did. Her brother Heinrich took her along to a medical congress once, in the early sixties. Heinrich was at that time the president of the German Gynecology Association. Their host in Rome was the president of the Italian Gynecology Association. Lene and Heinrich stayed in the Italian colleague's Roman palace and were given a marvellous tour of the sights and restaurants. My grandmother loved Rome, but what impressed her most was that Heinrich, who spoke no Italian, and his Italian counterpart, who spoke no German, conversed fluently with one another—in Latin!

30 | *The factory director*

The business my grandfather had been compelled to take over was Rudolph Koepp & Co., a small chemical factory in Oestrich, another town directly on the Rhine, downstream next to Hattenheim. By car, it was only half an hour from Oestrich to Wiesbaden, where the Wachendorffs resided on fashionable Gustav-Freytag Street, in a *belle époque* villa full of nooks and crannies, including the aforementioned turret where my grandparents had what probably was their first unsupervised encounter as bride and groom.

One of my great-grandfather Hermann Wachendorff's brothers had married the daughter of the factory's founder, Rudolf Koepp. When Koepp was elected to the Reichstag, my great-grandfather took over the company's directorship. Koepp became the largest European producer of oxalic and formic acids, both used for all kinds of purposes at the time, from industrial tanning and bleaching to food conservation.

Many years later, when I was living in Canada, I was reminded of this curious combination of purposes when I was told by one of my Monday-night doubles tennis partners, a chemical engineer, that he had just lost his job now that the last of the tanneries in Kitchener, Ontario, had closed. He had already found a new post, with Schneider Foods in the same city, and his job essentially would be the same it had been in the tannery.

On 12 August 1918, two months before his wedding, my grandfather Alfred joined the company, beginning his career there under his father's critical stare. It was also his father who, driving through Hattenheim on his daily trips from the villa in Wiesbaden to the factory in Oestrich, had found the house that he bought and gave to his son and daughter-in-law as a wedding present. Great-grandfather Hermann did not relinquish the directorship of the company until he died in 1940, almost ninety years of age. Only then did my grandfather, nearly fifty years of age himself, become the undisputed head of the Wachendorff family and the director of the factory.

Five years later, in 1945, the factory was occupied by American soldiers and closed. A chemical factory is full of equipment made of glass. Most of it had already been destroyed by an aerial mine the Americans had dropped (in all likelihood accidentally) during the last days of the war. The occupying American soldiers joyfully smashed the rest. This turned out to be a great piece of luck. As the Second World War seamlessly turned into the Cold War confrontation between Americans and Soviets, the Americans made the reindustrialization of West Germany a priority. My grandfather's factory started operating again in 1946. With the help of American money, it was refitted with the latest equipment and technology.

What irony. Here were the Germans, who had brought unspeakable horrors to the peoples of Europe and who most deservedly had lost the war in the end. But because of the Cold War, their economy was being rebuilt rapidly, aided by the American victors, who rather quickly allowed most of the convicted and imprisoned war criminals among the entrepreneurial elite to assume their former positions at the helm of West Germany's large corporations. Within a decade of defeat and humiliation, West Germany once again had become Europe's industrial and economic powerhouse.

And then there were the Brits, whose cities had been attacked by Hitler's Luftwaffe and the infamous V-2 missiles; who had fought bravely; and who had been on the winning side. But because nobody had bombed their industries in a timely fashion, they found themselves stuck with an aging and outmoded industrial infrastructure. While Britain turned into Europe's economic basketcase, the Germans soared to renewed European economic glory. What Hitler had not accomplished with his stormtroopers, one disgruntled British observer commented later, the Germans were now accomplishing with their Deutschmarks.

My grandfather Alfred was not a war criminal. He had been born in London, where his parents were staying on an extended business trip at the time. When the First World War broke out and he enlisted for combat duty, the Brits condemned him to death *in absentia* because according to their rules he was one of them and therefore guilty of treason. Consequently, he could serve only on the Eastern Front so that he would not fall into British hands and be executed. In the east, of course, grenade shrapnel ended his military career after a few months.

He had marched into that war "happily whistling," as his mother sadly noted in her diary. He still whistled in his old age. One day during the 1960s, at the end of a weekend, when I said my goodbyes to my grandparents to return to my military duties, I was in my grandmother's bedroom when we heard my grandfather whistling as he got up in his adjacent bedroom. "Listen to that," my grandmother exclaimed with indignation, "he does that every morning as if he didn't know that his life will not last much longer." She was very much afraid of dying. He never thought about it.

In 1919 my grandfather resented the defeat and the stipulations of the Versailles Treaty, like most Germans. As a nationalistic and conservative businessman, he might have harboured admiration for Hitler and the Nazis. But he couldn't become an active Nazi, at least not without jeopardizing the lives of his wife and children—because this wife of his, the beautiful blond Lene, turned out to be Jewish. He protected his family by carefully abstaining from joining all kinds of Nazi associations (business associations, veterans' associations, and the like), for doing so could have forced him to prove the Aryan purity of his family. His excuse was that he was a handicapped war veteran and therefore could not attend gatherings and meetings. He kept his profile low and his family safe. In the terminology of my other grandfather, he was decent (*anständig*).

So in 1946, his career as *Fabrikdirektor* (factory director) finally took off. Over two decades the company regained the glory it had first achieved under great-grandfather Hermann. I knew this first-hand because I collected stamps as a child. The ones I got from my grandfather came from more than fifty different countries and colonies. They were my first great lesson in colonial history and world geography. I remember as particularly beautiful the stamps from Iran, the British colony of Aden, Peru, Bolivia, and Tanganyika (then still a British protectorate of what had been German East Africa). The factory had its own loading crane directly on the Rhine, and after being loaded, the barges would sail to Rotterdam, where their cargo would be transferred to oceangoing vessels and shipped all over the world.

The company's glory years did not last forever. During the 1960s, the chemical industry underwent a tremendous process of global amalgamation, and only the largest corporations stood a chance to survive. By then, my grandfather had already been replaced by his son Rolf in the leadership of the company. Rolf tried to diversify, starting the production of synthetic foam (for years we all slept on Koepp foam mattresses). But it only prolonged the agony. Because my grandfather still thought of the firm as a family enterprise, he sold the company shares too late and at a fraction of the price a more prudent sale some years earlier would have achieved. At least implicitly, my grandfather blamed his son, intoning the usual line: my father ran the company sucessfully, I ran the company sucessfully, and under my son it was run into the ground. Nothing could be further from the truth. My uncle Rolf did the best he could under the circumstances. Almost at retirement age himself, he then started all over again, founding a successful electronics company together with his sons.

When my grandfather retired, in 1956, a street in Oestrich was named after him. Of course we all showed up for the occasion. He was also asked whether he would like a bust of himself put up in a public park by the river. The park consisted mainly of a mini-golf course. We all giggled at the thought of him in the middle of it all, as a bust. Needless to say, he politely declined. He was embarrassed again. He was also embarrassed when he developed pains from what turned out to be prostate cancer, so he did not tell anybody until it was too late to operate. From a nearby hospital, in Rüdesheim, when he knew his end was approaching, he called his wife and asked her to bring a bottle of *Sekt*, the German variety of champagne. She did, and they toasted each other one last time.

A few days later, in 1978, in his eighty-seventh year, he died peacefully. I was living in Italy at the time and could talk to my grandmother only from a public phone at the railway station in Florence. When she followed him two years later, in 1980, I was away again, on a lecture tour through the United States. Cousin Chris called me from Portland. I was in Berkeley. My daughter Hannah was born a few months later that year.

31 | *The gardener*

If there was anything my grandfather was more passionate about than photography, it was gardening (needless to say, there were as many photos of flowers as of his youngest daughter Ursula). He had three gardens, two in front of the house in Hattenheim and one adjacent to the factory in Oestrich. The Hattenheim gardens were connected by a wooden bridge over a narrow cobbled street. In the upper garden, children were allowed to play. In the lower garden, they were admitted only in the company of grown-ups. We were allowed, though, to sit on the bench at the top of the bridge and count the cars going by on the highway that had been built during the 1930s between the lower garden and the river. During the 1950s, sometimes our count had not gone beyond twenty by the time we were called for dinner. Today, there is a steady stream of cars, mostly commuters to the neighbouring cities of Wiesbaden and Mainz. The traffic and its noise never stop entirely, even during the night.

The upper garden still was an impressive concoction of lawns, flowerbeds, shrubbery, and a large tiled terrace in front of the house. It centred on a huge tree, a sophora (*Sophora japonica*). There also was a goldfish pond. Grandchildren were paid fifty pfennigs for every dandelion or other weed they found growing on the lawn. Over the course of a summer vacation, one could perhaps find three or four. From the terrace, one could see the ships go by on the Rhine. The sophora had to be felled later, and my grandmother had a piece of furniture made from its wood for each of her children. My mother got a little two-shelf cabinet, which we used to store sheet music.

The lower garden was one of the most beautiful in southern Germany and acknowledged as such in various articles and photographs that appeared about it in garden magazines over the years. People spontaneously (sometimes dangerously) stopped their cars on the highway in order to take pictures. There was a huge rose garden and an entire field of carefully arranged beds of irises, some cultivars of which my grandfather had developed himself. There were several more goldfish ponds.

Pathways through old-growth trees were lined with seasonally changing flowerbeds. In the middle of it all stood a gigantic copper beech. At one end was a small stand of fur trees. At the other end was a cherry tree carrying a huge load of the sweetest fruit every year. Against the back wall, at the warmest spot, my grandfather had successfully planted a fig tree, which on occasion even bore fruit—a handful of figs that only he was allowed to pick and eat. The rest of us had to watch in admiration.

The third garden surrounded the beautiful baroque building that served as the company's administrative headquarters in Oestrich. That garden was much more than just a garden, though. It contained an entire vineyard that supplied the family with delicious bottles of Rheingau Riesling. It also produced all the vegetables the family needed over the course of the year, and the fruit trees and berry bushes were so plentiful that according to the careful labels my grandmother attached to glasses and jars, the jams and preserves we ate were often several years behind. My grandmother would come with a new jar from the pantry, say, in the summer of 1956, and announce: "We just finished 1955."

My grandfather came home for lunch every day. Whenever I was visiting as a young boy, my duty was to open the garage doors leading out to the village street a few minutes before one o'clock. From the sidewalk I then watched the Mercedes swing into the garage with my grandfather honking the horn at me. My grandmother, the cook, and whoever else was on hand would then open the car's trunk, where baskets of fruit and vegetables had been placed by Oestrich's gardeners.

One of my favourite pastimes during those summer vacations in Hattenheim was to walk to Oestrich, about half an hour by the old towpath along the Rhine. Before meeting my grandfather at his office—perhaps picking up some new stamps and then riding back to Hattenheim with him in the Mercedes—I would always make sure I had time to pay a visit to the garden, where I would stuff myself with all kinds of fruit. It was like a paradise garden. You could sit on the grass in one particular spot and with your arms, without ever moving, you could reach peaches, raspberries, gooseberries, and whatever else you wanted to try.

Except for the upper garden in Hattenheim, which has been maintained in a simplified form by Gerda, none of this exists anymore. The maintenance of the gardens was possible only because of the full-time employment of several gardeners on the company payroll. This regime had been established under great-grandfather Hermann, who was particularly fond of a certain type of apple grown in Oestrich. It was called Calvill and seems to be extinct now. It had legendary status in the Wachendorff family because once a year, when the apples were still small, great-grandmother Hedwig would come from Wiesbaden and tie every single apple into a little parchment pouch so that the bugs could not get to them. And whoever later harvested the apples had to wear gloves to avoid leaving blemishes.

As long as Koepp & Co. was a family business, there was nothing wrong, of course, with diverting some of its resources to gardening and agriculture. But when Koepp & Co. was turned into Koepp AG, and hence into a publicly traded company, the private use of company resources was no longer appropriate. I don't think this ever crossed my grandfather's mind, but when his son took over the company, so did a new spirit of corporate correctness. Much of the garden in Oestrich, including the entire vineyard, gave way to a new administration building (much uglier than the old one, the rest of the family griped). Gustav, the trusty old gardener, was still allowed to tend the gardens in Hattenheim, for a clearly defined number of hours per week, but my grandfather now had to pay him out of his own pocket. And there no longer were heaping baskets of fruit and vegetables.

Most regrettably, at least for some, there was no more wine. The vineyard was gone. For some years, there still were old bottles in the wine cellar, behind the garage in Hattenheim, and whenever various family members visited, they would take off with a case or two. When I was doing my military service in Mainz, during the spring and summer of 1967, I descended into the old vault to grab a few bottles now and then. I did not drink them myself but used them to bribe my corporals. Many of them were sons of local wine growers and got a tremendous kick out of this wine, which by then was about ten years old and overmature. To them it was like tasting local history.

The military base in Mainz was a regional supply centre, stocking and dispensing everything from truck tires to ammunition. As an officer candidate, I was in charge of supervising a number of enlisted men doing all the real work. With the wine, I bribed them to do this work on their own, without me looking over their shoulder. Instead I went playing tennis. My grandfather would have been horrified had he known that the success of his grandson's short and compulsory military career depended on his wine rather than virtue and bravery.

The full extent of expense, diligence, and attention these gardens commanded became obvious to us—rather drastically so—only after my grandfather died. Since his retirement, he had spent hours in those two Hattenheim gardens every day. And since nobody was now paying for

Gustav any more either, the lower garden, this horticultural gem of the Rheingau, turned into an impenetrable mess of brambles within a few years: no way to get to the cherry tree at the far end ever again; the ponds so overgrown that it was impossible even to locate them any longer; no traces of roses or irises anywhere to be found; even the huge copper beech succumbed to parasitic overgrowth and turned into a mournful skeleton of bleached and broken branches. Rolf's youngest son Robert and his family, who now live on the second floor of the old house, cannot remember the lower garden otherwise. A few years ago, I took out some of our grandfather's old slides and scanned them into my laptop. The junior Wachendorffs were speechless when they saw what that jungle down there had once looked like. Gerda does not mind the wild growth so much because it shields her from the ever louder traffic noise. She returned to the old house after twenty-five years in America and now occupies the ground floor.

32 | *Tyrant and charmer*

It was not all roses with my grandfather Alfred. He was a controlling tyrant. It was not exactly that he *asked* to have the garage doors opened when he came home for lunch. They *had* to be open, and on time, and when he honked, everybody had to sprint to the garage to receive the orders of the day. Sitting at the head of the table at lunch, facing the big window overlooking the Rhine, he would comment on the ships going by. The children or grandchildren, sitting at the other end of the table and with their backs to the window, were forbidden to turn around. After lunch, he would retreat to his big armchair in the middle of the room and read. Sometimes he would also play some paramilitary game with us, alternately commanding us to "lie down ... get up ...," whereupon we had to throw ourselves to the floor and then jump up just as quickly again. Being somewhat naive, perhaps, I actually liked that game. My brother Michael hated it. And because my grandfather knew that Michael hated it, he would constantly get at him about it. According to my mother, Michael developed a tendency to fall ill whenever we visited Hattenheim.

My cousin Chris (Christian) also did not much like it in Hattenheim. He lived there for the first nine or ten years of his life, with his mother Gerda, after her divorce from the father he never really knew. My grandfather thus became an overbearing substitute father for him. Again according to my mother, because of circumstances relating to the war and the divorce, the dinner table where the family had their meals was actually part of Gerda's dowry. So when Christian knocked over his drink one evening, my grandfather said to him: "Doesn't matter, since it isn't our table." Little Christian was so upset that from then on, and for a long time, he knocked over his glass almost every other dinner, always in fearful anticipation of his grandfather's smirk and that dreadful remark reminding him that it was his mother's table he was spilling his drink on. Chris must have sighed a big sigh of relief when he emigrated to Portland.

Chris now seems to look back to his Hattenheim years more fondly (and so does my brother Michael). Either they have forgotten (we all tend to block from memory our less pleasant experiences), or I got wrong what my mother told me. After all, I am writing down now what I heard (for the first and the last time) when I was maybe ten years old. But the fact that I still remember it so vividly is at least testimony to the fact that it very much must have preoccupied my mind at the time.

Our grandfather was a victim of his own education. While his mother pampered him as the male heir to the family throne, he suffered under his father's impersonal harshness. Again according to my mother, he was never allowed to feel he was living up to his father's expectations. Strangely but typically, he would later do to his own son what his father had done to him. After being wounded, of course, he quickly got used to everybody around him catering to his every whim, and that included his bride and future wife, who met him when she was very young and impressionable. My mother told me that he threw incredible tantrums whenever anybody disagreed with him, banging his head against the wall until he got his way. As so often when I was little and quite impressionable myself, I was not quite sure whether this was meant figuratively or whether it was a literal description of his antics.

Yet our grandfather did have a sense of humour, which on occasion he even directed at himself. A legendary story that we heard (and wanted to hear) many times over was the one about the soft-boiled egg. My grandfather loved soft-boiled eggs, and they were a supper staple. There was in the family even a Swiftian debate about how to open soft-boiled eggs. At issue was not from which side of the egg—round or pointed—this had to be done, but rather with what kind of utensil: some in the family (I think including my grandfather) used a small knife, others insisted on an egg spoon. Meanwhile, the children (whichever children were at the table, we all did it) had developed the routine of putting the empty shell upside down in the egg cup and declaring that they did not want to eat it. Grandfather would then grab the egg, pretend to be angry, exclaim, "What, are you not eating your egg again?" and hit down on the egg with his fist. When it turned out that the egg was empty, everybody laughed. As the story went, little Rolf once had not eaten his egg for real, and when his father slammed his fist down on it, the yolk splashed all over his clothes. Grandfather liked telling this story, but he made sure not to let it happen again no matter how many times we tried to foist a full egg on him.

The egg incident probably was symptomatic for Rolf, who had to steer a cautious course between proving he was a real boy ("little rascal," grandfather would say admiringly when he heard of a good prank) and avoiding the ire of a father for whom the parental relationship was always a power game. Rolf had problems in school and was eventually sent to a boarding school some hours away, the Odenwaldschule near Heidelberg, farther up the Rhine.

The Odenwaldschule belonged to a worldwide progressive-education movement and enjoyed an international reputation for its liberal spirit and racial tolerance. At the time, it also was the first coeducational boarding school in Germany. What my grandparents probably did not know is that the Nazis had targeted it early as a school for "communists and Jews"; that after brutal raids in 1933 and 1934, the founders, Paul and Edith Geheeb, had emigrated to Switzerland; and that by the time Rolf entered the school, at the age of twelve in 1937, liberal spirit and racial tolerance had both been suppressed by the Nazi faction among the teachers. As he told me, the students did not notice much and sang the Nazi songs "without any awareness that it was all part of a terrible scheme."

Rolf quickly got himself into trouble again, or so my mother told me. He and some friends used a street sign for stone-throwing practice. The sign turned out to be a sign for the local branch of the Nazi Party. Hence assurances had to be provided to the local Party that this had not been a deliberate anti-Nazi gesture but only the harmless prank of a bunch of rambunctious boys. For a family with Jewish members, this was a dangerous encounter with the authorities.

Rolf graduated from the Odenwaldschule with a *Notabitur* (accelerated war graduation) in 1943 so that he could be thrown into Hitler's war at the age of seventeen. He fought in Italy and later found himself in northern Germany, somewhere to the east of the Elbe river. By May 1945, the German army had capitulated. The Americans caught up with his regiment, and Rolf, being the youngest officer in it, was ordered to ride towards them, on his horse, across a bridge, holding up a white flag. Then the Americans retreated across the Elbe and what had been a relatively mild experience of imprisonment under the Americans turned suddenly into much harsher treatment under the Russians. Rolf and a few comrades managed to escape. Swimming across one of the canals linking the Elbe with other waterways, they reached the British occupational zone. Exchanging his uniform for a farmer's outfit, he tried to move farther west. But when he tried to swim across the Elbe itself, a patrol caught him and he ended up a prisoner of the British.

By this time, his parents had not heard from him for many months and had no idea of his whereabouts or whether he was still alive. With another soldier who had been released earlier from the British internment camp, he managed finally to send a note to his aunt Erna in Wiesbaden—the same Erna who had once nursed her brother Alfred back to life one world war earlier. With no means to communicate the good news to her brother and his family, no trains running, and no gas for the car, Erna immediately walked all the way to Hattenheim, twenty-three kilometres.

Rolf made it back a few months later, in time for my parents' wedding in October 1945. Half a year later, he also travelled to Ebenhausen to attend my baptism and become my godfather. He also lived it up for a while. True or not, I heard a story that he and some friends celebrated their survival by trying to jump an old car over a ramp and through the open doors of an abandoned railway cattle car.

Because the German universities did not recognize the *Notabitur* after the war, Rolf undertook a number of apprenticeships before entering his father's company. Even though he became a much more devoted (and talented) businessman than his father ever was, he was never quite forgiven that it was under his aegis that the family shares were finally sold, and at a loss. He was a good godfather during those years as factory director. He gave me summer jobs and a company car to drive, and he hardly blinked when I put a dent in that car.

Rolf had other reasons to resent his father. Grandfather Alfred had a lifelong string of romantic relationships with all kinds of lady friends. It seems that right from the beginning, there always had to be one other woman apart from his wife whom my grandfather drooled over. Often, these relationships were formed during vacations, and these women then came to visit him in Hattenheim. My grandmother's strategy seems to have been to render them harmless by befriending them herself. There is no single hard piece of evidence that any of these relationships were ever sexual. To this day, though, Rolf insists that at least some of them were. He tells the story of how he and his two sisters, Gerda and my mother Renate, well before the war when they were little, were picked up from a swimming pool in Wiesbaden, and how they had to wait in the car, wet and cold, for

Favourite grandson: my grandfather Alfred and I.

half an hour while their father disappeared somewhere upstairs to "see" his lady friend of the day.

My own father also believed there was more to these encounters than courtly flirtation. Whenever he grew angry at his father-in-law, which happened with semi-regular frequency, he would sooner or later repeat the story of how grandfather Alfred, much later and after the war, had cut a bouquet of flowers in the upper garden for his current lady friend of the day, whom he was about to visit in Wiesbaden, and how he had quickly tossed that bouquet over the garden wall and into his cabriolet parked below when his wife Lene unexpectedly appeared on the terrace. That particular lady friend was Frau Schaefer, who owned and ran an art shop, Kunst Schaefer, in Wiesbaden, where my grandfather had his prints and pictures framed. In Julia's study, there are two beautiful large floral prints from the house in Hattenheim, one a blue iris, *Chamaeiris latifolia*, the other a reddish anemone, *Anemone hortensis latifolia*. On the back of each print, the Kunst Schaefer label is still attached and without blemish. By now, probably every member of the family has at least one piece hanging on a wall that has the Kunst Schaefer label on the back. With the possible exception of Rolf, we all giggle when we see it.

The truth is that my grandfather was a tremendous charmer. Even though he had lost most of his hair by his mid-twenties and was increasingly heavy-set because of his impaired mobility, women found him immensely attractive and flocked to him like those young ladies and pretend-nurses of society who had long ago gathered around his hospital bed in Wiesbaden. Most of these lady friends eventually withdrew, finding him overbearing. This is true even of his youngest and belated own daughter Ursula (Ulli), who suffered through years of overprotective attention, which included having to pose for his camera literally thousands of times. But it's the men, as a group, who somehow hold a more serious grudge. Among these, it seems that I am the only one who for the most part remembers him fondly.

Maybe I was his favourite grandchild because I never felt threatened by his demands and overbearing demeanour, or because I was the oldest one after Christian left for America. Grandfather always treated me with fairness and generosity. When I was about ten I spent the summer vacation in Hattenheim with another child, slightly older—Ludwig Matthes, a more distant relative of the family, if I remember correctly. Ludwig collected stamps, as I did, and he did so in a much more serious way, with an impressive album and stamps I had never seen or heard of. I stole some of them. When Ludwig noticed and complained that they were missing, my grandparents did not say a word. Of course they realized that only I could have been the culprit. But they wanted me to make the first move. The following night, lying in bed in the same room as Ludwig, I broke down and tearfully confessed to him. The next morning, I had to face my grandfather. He did not yell, and there was no punishment. After I told him what I had done and that I was sorry, he put his arm around me and gave me a speech. He said that stealing was a common temptation, and particularly so among stamp collectors, that it was good that I had realized on my own that it was wrong, and that I should never forget the awful feeling of guilt and bad conscience because it would stop me from doing it ever again.

33 | *Possible encounter*

According to testimony from various older family members, great-grandfather Hermann Wachendorff was a bore, and what came before him on the Wachendorff side of the family was hardly worth much dwelling on either. Supposedly, the family had originated on some castle hill during the Middle Ages (who hadn't, in a country where the better families built fake castle ruins for themselves along the Rhine during the nineteenth century?). As my father laughingly pointed out whenever there was an opportunity, the family even claimed that it had been of noble origin but had renounced its title at some point and for whatever reason.

Again, the more interesting side of my grandfather Alfred, the one from which came the spark getting him into trouble with his father, was his mother's side. This mother, my great-grandmother, Hedwig Wachendorff, née Overbeck, was a resolute woman of principle. She had a strong social conscience and gave freely and generously to charity. The poor in Wiesbaden knew that when they showed up at the house on Gustav-Freytag Street, they would likely get five marks, a considerable sum of money at the time. Family legend has it that the the house had even been marked somehow by some of the regular beggars so that others would recognize it as a generous one.

Less developed than her social conscience was her interest in men. The story goes that when Hermann courted her she had to be told by her parents what the purpose was. "So I went and got myself engaged," she said, according to family anecdote. Also according to family anecdote, she was still convinced shortly before giving birth to her first child that it would appear through her navel like a beautiful flower. She would eventually give birth to four children: three girls, Gertrud (Gertie), Erna, and Herta, and one boy, my grandfather Alfred.

She would later have four grandchildren, all girls. Two would be from Erna (Lore and Irmela), and two from Alfred (Gerda and my mother Renate). Finally, when the first male grandchild was born, Rolf, she was driven to Hattenheim and led into the room where the newly born male heir to the family throne was ceremoniously laid out on his diapers. She looked at his nakedness and calmly remarked: "I had entirely forgotten how ugly this is." No wonder, then, that she remained clueless about the sparks flying between her son and young Lene Martius during those summer vacations of 1917 and 1918.

A number of Hedwig's other diary entries are quite revealing as well. When Erna stayed in Poland to care for her wounded brother, Hedwig noted that her poor daughter had to work "under terrible conditions," which she then specified in brackets: "(only men!)." And when she witnessed how her convalescing son Alfred was surrounded by the aforementioned brazen ladies of society in Wiesbaden, she expressed how much she disliked that entire scene but how she should put up with it since it was a nice compensation for all the hardship her Fred had gone through.

Her oldest daughter Gertie never had children. Indeed, she spent her entire life in the company of other women. These relationships were mostly intellectual, but then again, perhaps not *only* mostly. Nobody talked about it, of course. According to my aunt Gerda, when Gertie made one of her rare visits to Hattenheim and saw the menagerie of children there, she remarked that it would be nice to have a few of those around "if there just weren't that thing with men first."

Hedwig came from a family of wealthy industrialists in Dortmund, the Overbecks. The family firm produced stearin candles. Just before Christmas a parcel would arrive at Ebenhausen, via the grandparents in Hattenheim, containing several sets of Overbeck candles for the Christmas tree. The founder of the candle enterprise, Wilhelm Overbeck, my great-great-great-grandfather, a *Kommerzienrat* again, was nicknamed "the

Dortmund king of lights" and later became an honorary citizen of that city. His son Julius Overbeck, also a *Kommerzienrat*, married Maria (or Marie) Simon, the daughter of the widow of a radical democrat and painter from Stuttgart, Carl Simon. Marie and Julius had nine children, one of whom was my great-grandmother Hedwig.

Another one was Ewald, who died of indigestion at the age of ten after winning a bet that he could eat one hundred walnuts. As children, whenever we ate walnuts in Hattenheim, from trees that grew in the garden at Oestrich, we were told this story and admonished not to eat too many. Maybe it ran in the family. One of Hedwig's daughters, Herta, died at a young age from a tobogganing accident on one of Wiesbaden's hilly streets.

But it was the Simon family that added colour—and, judging from Ewald's story, craziness—to the family tree. Carl Alexander Simon (1805–52/53) was born in Frankfurt an der Oder, the other German city of Frankfurt, almost on the Polish border. He studied painting in Berlin and, according to some sources, also with the famous painter Peter Cornelius in Munich. Besides being a painter, he was a philosopher, historian, economist, critic, radical democrat, and poet. At least one of his poems, "Die Heimkehr" (The Homecoming), was set to music by Carl Banck, a contemporary of Schubert. I could verify only its opening line: "Der Mond schlich überm Hügel her" (The moon was slinking along the hill). According to the Internet, the composition is still available as sheet music in some collections of nineteenth-century Romantic German songs.

Between 1829 and 1831, Simon made an extended tour of Italy that took him to Rome and all the way down to Sicily. Back in Germany he must have gotten married, because a couple of years later, in 1833, his oldest daughter Marie was born. This is the Marie who would later marry Julius Overbeck. Carl Simon therefore is my great-great-great-grandfather. Marie was born in Frankfurt an der Oder, but by 1835 the family was in Weimar, where Carl participated in decorating some of the rooms in the Wartburg castle there. (This was the famous castle where Martin Luther had once translated the Bible.) Devoting several years to painstaking historical research, he also developed plans and sketches for a somewhat grandiose reconstruction of the Wartburg as a temple of German culture.

Not much came of any of this, and the ever growing family moved on to Stuttgart, where Carl hoped to find employment at the art academy. Since he almost immediately began to criticize the works of the entire artistic establishment in Stuttgart for their various shortcomings, such employment was not to be had. Instead, Carl drifted towards the radical circles of those who would a few years later be the ringleaders of the 1848 revolution. He had to leave Stuttgart briefly in 1847 when he co-signed a manifesto protesting the military's brutal crushing of a bread riot that year. As he was from out of town, he was the only one expelled from the city. After the 1848 turmoil, finally, he fled, leaving his family behind.

Over the winter months of 1848–49, Carl Simon and a few like-minded companions travelled through France, mostly on foot and all the way down to Marseille and back. He kept a diary. It is a deeply moving document of despair and hope, romantic descriptions of landscapes—the cold east is associated with tyranny, the mild south with freedom—self-beratings for having left his family behind, vehement outbursts against the social injustice of the world, and emotional conjurations of a better future to come.

The travellers lived mainly off charity. Sometimes they were taken in by farm families, who shared their food with them. More often than not, they begged in the streets. With the few pennies they received, always from people who seemed almost as hard up as themselves (as Carl noted scornfully), they bought stale bread and cheap wine in local inns along the way. Most stomach-churning in the diary are the descriptions of how the food smelled that they could not afford in those inns. In Marseille, Carl found a little pouch with money lying in the street. He immediately sent most of it to his wife Charlotte in Stuttgart.

When I mentioned this diary, over supper, in our beautiful and well-appointed Canadian dining room, Julia asked whether I would be including its most depressing parts in my family tale. At that point our twelve-year-old son Jacob glanced up from his plate of seafood risotto and calmly declared: "There should be a part of the book that people cry over." Carl Simon's diary would be that part.

When he heard of the election of Louis Napoleon as president of the Second Republic, on 10 December 1848, Carl noted: "So it happened! The majority of France bribed by dynastic money!" A few days later he admonished his daughter Marie, in a letter dated 14 December 1848, to become a diligent student of the arts and sciences, including geography, physics, chemistry, and "everything that goes with it." He warned her to be wary of the spirit of the aristocracy, which is characterized by pride and conceit and aims only at outward splendour.

On the way back to Germany, in March 1849, Carl Simon stopped for a few days in Geneva. He had a brief reunion with a democratic association of other exiled Germans, 108 in number, and he generally enjoyed the city's republican spirit. What if this radical great-great-great-grandfather of mine met my radical great-great-grandfather there, Jean Marc Baud, who was at the time twenty-one years old, also a painter, and surely involved in the affairs of the time? There is no evidence, of course, that this encounter ever took place. The two families would not become related for almost one hundred years, in October 1945, when my parents got married.

34 | Another Chile connection

Towards the end of Carl Simon's diary, there appears the idea that a better life and future would have to be sought elsewhere, in the Americas. Hardly back in Stuttgart, he left again, in November 1849, with his oldest son, also named Carl. Their destination was Chile—specifically, the Chilean town of Valdivia, where a small community of exiled German democrats had gathered in the hope of building a new utopia of equality and freedom. His brother-in-law seems to have been involved in organizing this radical emigration movement, and he probably supplied some financial assistance, both to the voyagers and to the family left behind. For months, the two Simons hung around various North Sea ports, unable to find passage. None of the South America–bound ships seemed to want to stop in Valdivia. Then the harbours froze shut due to a particularly harsh winter. Letters went back and forth between Carl and his wife. Charlotte was now quite bitter at times, and she clearly expressed that she did not fancy at all starting a new life in Chile. But she assured her husband of her eternal love. He was apologetic but determined. He managed to send money now and then, God knows from what sources. In one letter, Charlotte acknowledged receipt of a small sum of money and added that she would have the piano tuned with it.

They would never see each other again. Carl Simon finally found a boat that would take him to Chile—without his son, it seems—and he arrived in Valdivia some time before June 1850. In one of his last letters, he complained that there was no work for a painter there, adding that he would ask his family to follow him only once he was able to provide for them a better and more stable existence. That never happened. In his struggle to survive, Carl Simon joined various expeditions into the Chilean hinterland. Before the age of photography, he served these expeditions as a sketch artist. Towards the end of 1852, he and, according to some sources, the governor of Valdivia did not return from one of these expeditions. Somewhere down south, in Tierra del Fuego, near the Strait of Magellan, they had met a violent death visiting an indigenous tribe known to be hostile towards intruders.

The artist and romantic dreamer, my great-great-great-grandfather, said of himself: "Eine Skizze bin ich und Skizzen habe ich geschaffen" (I am a sketch, and sketches are what I have created). This quote was the title of an exhibition of Simon's sketches, paintings, and architectural plans for the Wartburg, commemorating his two hundredth birthday in 2005. In Chile, Carl Alexander Simon is recognized as one of the country's important early artists, and a number of his sketches and delicate landscapes hang in Santiago's Museo de Bellas Artes.

The real mystery is how the daughter of this political radical and social misfit, my great-great-grandmother Marie Simon, got to marry into the entirely bourgeois and stinking-rich Overbeck family. One can only guess that opposites attracted.

35 | Hattenheim

My grandmother Lene Wachendorff, née Martius, came from a well-established academic family. The Martiuses had far less money than the Wachendorffs, of course, but they were comfortable enough. Lene's father Friedrich Martius was a university professor and had been personal physician to the Grand Duke of Mecklenburg. Her mother Martha Martius was an incessant writer of poems, plays, and essays, some of which were published.

Lene's move from Rostock to Hattenheim must have felt like a move from the height of bourgeois civilization to homesteading in the wilderness. The new house her father-in-law had bought was in fact a very old house. The previous owner had died, and obviously he had long before lost the energy, or lacked the money, or both, to look after the place. The plaster was peeling from the walls everywhere, and one of the front rooms did not even have a floor. The house was an enormous complex consisting of the main building and several attached side buildings—some forty rooms in all. But only two of these had a coal stove for heating. The two gardens were in even worse shape. They needed clearing rather than gardening.

On the other hand, it was a little baroque palace. Goethe had made note of it in his diary when he travelled through the Rheingau on his way to Italy more than a hundred years earlier. The formal front rooms facing the Rhine had twelve-foot ceilings and nine-foot windows. My grandmother did not complain—not about the task ahead, and not about her husband, who expected to be pampered, poor *Fredebumschen*, as he was sometimes called, with his lost leg and all. As she told me once, much later, when we had long conversations during the time I was in military serv-

The house in Hattenheim, with my grandmother in profile, and the sophora tree still standing.

ice and hence in the neighbourhood, she had been educated to serve, and she (almost) never questioned it.

While Fred escaped to his new job in his father's factory in Oestrich every day, Lene, pregnant almost immediately and not exactly blessed with practical talents, was left behind with the mess. A lot of the inside clearing renovating was in the end owed to her mother-in-law. During the first year or so, Hedwig came out to Hattenheim almost every day. She was probably simply dropped off by her husband Hermann on his way to Oestrich, then picked up again at the end of the day.

Of course the women did not have to do any physical work themselves. Their men would send the factory workers from Oestrich—plasterers, plumbers, electricians, and carpenters, not to forget gardeners. Koepp & Co. had it all. Even while I was a child in Ebenhausen, those factory workers would sometimes be detailed for family service. The furniture my mother received when she finally got her own dining room under the roof in the villa was made in Oestrich, and so were the little cabinets my grandmother had made out of the sophora tree.

Central heating came along only with the birth of my mother's youngest sister, Ursula, in 1936. When my mother left the house in 1945 to start her own family, there were still quite a few rooms that she had never entered. There was the main building, with the two gardens in front of it. To the west were the outbuildings, with an enormous separate yard in front of them. That yard served as additional parking; it also contained a tool shed, rows of laundry lines, and a concrete basin for composting garbage. It also was the main playground for children and had a large sandpit. Once, during the 1930s, when my grandfather brought a business partner home for lunch unannounced, he found his wife in that yard, tied to a pole with her hair open and hanging down to her hips, and his children dancing around her dressed up as Indians.

Apart from the formal front rooms, the most impressive part of the house, as in Ebenhausen, was the entrance hall, with its broad staircase leading to the upper floors. There was a mirror, and a huge wooden chest that for some strange reason mostly contained dress-up clothes. Next to the chest was a chair. When my grandfather's slim leather bag was lying on it, he was home. When the chair was empty, he was out. There also was a large oil painting of great-grandfather Hermann, in profile, with his large nose, which I have inherited. I can still remember how wonderfully cool that entrance hall was even during the hottest summer days.

A particular feature of life in Hattenheim was that the rooms often changed their use. Gerda later claimed that there was not a single room in the main building that she had not at some point lived in. When I was a boy, the first floor downstairs was occupied by a combined dining room / music room, which housed a Bechstein grand piano that had a more brilliant tone than the mellow Blüthner in Ebenhausen. That room was flanked by my grandmother's salon on one side and by a guest room on the other. There was also a large kitchen at the end of a long corridor, on the way to the garage. The second floor contained the various bedrooms and my grandfather's large den, where mostly men were entertained with cigars and brandy. Before building their own house in nearby Johannisberg, Rolf and his family occupied the third floor.

Later, when the grandparents grew old and began to fear the steps, they moved downstairs entirely. The kitchen was transformed into two bedrooms and a new kitchen was built next to the guest room, which itself became a dining room. The dining/music room now served as the general living room. The second floor became entirely for guests. The grand piano occupied grandfather's old den. The third floor remained mostly empty until Gerda and her husband Hans-Erich returned from Portland and reclaimed it.

When my mother grew up in the old house, there was only one bathroom, on the first floor, next to her parents' bedrooms. It had to be used by everyone, including visitors. Its most peculiar feature was a large frosted-glass window towards the staircase landing. According to my mother, the children (and sometimes even grown-ups) would gather on the landing whenever someone took a shower and watch the silhouette through the frosted glass.

My grandmother did not spend all that much time in her various kitchens, except to supervise the cooks, who came and went over the years. No matter who they were and how long they stayed, they all were resentful of my grandmother poking into the kitchen, full of advice, planning the menu from various old family cookbooks but without ever doing much herself. One of my grandmother's legendary pieces of cooking advice was: "When in doubt, double the expensive ingredients."

The presence of various household staff mingling with the family certainly was another peculiar feature of Hattenheim, at least for a visiting boy from Ebenhausen, where not even the grandparents were much of a presence in our lives, and where the meals were brought from the nearby sanatorium. I remember a whole string of housekeepers who doubled as cooks. They were all young women: Else, Hannelore, Anneliese, and a few others whose names I have forgotten. Some, like Else and Hannelore, stayed for years and became all but members of the family. Else and her family continued to live in the house even after she no longer worked for my grandmother. I played with her children. Gustav, the gardener, was my particular friend. I loved to follow him around in the garden. He and his wife lived in one of the side buildings. So did Anton, who did various jobs for the family and whose wife was revered by all the children for the pancakes she made. There was also Frau Claudi, the seamstress, who appeared regularly to do all the sewing and mending. During the lean years after the war, that job included altering all kinds of used clothes for various grown-ups as well as children.

I loved to hear stories about all the people who had been in the house before my time. Many became regular bedtime stories. My favourite one was about a particular housekeeper, during the 1930s, who was a compulsive baker. Every few days she would say: "There always must be cookies in the house!" and then retreat to the kitchen. According to my mother, she then left little platefuls of these cookies in every room. The Wachendorffs, and the children among them in particular, had no problem with this part of her personality. But when she attacked my grandfather with a kitchen knife, the police had to be called, reluctantly, because of rumours about what the Nazis did to the mentally ill.

36 | *The Rhine*

The Rhine has been the main border between Germany and France for more than a thousand years. Whenever hostilities broke out between the two countries, it meant one nation crossing the river to invade the other. In the late nineteenth century, the railway on the eastern bank was built like a demonstration of Prussian might, with viaducts and tunnels made of large blocks of stone like fortresses. It was a demonstrative nation-building exercise not unlike the railway stations and hotels built by the Canadian Pacific Railway in Canada around the same time along the transcontinental tracks.

The Rhine generally flows from south to north, with navigation on its internationalized waters possible from Basle in Switzerland to Rotterdam in the Netherlands. But blocked by a low mountain range, the Taunus, on its long descent from the Alps to the North Sea, it flows east–west for some thirty kilometres, between Wiesbaden and Rüdesheim, with Hattenheim, Oestrich, and a few more wine villages in between. What is called the Rheingau consists mainly of the hills north of the river on that stretch, which rise to the heights of the Taunus, facing south and thus exposed to the sun all day long. Legend has it that none other than Charlemagne noticed the almost Mediterranean microclimate and ordered the first vines to be planted there.

Praying for good weather and harvests, the local farmers put up madonnas statues in the local churches and sometimes even in the vineyards. Here, incidentally, is another similarity between my grandfather Albert in Ebenhausen and my grandfather Alfred in Hattenheim: while

Albert collected antique madonnas and placed them on pedestals in his villa, Alfred spent hours photographing madonna statues and images all over the Rheingau and then showed them in his slide shows. Neither man was even remotely religious, by the way. Neither am I. But in our Canadian home we have assembled an entire array of religious images, a nineteenth-century painting of a black Bohemian madonna among them. We refer to her as the "wine queen" because she holds in her hand what probably is some Holy Scripture but, with a little imagination, can also be interpreted as a glass of wine.

For vacationing children, the Rhine was endlessly fascinating. I would wake up in the early morning and lie still in my bed, listening for the hooting of the Rhine freight ships as they lifted anchor. I sometimes even did that back home in Ebenhausen, hoping that I would be in Hattenheim when I opened my eyes. Before these Rhine freighters were equipped with modern radar, they had to anchor for the night. The hooting signals were necessary because the most common mode of transportation on the Rhine at the time was barges—as many as six at a time towed by a strong tugboat or head freighter. Getting ready for the day and lifting the anchor therefore had to be coordinated acoustically. My mother often took me on a walk to the Rhine in the evenings so that I could see whether one of these convoys would anchor right in front of us. One time—I could not have been more than five or six—I even struck up a conversation with the captain of one of the ships. He was from Mulhouse in France, and he promised to write me a postcard once he reached his home—which, to everyone's surprise, he did.

Then there were the passenger ships, huge white paddle steamers generically called *Köln-Düsseldorfer* after their port of origin. In the 1950s they still provided basic transportation on the Rhine. Quite a few people in Hattenheim, for instance, would take the morning boat to commute to their jobs elsewhere, then come back in the late afternoon. The six o'clock *Köln-Düsseldorfer* from Wiesbaden was always full and let out a whole bunch of people during its stop at Hattenheim. As children, we loved to hang out down there at the *Dampferanlegestelle* (one word!), the pontooned pier sticking out into the river where the ships would come and go in a steady stream. There also were express steamers connecting only the larger towns and therefore not stopping in Hattenheim. It was our particular thrill to watch the next ship steam around the river bend and then to guess whether it would stop or not. The local stationmaster, known as Bock Martin, who resided in a small building next to the pier, became a friend to all children. He must have been a very patient man.

Even more thrilling, of course, was to be taken on board one of those ships for a Rhine excursion. My grandmother often took us. One of her favourite summer activities with us combined a boat ride with a chairlift and a hike. First we would board the steamer for a brief downriver cruise, from Hattenheim to Rüdesheim. There, a gondola would take us up to the heights of the Niederwald, the westernmost point of the Taunus and hence of the Rheingau. Each of the little open gondolas seated four and would silently glide across vineyard after vineyard right past the monastery where Hildegard von Bingen once lived.

This would be followed by a leisurely stroll, lasting an hour at the most, through a beautifully cool forest interspersed with dramatic views down to the Rhine, with its ships glistening in the sun, and, in the middle of the stream, the Mäuseturm (Tower of Mice), a medieval structure that once had been used to collect the toll from passing ships. Of course, grandmother had to retell the gruesome story of the Mäuseturm: Once, during the Middle Ages, there was a severe famine. The evil Archbishop of Mainz hoarded all the remaining wheat, and went with it to the tower, where he thought he would be safe from the anger of the starving people. But all the mice swam across the river and ate not only all the wheat but the archbishop as well.

Halfway across the Niederwald we would inevitably come to the Niederwalddenkmal (one word again). This was one of those gigantic monuments the Germans built during the Second (Bismarck) Empire's founding years, thirty-eight metres high and visible from almost everywhere in the Rheingau, an eyesore really, but immensely popular with tourists from all over the world. The tourists do not come up with the gondola lift, of course, but are driven up the road by the busload, usually by then already filled to the brim with the Riesling wine they have first imbibed collectively in the many taverns along Rüdesheim's narrow cobbled streets.

At the centre of that monument towers the figure of Germania, a kind of Valkyrie, eleven metres tall, meant to symbolize the belated unity of all German tribes. Germania was the best-known symbol of German nationalism during those founder years. She also was the image on nearly all German stamps at the time. When Wilhelm II ascended to the Imperial throne in 1888, the assumption was that his image would replace that of Germania on those stamps. But it didn't. As the joke went, he abstained because he did not want to be licked from behind and stamped in front.

On the west side, below Germania's feet, a huge iron plate is attached to the pedestal. On it are engraved the words to "Die Wacht am Rhein"

(Watch on the Rhine), a notorious nationalist hymn especially popular with the Nazis later on. It has been immortalized in the movie *Casablanca*, in which it is sung in Rick's Bar by a party of Nazis before being drowned out by French locals singing "La Marseillaise." The same plate contains a relief showing German soldiers departing from their women on the eve of the Franco–Prussian War of 1870–71. According to family legend again, one of the women was modelled after Martha Martius, grandmother Lene's Jewish mother (the family was acquainted with the sculptor who designed the monument). There were giggles, of course, when the grown-ups imagined how Nazis had pranced around in front of that monument, celebrating what they thought was their Germanic superiority, with a young Jewish woman all the while calmly looking down at them.

None of this was on the minds of us children, of course, when we walked past that monument on the Niederwald with our grandmother. What *was* very much on our minds was that we were heading to the café at the other end of the forest, where we would be treated to strawberry cake and lemonade before taking a steep chairlift down to Assmannshausen. From there, we would then take a longer boat cruise back upstream to Hattenheim.

A few of the old Köln–Düsseldorfer steamers still travel up and down the Rhine, but they no longer stop at Hattenheim. Many ferries, though, still go back and forth across the river. We often took those during my sabbatical year at the University of Mannheim in 1997–98, a time when our three-year-old son Jacob spoke better German than English for a while. Once, during an excursion with Gerda, we crossed the Rhine at Kaub, where the ferry steams past the picturesque Pfalz, a medieval structure that once served, like the Mäuseturm, as a customs station. Just as we were passing the old fortress, right in the middle of the river, the ferry inexplicably made a 360-degree turn. It felt like being on a merry-go-round in the middle of the river. We all danced around on the ferry's wooden planks, Gerda, Julia, Jacob, and I, and of course, as usual, we all giggled.

The middle Rhine's landscape includes valleys carved into the Taunus by various streams. One of the most beautiful of these is the Wispertal, where my grandfather loved to take us for Sunday picnics. I have vivid memories of how my third birthday was celebrated, on a green meadow surrounded by trees at the edge of the water, complete with cake and candles, during one of those picnic excursions into the Wispertal. Often these excursions were part of one of those controlling games that my grandfather loved. He announced that we would do a "trip into the blue," which meant that everyone in the car (except him of course) had to close their eyes at intersections so that the final destination could only be guessed.

My grandfather was particularly fond of another valley, the Grohlochtal, which branched off from the Wispertal. The little wooded spot where it begins is the one where, according to my grandfather, fox and hare say good night to each other. When the whole area was declared a nature park, the access road to the Grohlochtal was closed at either end with a gate that only the local foresters could open. My grandfather was quite devastated. He could not walk long distances and depended on a car to reach his favourite places. A few years later, however—on his seventy-fifth birthday, I think—the local authorities presented him with a key and lifetime permission to open that gate. When I visited Hattenheim during my student years, and my grandfather no longer liked driving himself, I would chauffeur him and grandmother through the Grohlochtal a few more times.

When I brought Julia to Hattenheim for the first time, I planned the trip carefully so that we would approach the Rheingau from the north, driving through some of those lovely valleys along the Taunus. Alas, the previous evening, spent with some academic friends in the old university town of Marburg, and probably occasioned by the fact that she could not follow the conversation, which was mostly in German, Julia had imbibed far too much Riesling, and the Taunus drive was overshadowed by a considerable hangover. We did manage to have a picnic. It mainly consisted of raw marinated herring sandwiches that we had bought in a town along the way, which are said to have a sobering effect.

Then there was the Ley, as in "Loreley." *Ley* means "rock" in local parlance, and *Lore* is cognate with "lure." Loreley, then, is the lovely girl sitting on top of a steep cliff, combing her blond hair and bewitching the sailors until they run their ships onto the rocks that line the sharp bend in the river below. Loreley lures them onto the rocks, so to speak. My grandfather never took us to the real Loreley. He thought it was a tourist trap, and he was right. When I went there by myself, later, with an American friend who insisted on the visit, I found that the first thing one encounters when approaching the famous rock is a Coca-Cola machine.

My grandfather had his own Ley. As it flows down its narrow valley, the Rhine is lined with similar rocks and lookouts. "His" lookout was not as dramatic as the famous one, but it had better vistas, from a photographer's point of view, up and down the river valley with its towns, ships, and the railway tracks on either side. We also mostly had it to ourselves. Many family picnics were held on our Ley. But my grandfather insisted that only he had the right to take us there, preferably with our eyes closed at all intersections.

Later, when I was grown up and had a car, I once asked him for directions because I wanted to show the place to some friends. He was quite offended. Later again, when cousin Chris visited from Portland and wanted to go there, we did so secretly, without telling him. Meanwhile, Julia and Jacob have been there, too. A gazebo has been built on the site, and one is less likely to have the place to oneself. But it is still a magical place.

37 | *Freie Heimat*

I loved my visits to Hattenheim, more so, I think, than any other member of the family. The house in Ebenhausen was dark. The one in Hattenheim was full of light. The grandparents in Ebenhausen were not much fun. The ones in Hattenheim were. Long before I had my own room at home, I had one in Hattenheim, and a radio to which I could listen before falling asleep at night. Obviously I loved the excursions and the entire idea of going somewhere else and having a good time. One could do so many things in Hattenheim that one simply could not do at home.

Like playing dress-up, for example. I liked to don my grandfather's big old hats. My other grandfather in Ebenhausen would have been aghast had he caught me wearing one of his precious Borsalino hats. Several old Hattenheimers still remember the day I appeared at the open front door, maybe three or four years old, donning one of those hats. The public school was right across the street. In no time, windows full of schoolchildren were looking at me and laughing.

When I was a little older, I was sent to Hattenheim for the summer by myself, by train, accompanied by a family friend going the same way. During that summer, my grandmother bought me a new pair of sandals. Like all new shoes, they hurt. My grandmother reported back to Ebenhausen that I firmly placed myself in front of her and declared: "This is my free homeland [*freie Heimat*], and here I am not putting on any constraining shoes against my will." More than half a century later, when I visit Gerda, Hattenheim to me still means *freie Heimat*.

I had quite a mouth, apparently. Again in Hattenheim, long before I started school, I was taken along to a dinner party, and as always quite attentively listened to the conversations going on. At some point, quite late, somebody looked at me and said it was remarkable how well behaved and quiet I had been all evening. All conversation stopped. Into the silence, with everybody looking at me, I calmly announced: "It is so boring here that I could puke."

On another occasion, when I was six, my parents took me to my first public concert, a performance of some of Bach's Brandenburg Concertos by a local chamber orchestra in Wolfratshausen, a small town near Ebenhausen. My father knew the conductor and most of the players. After the concert, we went backstage. Again I sat quietly on a chair while my parents chatted with the musicians. Suddenly the attention turned to me. One of the violinists, a young woman, had just asked me how I had liked the concert. My firm answer: "It was all far too loud." I had the entire orchestra laughing at me. In Hattenheim, at the dinner table, my grandfather decreed that nobody was allowed to laugh at my utterings and jokes. He feared I would turn into a complete clown otherwise.

38 | *Books and poems*

The heart and soul of Hattenheim, and of my visits there, was my grandmother. This may sound strange, considering that the household was so much dominated by an overbearing and self-centred grandfather. It was he who gave presents, took responsibility for decorating the Christmas tree, planned the excursions, and generally set the schedule and routine for each day. On the other hand, he spent weekdays in his office and much of the rest of his time in the lower garden, where children had only restricted access.

My grandmother and I shared an intellectual affinity right from the beginning, when I was a little boy. She and I talked a lot, about everything. She gave me books to read. Over the years in Hattenheim, I read all the children's books my mother had read before me. Those old books were the only ones with German content that I got to read as a child. Most of the new books my parents bought me were translations of American children's books. During the postwar years of de-Nazification, German book printing had been interrupted and delayed by American censorship.

I did love those American stories, about the orphaned boy from New York who ends up snowshoeing in New England, or about the young newspaper reporter delivering blankets and medications to an Indian tribe in the north. I got a clear impression from those books about North American geography. There was New York, then farther north there was upstate New York, or New England, and then, rather quickly, came the North Pole. Looking out the window in my Canadian study so many years later, it strikes me that none of those books ever mentioned another country lying between New York and the North Pole.

Early on, my favourite book was a collection of bedtime stories my grandmother had sent me, *Die schönsten Gute Nacht Geschichten* (The Most Beautiful Good Night Stories), first published in 1951. The stories had been collected by a Jewish librarian and children's book author, Jella Lepman, who had returned from British exile to her native Germany as "Adviser on the Cultural and Educational Needs of Women and Children in the American Zone." A newspaper campaign had yielded thousands of stories from all over the world. Lepman's selection was meant to convey to German children that there were mothers reading bedtime stories to their children everywhere in the world. My grandmother had a story in it, about the Handkerchief Queen. It was inspired by her youngest daughter Ursula, nine years old at the end of the war, and her habit of running around clutching a handkerchief like the *Peanuts* character Linus with his security blanket.

One particular effect of American censorship was the socially progressive character of most book publications early on. Authors with a proven anti-Nazi track record obviously found it easier to get past the censorship hurdle quickly. Such was the case with the books of Erich Kästner, a social critic even in his children books, who had refused to join the Nazi writers' organization, or to emigrate, even though he had been arrested by the Gestapo at least twice. My favourite Kästner story was *Pünktchen und Anton*.

Pünktchen (literally, little dot) is the daughter of a wealthy family living in a villa, and Anton is her working-class friend in the city. Both are about ten years old. Pünktchen's parents have a sinister housekeeper who forces Pünktchen to go out with her after dark selling matches while the parents are at the opera. So there we have Pünktchen, at some downtown intersection, with the housekeeper next to her. The housekeeper is wearing dark glasses and pretending to be blind. Pünktchen is holding up boxes of matches, crying out: "People, buy matches, it is for my poor little mother, so young and already gone blind." I forget what role Anton plays in the story, but he somehow looks after Pünktchen. The whole imbroglio is revealed when one evening it is her parents who stop to buy matches.

For years, I teased my mother by calling her "my poor little mother" whenever she seemed to be discontented with something in her life, which was not often. And whenever we encountered one of those people, of which there are many—the ones who constantly tell you how hard they have it in the world, even though they have it better than most—we would look at each other and say: "So young and already gone blind." And we would giggle, of course.

As I grew up, my grandmother and I began to discuss more advanced forms of literature. We both read Pasternak's *Doctor Zhivago* shortly after its first appearance in German translation. Then we went and saw the movie together. We agreed that it did not do justice to the book, of course. The book contains a number of poems. My grandmother probably was among the few who read those poems as attentively as the epic tale itself.

Like her mother, my grandmother wrote poems all her life, about everything. Two slim volumes of them still exist as private printings. The first of these, *Poems by Lene Wachendorff*, was presented to her by her "children and children-in-law" on her seventy-fifth birthday, 5 December 1972. The second one, *Old-Age Verses and Postscripts*, was added six years later, on 19 October 1978, when we all gathered to celebrate the grandparents' diamond wedding anniversary, only a few weeks before grandfather died.

In an early poem, dated October 1942, she mused that old age might be quite beautiful, like autumn, but only if the sound of children's quick steps in the garden never stopped. In a much later poem from the 1960s, she reflected on the difference between traditional and modern motherhood. Her youngest daughter Ursula had just become a mother. The poem's title says it all: "Young Mother of Today—Neither Pink nor Light Blue." Only some poems were written in rhyme; others consisted of elegant prose. Strangely missing from the collection is a pair of rhymed poems written on the same subject, side by side: "Madonna in the Vineyard." One side is written in regular High German, the other in the local Hessian dialect. Perhaps not so strangely: I once read those poems to a few local friends. Their reaction to the poem written in dialect was ridicule. The "children and children-in-law" probably felt the same way.

That is too bad, because my grandmother usually had her reasons for whatever she did, so she would have had one for the poetic experiment in dialect. She always insisted that some of the rhymed verses of Germany's most famous poet, Goethe, who came from the neighbouring city of Frankfurt and therefore was a Hessian, made sense (i.e., rhymed) only when they were pronounced in dialect. Indeed, there is undisputed biographical evidence that the most German of all German poets spoke with a strong Hessian accent all his life.

During my military stint in Mainz, my grandmother made me read Thomas Mann's *Zauberberg* (Magic Mountain). It was this time in the military that convinced me that Karl Marx was right after all: it is our material existence that determines our consciousness, not the other way round, as the Hegelians insisted. I spent most of my two years in the military either playing war games in some field or forest, or driving trucks into the dirt, washing them, driving them into the dirt again, washing them again, and when the paint was washed off, painting them.

Such mindless and repetitive activities, not entirely unlike what workers must endure on production lines or in sweatshops, quickly dull the mind. After eight or ten hours of that sort of thing, the brain cannot suddenly be switched to intellectual mode. I am convinced that this is why most of humanity prefers to read tabloids rather than serious newspapers. So did I in Mainz. But when I told my grandmother, she pulled out the two volumes of *Zauberberg*, with its endless if somewhat superficial discussions of art, politics, and philosophy, and she not only made me read the whole thing chapter by chapter but also insisted on written summaries, which I then had to bring to Hattenheim on weekends to discuss with her. I must have been a sight, sitting in the military canteen during coffee breaks, jokingly called NATO-breaks by the soldiers, reading those books, pen in hand, while everyone else read the main German tabloid, the notorious *Bildzeitung*. Thank God I had that wine from my grandfather's cellar.

Around this time, my grandmother also gave me the monumental Goethe biography by Richard Friedenthal, which had appeared in 1963. One evening over supper, we were discussing the finer points of Friedenthal's interpretation when my grandfather looked up from his dinner plate, turned to his wife, and asked with mild reproach: "Why did you not tell *me* to read this book?" Hardly interrupting her train of thought, she snapped: "Because you would not have understood it anyway." Without showing any signs of being insulted, grandfather turned his concentration back to supper.

During these later years in their lives, my grandparents almost switched personalities. My grandfather grew milder to the point that some of the old stories would no longer ring true to those who had not known him before this miraculous transformation; my grandmother became increasingly moody. As the poem about her youngest daughter's emancipated motherhood indicated, she had begun to resent what increasingly seemed to her a (partly) wasted life. She was jealous of her daughters' lives. Gerda had come back from America with an independent and successful career, and Ursula's marriage to an art historian had opened up what sounded like a marvellous life of gallery openings, intellectual stimulation, and artistic friendships.

During those last years, she sometimes reminisced openly about a choice she had faced early in her life, between accepting a writing job with a women's magazine that had been offered to her, or marrying Fred and leading what she knew would be a traditional family life. Of course she followed her heart in the end, and she never regretted it, but on occasion she wondered what she might have missed. Her sister Hedwig Conrad-Martius had gone through life as an independent philosopher and university teacher, and her brother was a famous gynecologist and author of numerous scientific treatises and textbooks. Many around my grandmother were certain that she could have been the brightest star of them all.

She could have been, but I am not entirely sure that is what she wanted. She had a rather passive personality and—as a common family saying went—was happiest lying on a deck chair on the terrace with a book a buttered piece of bread, and a glass of cocoa. She passed that personality on to my mother, who could stomp her foot and throw a tantrum when necessary but generally preferred to let things go as they went—which meant that my father made most of the decisions. It is always a mixture of nature and socialization. Life with my grandfather did not exactly invite expressions of emancipative thought. My father, for his part, was certainly not a tyrant, and my mother usually got what she wanted in the end.

It would also be a misrepresentation to suggest that Lene did not have a darned good time for most of the ride. There are stories of wild parties during the early years of my grandparents' marriage. On at least one occasion, mattresses for such a party were delivered to one of the best hotels in the Rheingau, the Oestricher Lenchen, no doubt by one of Koepp's trusty company trucks. Those parties are still the stuff of Rheingau legends. And as far as Fred's lady friend flirtations go, grandmother Lene does not seem to have been far behind. Gerda reports that on one occasion, as a young girl, she burst into the upstairs salon only to find her mother lying on the couch with another man kneeling in front of her.

That other man was Bertram Graubner, uncle Tram-Tram as we called him. He and his wife remained lifelong fixtures in the Wachendorff's family and social orbit, regularly invited to attend weddings, christenings, and other festivities. Uncle Tram-Tram had a golden pocket watch with an hourly chime that could be triggered by opening the golden lid and pressing a little button. As children we loved to press that button. Uncle Tram-Tram once drove my mother and me from Ebenhausen to Hattenheim. We stopped at a small restaurant on the Autobahn near Stuttgart and had pea soup with sausages. The next time uncle Tram-Tram came past that restaurant by himself, he sent me a picture postcard of it with a car exactly like his Mercedes in front of it.

Uncle Tram-Tram's postcard from the Autobahn restaurant, with the same Mercedes in front of it as his and my grandfather's.

Lene and Bertram would disappear for endless walks in the countryside, or so it appeared to the wondering children. They mainly seem to have read poems to each other. Ostensibly for the same purpose, and for at least some time, my grandmother would take off once a week for an evening, in her Adler convertible, to visit Bertram in Wiesbaden. Around that time, she had a second ardent admirer, Herr Enderli, a Swiss, also married like Bertram, and the director of chemistry at the Koepp factory. Herr Enderli was so jealous of my grandmother's weekly outings to Wiesbaden that he began to follow her in his car, waiting outside all evening while my grandmother did the poetry thing with Bertram. When he started following her on the way back, Bertram, who was worried, began to follow him, so that the weekly poetry excursions to Wiesbaden ended in a little convoy back to Hattenheim: my grandmother followed by Herr Enderli followed by Bertram.

During my military service in Mainz, in June 1967, the Six Day War broke out between Israel and Egypt. Some of the old German corporals and officers gleefully predicted that the Egyptians would wipe out the Israelis in no time. They were not really Nazis, or at least not any more, but they obviously still harboured the old prejudices about Jews, racial or otherwise. Were they in for a surprise! I was taking a course in military English at the time—I had volunteered for it, just as something to do—at a neighbouring American base in Wiesbaden, and I remember the copy of

Time magazine that came out when the war was over almost before it really had begun. The headline read "The Blintzkrieg," and the main report was interspersed with jokes like that Ralph Nader had demanded that Egyptian tanks be equipped with backup lights. It was then that I began to talk to my grandmother about the Jewish connection in our family, and, shortly thereafter, to wear a Star of David on a golden chain around my neck, not for any religious reasons whatsoever, but as a cultural tribute to my grandmother, who for me represented the very best in our family.

39 | *The Jewish question (II)*

On a warm, sunny day in July 1935, Adolf Hitler drove past a small lake near the southern Bavarian town of Berchtesgaden, on the way to his usual summer hideout in the mountains. At the lake he spotted four boys, all tall, blue-eyed, blond, and wearing the traditional *Lederhosn* of the region. The motorcade stopped. Hitler stepped out of his limousine, summoned his court photographer Heinrich Hoffmann, who happened to be part of the entourage, and had his picture taken with these boys. Over the next year or so, the picture appeared in nearly all German daily newspapers as well as weekly or monthly magazines, often with captions like "The Führer is greeted by German youth." Postcards of it were sold at kiosks. The four boys were my grand-uncles, the sons of Heinrich Martius and his wife Martha, and hence the nephews of my grandmother. They also were not entirely Aryan.

Much of what follows may sound incredible, but it has been painstakingly reconstructed and written down by the youngest of the four boys, Götz Martius, the one on whose shoulders Hitler's hands rest in the picture. I will tell the story as I heard it, and in *the way* I heard it, from my grandmother as well as from my mother. None of it contradicts what Götz researched and wrote down, but the emphases are a bit different here and there. Only on occasion will I rely on Götz's account, for greater accuracy in some places, and for the sake of including some anecdotal material that is just too good to leave out.

My maternal great-grandmother Martha Martius, née Leonhard, the mother of Lene and Heinrich, and the grandmother of the four blond boys, came from a family of Jewish merchants in Glogau, a small town in Silesia. Her grandfather was Samuel Raphael Levisohn. Her father was Emanuel Levisohn but became Emil Leonhard when the family converted to Protestantism in 1843 in order to surmount career and other civil restrictions

The infamous photo of Hitler and my Jewish grand-uncles.

imposed on Jews under Prussian law. A lot of Jews did that at the time, including the parents of Karl Marx at the other end of Germany, in Trier.

Emil Leonhard in turn married Antonie Gutike, the daughter of Paul and Mathilde Gutike, née Landsberger. It has always been clear that the Landsbergers were Jewish, but it seems likely that the Gutikes were as well and that like the Leonhards they had converted to Protestantism a generation earlier. Anti-Semitism at the time was a general phenomenon, and not just in Germany. Götz quotes the German political writer and literary critic Ludwig Börne (1776–1837), also a converted Jew, whose original name had been Juda Löb Baruch: "Some accuse me of being Jewish; others forgive me for it; a third one might even laud me for it. But they all think about it." Götz also provides a telling episode reconstructed from his grandmother Martha's diaries: In 1889 she accompanied the Grand Duke of Mecklenburg and his personal physician, her husband Friedrich, on a vacation to Biarritz in southwestern France, close to the border with Spain. One of her diary entries from that trip reads: "The Grand Duke opened the door to the dining room and let me enter first. The idea struck me like lightning: grand-daughter of a little Jewish merchant from Glogau."

All in all, this was the one moment in German history that the "Jewish question" might have begun to finally fade away owing to the willingness, on the part of many Jews, to assimilate into German society and culture. A generation later, the Nazis raised that question again. Survival often depended on how that question could be answered.

For all practical purposes, great-grandmother Martha Martius was Jewish. That made the blond boys on the shores of that little Bavarian lake one-quarter Jewish, like my mother. Technically, however, in terms of the blood flowing through her veins, if one believed in such nonsense, it could be claimed that Martha was only three-quarters Jewish because the Jewishness of the Gutike family remained unproven. This may explain why she remained unharmed even though, in a document retrieved from the Nazi ministry responsible for Aryan purity, the Reichssippenamt, after the war, there is a Jewish star pencilled in next to her name, which means that she had been singled out and classified as a Jew. In the legal gobbledygook of the Nazi bureaucracy, finally, Martha was classified as first-degree mixed race, and her children, Lene and Heinrich, as second-degree mixed race. People of partly Jewish descent in either of these two categories were not automatically shipped off to concentration camps for extermination. But they were always in danger of transgressing some other of the heinous Nazi laws restricting their lives that could lead to their incarceration, deportation, and possibly death.

Excerpt from the Nazi dossier on the Martius family, with a Star of David pencilled next to the entry for my great-grandmother, Martha Leonhard.

There is one more way of counting Jewishness that I cannot but include in this tale of bloodlines and other assorted forms of family descent hocus-pocus. Whenever I tell this story, anybody Jewish hearing it immediately points out to me that I could go to Israel and become a citizen right away because I am at the end of the female line—great-grandmother, grandmother, and mother—and because it is the female line that passes on Jewishness. In other words, the Jewish State of Israel has yet again constructed citizenship on principles of cultural-religious identity rather than civic community or what the German social philosopher Jürgen Habermas has propagated as constitutional patriotism: the idea that citizenship can be established only by a commitment to the sharing of common rights and obligations.

What ultimate irony: after centuries—if not millennia—of discrimination and persecution for their otherness as a people and as a culture, when Jews finally got a chance to build their own state, they turned around and built it on the same stupid—and ultimately tragic—principles that had done them so much harm in the world for so long. I know, I know—there are reasons for this, not least the hostile environment in which they had to build that state, surrounded as they were by an overwhelming majority hell-bent on their annihilation once again. But a stupidity it is nevertheless, and a terrible renunciation of one of the central premises of Western civilization worthy of universal recognition: the separation of religion and politics.

This is what my grandmother and I talked about, and agreed upon, on the occasion of that first in a string of Middle Eastern wars and conflicts, in 1967, when sympathies for obvious historical reasons still lay almost entirely with the Jewish side, and when hardly anything was known about the plight of millions of displaced Palestinians in refugee camps in the surrounding countries, where they were not really welcome either. Ironically again, and just as tragic, only the massacre of Jewish athletes by ski-masked Palestinian terrorists at the 1972 Olympic Games in Munich began to change that lopsided picture of Middle Eastern realities, albeit in a terrible and entirely destructive way yet again.

After a year or so, the photographs and postcards of my blond granduncles with Hitler were withdrawn from circulation. It had transpired that the boys were the sons of Heinrich Martius, director of gynecology and obstetrics at the university clinic in Göttingen. That Martius had "a Jewish mother" was common knowledge in the city. Clearly, then, the boys were not the shining examples of Aryan youth that the Nazi state wanted to brag about. Nevertheless, the Nazi court photographer Hoffmann sent a hefty bill of 250 Reichsmarks along with those copies of the pictures that the Martius parents received in the mail. Of course, the Martiuses could not say that they did not want the pictures. They paid.

At the end of the war, an officer in the British occupying forces in Göttingen asked Heinrich's wife Berta to his office. He had stumbled across the photo in the local Nazi archives and wanted to know what it was all about. He then left Berta alone in his office for some time, under the pretext that he momentarily had to look after some other business. Clearly, he was inviting her to look at the thick dossier the Nazis had kept on the Martius family. This she did, and among other things she learned that it had been some of her husband's jealous colleagues at the university who had first told the authorities who the boys were. Some of these same colleagues would come running to him after the war, begging him for help in whitewashing their Nazi past with a supportive letter. As far as I know, he wrote those letters. He did not really care.

Unlike his little sister Lene in Hattenheim, Heinrich Martius was utterly convinced of his own greatness. His son Götz reports a most revealing story about him. At the end of the First World War, when Heinrich returned from years as a field surgeon to the university clinic in Bonn, he complained to his parents about the "disgusting" democratic revolution in Berlin ("I do not think that a republic is the desire of a majority of Germans"), and he uttered pessimistic thoughts about the future of his country. But what annoyed him more than anything else was that the occupying Canadian (!) forces in Bonn had taken away his officer's sword, and that the Canadian officers demanded he greet them in the streets of the university city. "I'd rather stay at home," he wrote.

Nobody could touch him, and nothing could harm him. According to various family accounts, the Martiuses blasted BBC news reports, broadcast from London, through the open windows of their villa all through the years of the next world war, the Second, even though listening to enemy broadcasts was punishable by death. And just before the smashing and burning of Jewish shops and businesses during the infamous *Reichskristallnacht* (Crystal Night, or Night of Broken Glass) in November 1938, Heinrich's wife Berta had unabashedly made purchases from a Jewish company in Hannover, at a time when this was strictly forbidden. Potential disaster was averted only by Heinrich claiming that he had not known about his wife's purchases (most likely true), and by Berta insisting that she had not known the company was Jewish (most likely a lie: its name was Herzberg).

The greatest danger, however, arose when Heinrich Martius applied to the Nazi authorities in Berlin to have some of the anti-Semitic restrictions lifted that the Nazi laws had placed on his family. In particular, he was worried about his sons, who were about to be shipped to the Russian Front. They had had to sign sworn statements that they would retain their rank as officers only until the end of the war. Heinrich feared that this would lessen their survival chances. Soldiers singled out as "special," officers or otherwise, were often given the most dangerous assignments. Like his father before him in the First World War, Heinrich would lose two of his sons in the Second, one of them at Stalingrad.

Early in 1943, Heinrich Martius received a letter from a Karl Schofeld in Berlin, who advised him to withdraw his letter of application because it would doubtlessly rouse the suspicion of the Nazis in the Reichssippenamt (for which Schofeld worked) and might have consequences far more dire than the restrictions Martius wanted to have lifted. Schofeld volunteered to meet with Martius secretly, to discuss with him some way of getting out from underneath the Reichssippenamt's watchful eye, and to return to him his application letter in person. He also advised him to immediately destroy his (Schofeld's) letter. The meeting took place some time in early 1943, but Berta, once again in gleeful defiance of obvious danger, kept the letter. Götz found it among his parents' papers, and in 1989 he managed to locate Schofeld's widow in Berlin. It transpired that her husband had stashed away, in a basement cupboard, some sixty similar letters and applications from Jewish families to the Reichssippenamt—all of which he had withheld from further processing. "There was," the widow wrote to Götz, "considerable danger of life in what my husband did. But he did it anyway."

Heinrich himself always maintained that he had no idea why the Nazis never went after him and his family. As the family story goes, some well-meaning authority in Berlin must have held a protective hand over them, and that someone must have been higher up than Karl Schofeld, the brave little bureaucrat-turned-hero. Another family explanation is that the Nazis were reluctant to touch Martius because he was too famous in his field—a world-renowned physician. That explanation is hardly convincing, considering how the Nazis treated the far more famous journalist and pacifist Carl von Ossietzky even after he had been awarded the Nobel Peace Prize in 1936. By that time, Ossietzky was dying in a concentration camp. One could in fact argue the reverse—that Martius was not internationally renowned enough, and not *Jewish* enough, for the Nazis to bother making an example of him.

There is yet another, and nastier, possible explanation for how the famous gynecologist got away, not only with his carelessly displayed Jewishness but also with his hardly concealed contempt for the Nazis and his refusal to join the Nazi Party. One of the most hideous Nazi policies was the forced sterilization of women deemed to be carriers of—in the Nazis' own terminology—*unwertes Leben* (unworthy life). The victims mainly were those classified as mentally ill or retarded, but also included gypsies and homosexuals (or the mothers of homosexuals) until these unfortunate groups later joined the Jews in the extermination camps. At the time, forced or compulsory sterilization programs existed in many countries, including Canada (until 1972 in Alberta). In that era, the idea of eugenics was widely accepted as a kind of actively manipulated biological Darwinism. Only the Nazis, however, practised forced sterilization as part of a concerted effort to breed a superior Aryan race. In the United States, by contrast, according to Götz's research again, sterilizations were carried out only on mental patients already institutionalized. In Nazi Germany, the policy applied to the entire population. According to some estimates, about 400,000 sterilizations were carried out in Nazi Germany between 1933 and 1945—about fourteen times as many as in the entire United States during the same period.

Forced sterilizations were also carried out at Göttingen University's gynecological clinic, whose director was Heinrich Martius. About 150 of them (from an estimated total of 800) he performed himself. He even developed a new and less invasive method for the surgical procedure. One can at the very least speculate that the Nazis did not go after him, or heed repeated calls for his dismissal from the clinic by various of his ardent Nazi colleagues, because he was complying in a way that the Nazis expected him to comply as a gynecologist. Besides, he was only of "second-degree mixed race."

Heinrich Martius clearly was not a Nazi. First and foremost, he was one of the most gifted and innovative gynecologists of his time. His textbooks were studied by generations of medical students. He also wrote public health pamphlets with the explicit purpose of making pregnancy and childbirth easier for women by explaining to them in simple terms the changes and processes their bodies were undergoing. He was far ahead of his time in his least-invasive approaches to the treatment of gynecological problems. He was a scholar driven by the desire to improve medical treatment and operating techniques for his patients.

Yet he was also an unabashed patriarch. He named his clinic "New Bethlehem." He was convinced not only that his calling was to help women but also that it was up to him to decide what was best for them. "I will take care of your little problem," he reportedly used to say to the women looking up at him from the operating table. My mother, who belonged to the older generation, loved her uncle Heinrich. Her younger sister Ursula no longer did. In the 1960s she had gone to Göttingen for the birth of her daughter Sophie, and she resented what seemed to her his utterly inappropriate patriarchal manner. Caught in an age that believed almost universally in eugenics as a form of human improvement, Heinrich Martius probably really did think he was helping women with their little problems when he sterilized them.

40 | *Same subject continued*

My grandmother in Hattenheim had to deal with the Nazis as well, and she did so in her own incomparable way. While her son Rolf was stashed away in the Odenwaldschule, her daughters Gerda and Renate had to, and of course wanted to, join the local Nazi youth organization for girls, the BDM or Bund deutscher Mädchen. Lene was horrified but knew full well that a refusal was out of the question. What could she do? She volunteered to have the local BDM chapter hold its weekly meetings in her own house so that she could keep an eye on the girls and monitor what was going on. In doing so, she would also be signalling cooperation with local Nazi activities in the most harmless way possible. That room, one of the large rooms facing the village street, is now Gerda's beautiful kitchen. But it is still called the BDM-Zimmer (the BDM room) by most family members.

On another occasion my grandmother had to take on the system more directly, and with a more daring leap of faith. After the birth of her fifth child she qualified for a kind of Nazi mother Cross of Honour. The application arrived in the mail one day and of course it contained a requirement to provide proof of Aryan purity because the Nazis obviously did not intend to honour mothers for bringing Jewish brats into the world. My grandmother went to the village mayor and told him she could not provide that proof. The mayor looked at her and said: "Did not one of your children die? So you really had only four." Then he tossed out the application.

That episode invites us to rethink our assumptions about the totalitarian character of the Nazi regime. Totalitarianism is usually defined as a political system that controls not only the entire public sphere but also invades private space systematically and totally. I contend that the Nazis never had the means for that kind of control. They could not possibly control every village mayor, for instance. A village mayor therefore could either be a committed Nazi or not. The latter was obviously true in the case of Hattenheim's mayor at the time of my grandmother's close brush with the Cross of Honour.

I am convinced that the Nazi regime was in fact primarily a chaotic regime, driven by a small band of ideologically deranged leaders in Berlin and a few other strongholds, sustained by a population skilfully manipulated into widespread collaboration by the nationalistic propaganda machine. In all this, the Nazis were aided by the fact that most Germans had not had a chance to acquire any democratic or critical political skills since the collapse of their empire in 1918. What made the Nazi regime so dangerous for the general population was precisely this chaotic arbitrariness. Of course the Nazis did come close to succeed in achieving their own totalitarian ambitions in one particularly monstrous instance: the extermination of an entire people and culture in the Holocaust.

My favourite aunt Gerda was told about the family's Jewish ancestry by her mother when she was eighteen and about to leave home. Around that time she also met a young Prussian career officer, Carl-Otto von Hinckeldey, whom she married a few years later, in 1941, with the war already going on. Gerda recalls that she boasted about being Jewish to her friends and never thought this could ever have serious repercussions. Of course, Gerda also told Hinckeldey. It would not have mattered to him then. The army was proud of its tradition of staying out of politics, including, at that time, Nazi politics.

Some time after their son Christian (my cousin Chris) was born, however, Hinckeldey, already a General Staff colonel, took measures to join the *Waffen-SS*. Perhaps he was pressured to do so, perhaps he just thought it would be good for his career. As part of the army, the *Waffen-SS* was not the same as Himmler's infamous *Schutzstaffel-SS*. But it was of course meant to be a way for SS combat units, which had direct links to the Nazi leadership, to infiltrate the German Army proper. Seeking membership in the *Waffen-SS*, Hinckeldey now had to prove the Aryan purity of himself and his family.

Nobody has a convincing explanation for what happened next— except, of course, that the Prussian career officer turned out to have a rather flawed character. At the time, Hinckeldey was stationed on the Greek island of Crete. He would see his son, Christian, only once, as a little baby, during a short leave. There were rumours that he had an affair with the daughter of a wealthy local grape grower. In later retellings of this part of the family saga, this woman was mockingly referred to as the *Rosinenkönigin* (raisin queen), naturally followed by the obligatory round of giggles. In any case, a letter arrived one day in Hattenheim in which Hinckeldey suddenly began to express anti-Semitic sentiments to his wife, such as that it was horrible for him to think that Jewish blood was flowing through his son's veins. Why he wrote that remains unclear. Perhaps he just wanted an excuse for a divorce and a new life with the raisin queen. More likely, he felt trapped by the situation and panicked. Once connected to the *Waffen-SS*, his "Jewish connection" would be found out sooner or later.

For the first time, the family was scared for real. All letters from the military were of course censored. Somewhere—possibly in the hands of the SS—there was a record of the Jewishness of the Wachendorffs. But nothing ever came of it. Luckily, the war ended soon after.

And it was hardly over when who do you think appeared on the front steps of the Hattenheim house? Hinckeldey! He was now asking not only to be taken back into the family but also to be aided by the family with his de-Nazification—after all, had he not bravely married a partly Jewish woman? He never got to see Gerda and Christian. My grandfather took him aside, showed him the nasty letter he had written from Crete, and told him to sign the divorce papers and split or else this letter would go the American authorities. He signed and split.

41 | *Postscript*

In 1953, Gerda and Christian emigrated to Portland, Oregon, where Gerda's second husband Hans-Erich von Schmidt auf Altenstadt was already waiting for them. The move was occasioned by the job Hans-Erich had been offered at Portland's art museum, but it also had about it unmistakable signs of liberation echoing the title of Robert Graves's famous First World War memoir, *Good-bye to All That*. It was a goodbye to thirteen years of living under the shadow of the Nazis, to the memory of her marriage to the unsavoury Hinckeldey, and to her overbearing father. Only her mother sadly rhymed: "The day will come when your dark eyes will be close to me again, smilingly."

Grandfather Alfred had reacted violently against the new boyfriend. Gerda and Hans got married in a civil ceremony on their own, and when she brought the groom to the house in Hattenheim afterwards, she heard her father yell upstairs: "What does this bloke want here?" He then grudgingly opened a bottle of champagne. At the end of the day, on their wedding night, Gerda stayed in Hattenheim with her son Christian, and

Gerda and the "bloke" on their wedding day.

Hans-Erich took the last train back to Wiesbaden.

In Portland, one of the first things Gerda heard when she turned on the radio were the McCarthy hearings. That is when she almost had the breakdown that she had managed to avoid during all those dark years back in Germany. She had travelled eight thousand kilometres to get away from the country that had persecuted Jews as an inferior species, only to end up in a country that seemed immersed in yet another witch hunt, this time against communists, alleged or real. It did not help when she realized, quite soon, that while liberal Portland did not seem to exercise any form of discrimination against blacks, it apparently was not possible for Jews to buy property in certain neighbourhoods. This shocking realization came when one of her friends, Edith Carr, and her husband, both Holocaust survivors from Berlin, tried to buy a house in one of those neighbourhoods.

Then, of course, came Vietnam and Watergate. Gerda had moved from the most perverted dictatorship in human history to a deeply troubled republic. The difference was, as Gerda would be first to point out, that America, at least for the time being, always had the strength to find the road back to sanity on its own.

42 | *In from the cold*

The Hinckeldey saga is not over quite yet. First of all, Gerda insists that she knew nothing about Hinckeldey reappearing in Hattenheim at the end of the war, and she doubts that her father would have dealt with him without telling her. Did I, as a young and impressionable boy, misunderstand what my mother had told me? Did my mother, endowed with a vivid imagination herself, embellish the dramatic finale when she told her little son? We will never know. But Hinckeldey did sign, and he did split.

But that was not the last time the family heard of him. In Wiesbaden, he married again, this time to the owner of a nightclub called the Martini Bar. He became its manager. This must have been in 1954, when Gerda and Hans were already in Portland. My rather prudish grandfather feared that the family name might be dragged into an abyss of sleaze and dispatched to the bar a contingent of family members and friends whom Hinckeldey had never met before (including my father, if I remember correctly) in order to check it out. It appears that it was a rather harmless establishment.

Seven years later, news broke about Hinckeldey that was not so harmless. He had been arrested as a spy. He was back in the new West German army and had a desk job that gave him access to sensitive Ministry of Defence files. According to the German newsmagazine *Der Spiegel*, he had shared some of those files with a former comrade and superior, a General Feuchtinger, who now worked as a spy for East Germany and the KGB. Feuchtinger, by the way, had been best man at Gerda's first wedding.

Hinckeldey's involvement in West Germany's first postwar spy scandal turned out to be more hapless than sinister. Exploiting his connections with a number of former war buddies, Feuchtinger had moved around freely in the ministry, and Hinckeldey thought that the material requested was meant for the general's memoirs. In the end, Hinckeldey was sentenced to only six months in prison. And *that* is the last we ever heard of him.

But it is worth noting that Carl-Otto von Hinckeldey had a famous great-grandfather, Karl Ludwig Friedrich von Hinckeldey, who was the Police President of Berlin from 1848 to 1856 and who also, after 1853, had been the General Director of Police in the Prussian Ministry of the Interior. The older Hinckeldey not only put out successfully whatever radical fires were still burning in Prussia after the 1848 revolutions, but also formed the Polizeiverein (Police Union) for the purpose of coordinating the surveillance of liberal, democratic, and other radical elements across Germany and even Europe. Hinckeldey's agents carried out undercover operations in London, where Karl Marx in his British Museum library carrel was probably saved from the Prussian police chief's wrath only by the fact that the British police essentially refused to cooperate. At home, his attention was focused on two particular seedbeds of liberalism: newspapers and theatres. As William Grange, professor in the Johnny Carson School of Theatre and Film at the University of Nebraska, writes: "Hinckeldey's system of spies, identity checks, press seizures, and deportations became notorious in the 1850s." Ferdinand Lasalle, founder of the first

German Labour Party, at the time referred to Hinckeldey as the "white terror." The elder Hinckeldey died, like Lasalle, in a duel.

It is worth noting that the older Hinckeldey's career as Prussia's premier enforcer of law and order began precisely at a time when another member of our family, the painter and radical spirit Carl Simon, fled Stuttgart and eventually ended up in Chile. It is not entirely far-fetched to speculate that Simon's name cropped up in Hinckeldey's surveillance files. In the case of my cousin Chris, Gerda's son, this would mean that one of his great-great-great-grandfathers spied on one of his great-great-grandfathers.

The arrest of Carl-Otto von Hinckeldey as a spy in 1961 made the headlines in Portland's newspapers. Gerda was worried that this news about his biological father would upset Chris. It didn't. He had become an American citizen, thought of Hans-Erich as his real father, and called himself Chris von Schmidt. Later, after he had immigrated to Australia and become an Australian citizen, he adopted the Hinckeldey name again. Chris sells books—in fact, entire libraries of them—for Blackwell's in Oxford. Like his mother, he is at peace with the past. He and I are lucky. For the most part, we have been spared from having to make difficult choices of the kind our parents and their parents, grandparents, and great-grandparents had to make. When we meet, in Sydney or in Hattenheim, we speak English. We are both citizens of a new world now.

43 | *Favourite aunt*

According to my mother, who had a sharp tongue on occasion, her sister Gerda always had to have something special or different. That was her verdict on the Prussian career officer Carl-Otto von Hinckeldey as well: far too outlandish for the girl who would a few years later settle for the "little doctor." But my mother's favourite story about her sister Gerda was about the time the children were given money for chocolate and went across the street to Kling's bakery. Of course, Gerda had to have something different and chose a bar of *Eidotterschokolade* (egg yolk chocolate). It tasted horrible, and Gerda threw herself on her bed, sobbing. Ever since, in our family, when someone wants something different or outlandish, regardless of whether it turns out to be a disappointment or not, we look at one another with a knowing and resigned frown, and say: *Eidotterschokolade*.

Some time during the early 1960s, Gerda, who worked in the music room of the Portland Public Library, sent a recording of Bach's *Well-Tempered Clavier* played by a pianist then still rather unknown in Europe:

Glenn Gould. My grandmother played it for me. I did not like it. Gould's idiosyncratic approach to playing Bach, emphasizing rhythm and polyphonic drive rather than lingering on the harmonic structure, seemed to me a clear case of Gerda's *Eidotterschokolade* again. I was used to the romantic German interpretations of Bach with lots of pedal and emotion. Like much of the rest of the world, I eventually changed my mind. Gould's Bach not only became the yardstick for everyone else, but also foreshadowed the general trend to free baroque music from overly romantic performance practices. As so often, Gerda was one step ahead of everyone else.

At the time, we did not even know that Gould was Canadian. We found that out only when the news spread that he had renounced playing live concerts and had moved to the Canadian "north," to an unknown place called "Georgian Bay." For a long time I imagined the eccentric genius surrounded by eternal snow, pulled along by a team of sled dogs and playing the piano under the light of an oil lamp. I told Julia about this during one of our annual camping trips to Killbear Provincial Park, a beautiful spot halfway up Georgian Bay. As we lay in the sun, on the pink rocks of the Canadian Shield, gazing across the bay, with the blue water twinkling in the summer heat, we giggled.

I had no problems with something else Gerda sent from America: Chris's used clothes. I was a few years younger, and they usually fit me well after they had become too small for him. I probably was one of the first boys in Germany to wear blue jeans, and I especially loved a padded winter jacket, a kind of lumberjack coat complete with (fake) fur collar and a metal buckle in front. In rural Bavaria, I was the king of clothes among my schoolmates. Kids' clothing had not yet become a matter of relentless peer pressure and mass marketing.

Gerda was my brother Michi's godmother. Mine was Mucki. Gerda sent Michi birthday gifts from Amerika. I was jealous. Sometimes, for Christmas, she sent presents for all of us. Once, there were little ink-brush paintings of lobsters, quickly but skilfully dashed off by a street artist on Portland harbour. My brother and I did not even know what lobsters were. I still have two of them, now hanging in our Canadian kitchen.

From Gerda's letters, mostly to her mother, who then told my mother, who then told us, we got the impression that life in the New World was as exciting as it was exotic. My cousin Chris had abalone for supper! (When I finally arrived in Portland for a visit, some twenty-five years later, there was not a single abalone left on the Oregon coast.) Chris had not been a very adventurous boy back in Germany, and now he was playing high school football! The friends of Gerda and Hans were mostly painters,

A smiling Gerda during the years in Portland, Oregon.

whose works they collected and hung in their home. That home had a porch overlooking the city and snow-capped Mount Hood in the distance. Hans regularly fed "wild animals" at the back door. They were raccoons. The German word for racoon is *Waschbär* (literally "wash bear"). Hence I imagined Hans-Erich opening the back door to a couple of wild bears, who then demanded not only food but also a pail of water so that they could wash the food before eating it.

What we did not get from Gerda's letters—because she carefully avoided mentioning it to her parents—was that the von Schmidts in Portland at least initially had very little money. The house was rented and small. Besides the raccoons, two growing teenage boys had to be fed (by then, Hans-Erich's son Wolf was also part of the household). Once when my grandmother visited them, during the early years, they naturally took her on excursions, to museums, concerts, and restaurants. As Gerda recalls, not without some lingering resentment, her thrifty mother did not volunteer to pay for anything.

On the last day of her visit, my grandmother announced that she wanted to buy some souvenirs for her family. She went and bought one apron, and a second one only after Gerda had reminded her that she had *two* daughters back home. Then, on her departure, she triumphantly held in the air a whole wad of money and gleefully announced: "Fred will be so happy that I am bringing it all back!" Fred wasn't the happy one—*she* was. My grandmother had turned rather chintzty in her old age, in contrast to her husband, who had mellowed and become more generous. During my military stint in Mainz, he sometimes took me aside and gave me a hundred-mark bill, whispering: "But don't tell grandmother."

We were surprised, then, when Gerda wanted to move back to Hattenheim and share the old house with her parents. Everybody expected that the renewed confrontation between my grandfather and the "bloke," Hans-Erich, would lead to disaster. It didn't. The older and milder Alfred struck a warm friendship with Hans-Erich. And, perhaps for the first time, he developed a genuine admiration for his eldest daughter. That Hans-Erich and Gerda had returned from successful lives and careers in America was not lost on him. Gerda, though, had to deal with her increasingly more difficult mother, who had back her oldest daughter with the dark eyes, "smilingly," but who sometimes seemed to resent the presence of another woman in the house, one who was younger and also growing more resolute about what she wanted.

Gerda and Hans-Erich moved into the top floor. Now we could see all the art they had collected in Portland. It was a revelation. I had been surrounded by old madonna and landscape paintings most of my life and knew modern art only from museums. There also was a deck and roof garden where Gerda served delicious Indonesian food. I knew such food only from restaurants. And there was music. During her last weeks and months in Portland, Gerda had made tape copies of her favourite albums in the music library, hundreds of them, neatly organized and complete with her own cross-referenced catalogue.

A new pattern of social life developed in the Hattenheim house. Visitors came mainly to see the grandparents, of course. Gerda and Hans-Erich were expected to show up at least once a day. Usually, this happened after an early supper, when everybody gathered around grandfather's big TV (only he was allowed to use the remote control) to watch some of his favourite shows, like *The Avengers* (Diana Rigg as Emma Peel had replaced the lady friends he could no longer visit), or some opera broadcast (with Anneliese Rothenberger and Teresa Stratas being his all-time favourites). When the show was over, Gerda and Hans would say their good-nights and leave. The rest of us would politely hang around for a little while longer and then, after a few ostentatious yawns, retreat as well. But that did not necessarily mean bedtime. Instead we would scramble upstairs and join Gerda and Hans for a bottle of Riesling, music, and conversation that often lasted well into the night.

When my grandmother died, two years after her husband, Gerda and Hans-Erich moved downstairs. This is when the old BDM-Zimmer became Gerda's new kitchen. The grandparents had used it only as a storage room. Actually, it became kitchen and dining room in one because Gerda had it partitioned with a counter to match the large room's wood panelling. When Gerda came up with this plan, the family was skeptical. What on earth was she up to now? Was it another case of *Eidotterschokolade*? When it was finished, it became an instant success. The counter was high enough to hide the kitchen appliances from the dining area, but low enough to allow the cook to converse with her guests. It stretched three-quarters of the way across the room so that one could still walk from one part to the other. Dishes appeared on it before they were passed to the dining table.

Yet again, Gerda had been ahead of everyone else. She had successfully combined the idea of an open kitchen with that of a kitchen island long before either became common in Germany. The decorative stencil paintings around the edges of the room's ceiling remained untouched. They had been there when the little *BDM* girls milled around below.

44 | Hans-Erich

Perhaps because of Gerda's preference for the unconventional, Hans-Erich had developed a habit of always protesting everything before usually relenting. "You are totally crazy," he would declare with predictable regularity, and probably he had done so when Gerda first came up with the partition idea for the BDM-Zimmer kitchen. He was one of the nicest, gentlest, and most polite human beings I have ever met. He was a Dutch-German nobleman, a *jonkheer* or baron. If Gerda had reached for something special yet again, she surely hit the jackpot this time.

When my father wanted to tease Gerda (they liked each other a lot), he would exclaim, when she entered the room: "Ah, the baroness!" Yet Hans-Erich never once gave me the impression that his nobility made any difference to him one way or the other. It was just a family fact and name. The main thrill for Gerda seems to have been border crossings into the Netherlands. Several members of the von Schmidt auf Altenstadt clan had been in charge of the Dutch border police until quite recently, and when Hans and Gerda showed their passports to the inspecting officers, they would sometimes spring to attention and salute when they recognized the name.

Hans-Erich and Gerda were cousins by marriage. This raised (some) eyebrows as well as (more) giggles. My grandfather's sister Erna had married Theo Hengstenberg. One of Theo's sisters had married Hans-Erich's father. Gerda's best friends were her real cousins, Lore and Irmela, the children of Theo and Erna, who were also Hans-Erich's real cousins. There was an additional Hengstenberg aunt, by the name of Reni, who lived in the Austrian Alps and had to be visited annually. Gerda dreaded these visits. Reni had married an Austrian skiing instructor whom she had met as a young woman during one of the family vacations. I am not sure I remember this correctly, because it sounds almost too good to be true, but I think his name was Toni. (In German jokes about young ladies and their romantic adventures in the mountains, the name of the skiing instructor is always Toni.) As long as he was still around, Reni's skiing instructor was mostly drunk.

Reni was a proud and lifelong Nazi, the only one the family ever produced. During the endless and boring evenings during these annual visits, as Gerda recalls, there always arrived the moment when Reni turned to Gerda and proclaimed: "You know, I am an anti-Semite." And as even I can recall, she steadfastly insisted that the American moon landing of 1969 had been staged on a Hollywood film set. In a way, and inadvertently, of course, she exemplified the intellectual stupidity to which anti-Semitism, and racism more generally, belong.

Because of his father's marriage into the Hengstenberg family, Hans-Erich was a dual citizen: the Netherlands and Germany. He had been sent to school in Germany but otherwise grew up in Indonesia and became a tea planter there. Indonesia was a Dutch colony at the time. Whether the Schmidt auf Altenstadts owned or merely operated their tea plantations, I don't know. But I remember Hans-Erich talking about the variety of sambals his grandmother made and kept in the pantry. When Gerda served her Indonesian meals, the sambal was commercial and invariably from the Dutch Conimex company.

Hans-Erich was almost completely bald and had large ears with beautifully shaped lobes. While he was telling his Indonesian tales over dinner, every once in a while he would put a heaped teaspoonful of sambal directly into his mouth. The rest of us would gasp at the sight, but his only reaction would be two tiny drops of sweat dripping down his earlobes. Then he would remark that his grandmother's sambals had been much hotter.

When the Second World War broke out, he was on a ship sailing from Germany to Indonesia. When it anchored at Suez, the British pulled him off, accusing him of being a German spy. (That's how I heard it. Gerda insists that he was arrested in Indonesia and then shipped to India. I like my version better.) He spent the war in a British prison camp in India, building a tennis court for the first few years, playing on it for the remaining years. On special holidays, he was allowed to dress up and have a drink with the prison commander. (Gerda thinks that didn't happen, but I am sure I heard it from Hans-Erich himself.) It must have been a rather boring life, but ultimately his fate was of course much better—and a lot more harmless—than that of those millions who went to war and died. Fully aware of this, Hans-Erich never complained about these years.

At the end of the war, having been released from prison camp, he made it back to Wiesbaden. He did not have a job, and he could not go back to Indonesia. The Dutch colonies and their plantations were gone. Sukarno had declared Indonesia's independence in 1945. Someone in Wiesbaden told Hans-Erich that he might get a job with the Americans at the local Collecting Point. That was one of the places where the Americans were gathering all of Europe's displaced works of art. These included entire museum collections that had been hidden from the war and the bombing raids, as well as thousands of works of art that the Nazis had stolen from private Jewish owners. The Wiesbaden Collecting Point mainly handled museum collections from Berlin that had been recovered from salt mines in Thuringia and Hesse. The goal was to return them to their rightful places and owners—an enormous logistical task that involved finding, identifying, cataloguing, sometimes securing or even repairing, packing, and shipping.

So one day Hans-Erich walked up the steps to Wiesbaden's art museum, which was the local headquarters for the operation. Eventually, he found himself in a room where a bunch of Americans in uniform were standing around the famous bust of Nefertiti. The fragile sculpture had to be transferred to a different room, and nobody dared touch it. There are different accounts of what happened next, but the way I remember hearing it is this: Hans-Erich, sensing his opportunity, stepped forward, picked up Nefertiti, and carried her to her destination. He had a job.

Nefertiti made it safely back to Berlin. In 1995, Julia and I visited her. While entirely regal, she seemed a bit indignant about her fate as an itinerant Egyptian queen. Five years after the fall of the Berlin Wall, she found herself still on hold in a temporary collection, awaiting final transfer to the New Museum in former East Berlin. It was a sombre occasion. Hans-Erich was dead. I could not tell him that I had finally caught up with his queen. We had just come from the spot nearby where another regal woman, Rosa Luxemburg, had been murdered and tossed into the waters of the Landwehrkanal by facist thugs in 1919. I thought of the heroic and tragic life that feminist and socialist had led, and I remembered the stark and moving images from Margarethe von Trotta's 1986 docudrama with the congenial Barbara Sukowa in the title role.

Later that day, our visit to Berlin took a decidedly lighter and more festive turn when we visited the Reichstag, which had been just been wrapped by Christo. All day and night during this monumental two-week artistic happening, hundreds of thousands of people milled about the huge shrink-wrapped building. It was a fantastic time—a people's festival and fair with musicians, jugglers, bratwurst stands, and streams of beer. Had Hans-Erich been around, he would have enjoyed every moment of it, even though his initial reaction would have been that Christo was "totally crazy."

Hans-Erich kept his job at the Wiesbaden Collecting Point until the early 1950s. He eventually wrapped up most of the work more or less by himself, after the Americans left. Then he was out of work again. Obviously, there weren't any tea plantations around the corner, and the Germans, back in charge with their usual bureaucratic rigour, did not offer him any museum jobs either, because he did not have formal qualifications such as a degree in art history. The notion of employing a former tea planter for a museum job was outright preposterous. So what if he had carried Nefertiti? And so what if he had handled at some point or other just about every piece of art belonging to all the museums of Berlin combined? He wasn't qualified, period.

Fortunately, the Americans did not think so. They were willing to recognize talent and dedication when they saw it, regardless of title and certificate. Among the officers huddled around Nefertiti when Hans-Erich first encountered her was Tom Howe (Thomas Carr Howe), director of the Fine Arts Museum of San Francisco in civilian life. Back in San Francisco, when he heard about Hans-Erich's predicament, he helped him find the job in Portland.

Probably because he was a heavy smoker, Hans-Erich developed emphysema. The last time I saw him, I had already moved to Canada and was on a pre-Christmas visit back to Germany, which as usual included a brief stopover in Hattenheim. As it happened, I was to accompany Gerda and Hans on an afternoon visit to the Kronzuckers, next door. Dieter Kronzucker was a TV journalist who had just returned from a five-year stint as a German TV channel's chief Washington correspondent. While Mrs. Kronzucker served tea and Christmas cookies, her husband entertained us by holding forth on his views about America. These turned out to be exceptionally simplistic and superficial. Kronzucker had obviously seen Ronald Reagan's America only from behind the tinted windows of an air-conditioned limousine.

Towards the end, and finally out of breath, Kronzucker looked at me—for the first time, really—and asked: "And what, may I ask, are you doing?" Very deliberately, I replied: "I am a professor of political science in North America." There was a long and rather embarrassed silence. A little later we slowly walked back to the house. Of course, Gerda and I giggled. Hans-Erich never giggled. He only chuckled. It must have been one of his last chuckles. He died very soon afterwards.

45 | *Family reunions*

In October 1968, we celebrated the grandparents' golden wedding anniversary. Everybody came: the Hüglins from Munich, and Rolf and his family from their new home in neighbouring Johannisberg. Ursula came with her little daughter Sophie from Essen, where her husband was curator of the Folkwangmuseum. Gerda and Hans-Erich came all the way from Portland. There was an assortment of family friends, including even some of my grandfather's former lady friends, who had long since become fixtures in the extended family. There were local dignitaries coming and going all day with speeches and flowers. The day began with a champagne breakfast and a concert by the Oestrich volunteer fire-brigade brass band on the lawn of the upper garden. The festivities continued all day with more food, speeches, and champagne—or rather, *Sekt*, the Rheingau variety of the bubbly—and it ended with everybody sitting around in small groups reminiscing not only about the day but about the entire family history.

Reunions were and still are a central part of family life. Grandfather Alfred loved them because he usually was the centre of attention. Grandmother Lene organized them. We went whenever there was one, occasioned by a special birthday, a wedding anniversary, Christmas, or even Easter. The earliest one I can remember was Easter 1954. Grandfather had hidden so many Easter eggs in the lower garden that his wife had to draw a map of their locations. After several hours, we still had not found them all. Later that year, in October or November, a letter from my grandmother arrived in Ebenhausen telling us that during her walks in the garden, some eggs were still glittering at her through the fall leaves.

With Julia and Jacob, more than forty years later, during my Mannheim sabbatical, we had another of those Easter-egg hunts in Hattenheim. It took place on Gerda's terrace, with the children of my cousin Robert, Rolf's youngest son. With his family, he now lives above Gerda in the old house.

Most of these family reunions included musical or theatrical peformances. Both my grandmother and my father played the piano; my mother played the recorder; her sister Ursula was an accomplished violinist. Music usually did not involve us children, but on one occasion there was a performance of some classical piece that included cuckoo calls—by Josef Haydn, I think—that I played on the recorder. More often, the assembled grandchildren were called upon to participate in brief sketches that my grandmother wrote, usually as a birthday surprise for grandfather. There had to be secret rehearsals before the performance itself in front of the family. I remember one that involved a phone call to the missing oldest grandchild, Christian, in Portland, but I have no idea what the rest was about. It was just so exciting to actually talk to Chris over the phone and across such a long distance before passing the receiver to our grandfather. I loved these performances. I had always wanted to become an actor. Strutting about and holding forth in front of a large class at the university has become my substitute theatrical activity.

Long-distance phone calls, let alone transcontinental calls, were still very expensive back then. Gerda says that during all those years in Portland, she called her parents only twice. And the parents never called her. She and her mother instead exchanged hundreds of letters during the twenty years they were separated. Gerda's letters are all in a drawer at the house in Hattenheim, neatly bundled and kept by my grandmother. When I asked Gerda whether she ever felt like reading them again, she sighed and said that the letters would give only a one-sided picture of their lives in Portland. She had written to her mother only about the exciting and positive things. The rest she left out.

After I moved to Canada, attending these reunions became more difficult. The European members of our family don't quite understand that. They always expect us to quickly hop across the Atlantic for this, that, or the other occasion, but when we ask them when they might show up in Canada for a return visit, their usual answer is: "To Canada? We'd need at least four or five weeks …" Few of them ever come.

The main event in Hattenheim now is Gerda's birthday. But it is in October, when Julia and I both teach and Jacob is in school. So when a large party was planned for her eightieth birthday, we had to decline. At the last minute, however, I bought a ticket and flew over for three days, not missing a single lecture. Gerda's face, when I stood at the door unannounced on the morning of the party, was ample reward for the considerable expense and a sleepless night on the plane.

My father was still alive for that occasion, and he had come with my sister Andrea and her husband from Munich. He was already frail, never really having recovered fully from the loss of his wife, but he had a good time, still wearing the old tux he had worn all his life for festive occasions. It was a grand occasion with a catered buffet, streams of Riesling and *Sekt*, of course, and the octogenarian tirelessly on her feet for twelve hours or more.

Naturally, there was a musical performance. We all spilled into the entrance hall, where Ursula's daughter Sophie, halfway up the first flight of stairs, sang Turkish songs. Tall and blond, she had grown up in a Turkish neighbourhood in the North German city of Bremen. She speaks Turkish fluently, and she has been lead singer in a Turkish rock band for a number of years. It was the last concert I ever attended with my father. But it was not the last concert in Hattenheim.

For Gerda's eighty-fifth birthday in 2004, Julia and I did take a week from our academic duties and flew to Germany, leaving Jacob at a friend's house. Because my father had died a year earlier, I felt I needed to continue the tux tradition, so I bought one, at Tuxedo Royale in the Kitchener Fairview Mall. The somewhat hapless salesperson, himself looking like a shop-window best man, could not quite believe that I was there to buy a tuxedo rather than rent one, and that it was not even for a wedding. This time, the buffet was assembled from various family contributions. We had brought smoked salmon from Canada. Sophie sang again. A young Turkish woman, hired for the day to help out in the kitchen, had tears in her eyes. She was the only one besides Sophie who could understand the words.

Three years later, the family organized another party for Gerda's eighty-eighth. I could not get away, and we decided it was Julia's turn to represent the Canadian branch of the family. Gerda's ninetieth is already looming. With Julia busier than ever at the University of Waterloo and Jacob in his second year of high school, it looks like it will be my turn again for a three-day dash across the Atlantic.

46 | Gamelan meets baroque

In 2006 we also had a reunion on the Spanish island of Mallorca in the Mediterranean, about eight boat hours from Barcelona. After her divorce from the art historian and her retirement from an active career as a baroque violinist and music teacher in Bremen, Gerda's youngest sister Ursula had bought a farm there. The occasion was Ursula's seventieth birthday, which coincided with my sixtieth. The idea came up when we all sat around the table in Gerda's kitchen after the festivities for her eighty-fifth were over. I promised I would honour tradition and wear the tux again, no matter how hot the Mallorca sun.

Because Ursula's birthday falls in early summer, we all could go. It was an amazing event. About sixty people came, half of them family from all over the world, half of them Ursula's new Mallorcan friends. The main culinary event was a huge *paella*, the traditional Spanish dish consisting of saffron rice, seafood, and vegetables, cooked on an open fire in a round pan about a meter and a half across. Naturally, we expected musical entertainment as well, in the form of a little concert by Ursula and her friends. As it turned out, there were two concerts that day.

We had hardly arrived at the farm in the morning when about ninety minutes of gamelan music commenced, in the blazing sun—precise performances of various traditional pieces with Ursula the unquestioned leader of a group of Mallorcan musicians. Indeed, she had trained them all. Her interest in Indonesian music dated back to her time in Bremen. Before moving to Mallorca, she had travelled to Indonesia, where she had selected, bought, and had shipped to Mallorca the instruments for an entire gamelan ensemble, all kinds of xylophones, drums, and gongs.

Then came the *paella*, and with it streams of local cider and wine. After that, everyone retreated for a well-deserved siesta, except the Canadians—Julia, myself, and Jacob. Having arrived only the previous evening, and still without supplies for our rented apartment, we had to go shopping. My daughter Hannah came with us. In the next town, while looking for a supermarket, I drove too close to a curb and hit a sharp metal tube sticking out if it. We had a flat tire. After endless and useless phone calls to the car rental company, I finally changed the tire myself. Julia was most impressed. With my two left hands at home, in our 150-year-old Canadian house that constantly needs fixing, she would have never guessed that changing a tire was something I could do. Possibly, this was the only time anyone had ever changed a tire in Mallorca wearing a tuxedo with striped pants and patent-leather shoes.

We returned to the farm just in time for everyone to get ready for the second concert of the day. This time around, Ursula pulled out her trusty old baroque fiddle. Accompanied by a local harpsichordist, she played a series of early sonatas, and she played them very well. Obviously she had practised a lot. There were other performances. Madrigals were sung by an *a capella* choir that included Ursula. Sophie sang again. But it was Ursula who carried the day. She had played gamelan for over an hour in the morning, she had looked to her guests all day, and in the evening she had the strength, and the joy, to entertain them with another hour-long performance as precise and impressive as the one in the morning. Not bad for a seventy-year-old aunt.

47 | *Reborn*

This is the clan my mother Renate Hüglin, née Wachendorff, belongs to. She was born into it on 19 November 1923. She was named Renate, which means reborn (*re-nata*) in Latin, because she came a year after her mother had given birth to a baby girl, Marianne, who died almost immediately. So after Gerda and poor little Marianne, my mother was the third girl in a row. At her christening, assuming that the Wachendorffs had been hoping for a son and heir, the minister said: "It should have been a boy!"

I was reminded of this story when Julia and I prepared for our Canadian wedding. We had read the entire Bible in order to find some appropriate verses that were neither sexist nor implying naive faith—a difficult task indeed. We settled on the Song of Solomon, an obvious choice for those who want to celebrate love rather than original sin and redemption. We handed our verses to the minister, a friend and drinking buddy of Julia's from her undergraduate days. We instructed her, and she agreed not to stray from our choices. But then she betrayed us, cold-bloodedly, and obviously sober, by adding some cute story about baby Jesus to her sermon.

The story of aunt Ursula's wedding many moons ago also crept into my mind. There she stood at the altar, young and beautiful, all in white, next to a handsome groom, with a radiant smile on her face, and what did the minister say? He embarked upon a lengthy diatribe about how it was easy to be in love healthy and young, and how it would become much more difficult when the first wrinkles appeared on her face (I am not making this up). This minister probably jinxed Ursula's marriage there and then. My father obviously knew what he was doing when he left during the sermons all those years he played the organ on Sundays in Ebenhausen.

A case can be made for civil ceremonies. At least sometimes, secular authorities seem to have a better sense of what the situation calls for. When Gerda read this part of the first draft of the manuscript, she told me the story of her own wedding to Hans-Erich. It was a second marriage for both of them, she was a young mother, and both of them had just survived war and—in Hans-Erich's case—years of imprisonment. I will let her tell what happened in her own words: "The civil registrar began with the usual marriage gibberish. Then he interrupted himself, looked at us, and happily declared: 'Well, I don't think I need to tell you all this.'"

It was a second marriage for Julia and me, too. The obvious question is why we decided to get married in a church yet again. That question did cross my mind at the time, and it reminded me of yet another conversation I had with my grandmother, when I was fourteen and about to be confirmed. After attending church for a year as required, I had doubts as to whether I really believed all that baby-Jesus stuff. The wise and not so Aryan woman gave me a speech about the Judeo-Christian tradition, how it was part of our family culture and tradition, and how we had a right to pick from it and for ourselves whatever part we wanted. She then gave me the score of Bach's *St. Matthew Passion* as a confirmation gift. On Good Friday that year, I sat glued to the radio for two hours listening to a broadcast of this magnificent oratorio, reading the music along with it.

Our Canadian wedding was a smashing success, by the way. The immediate occasion was the rather imminent arrival of our son Jacob. Invitations for a shotgun wedding were sent out. It was the only time my father came to Canada. In church, my lawyer friend Julie Thorburn sang "Me and Bobby McGee," the Kris Kristofferson song of Janis Joplin fame. I had first heard it sung by Julia's four-year-old daughter Christian. She had a habit of singing it standing on a table in Janis Joplin pose. I had a maid of honour, Alison Wearing, who despite being a former student of mine had become a successful writer. Her first book, *Honeymoon in Purdah*, is an insightful and funny account of her travels through Iran. Julia had a best man, Jeff McNairn, a friend and colleague who went through the Ph.D. program in history at the University of Toronto with her. Our two daughters, one each from our first marriages, respectively, were the flower girls. At the reception, with a catered Lebanese buffet and streams of Spanish bubbly, Julie Thorburn danced with my father. A photo of the two of them is still pinned to Julie and her husband's fridge at their cottage up north.

Apropos second marriages: years later, when my cousin Peter remarried, renting an entire castle on the Rhine for the occasion, a grand occasion we missed owing to the usual Canadian scheduling problems, his eight-year-old niece Berenike snuggled up to her great-aunt Gerda a few days later and declared: "I think my big wedding will be the second one."

My "poor little mother" died suddenly at the age of sixty-nine, younger than most in our family, a year before Julia and I got married, and a year and a half before her grandson Jacob was born. It seems to be the fate of my children. My daughter Hannah was born a month after her maternal grandmother died. My mother was eight years younger than my father. Something she always used to tell him jokingly was in fact one of those family sayings that nobody can remember where it really came from: "Regardless of which of us dies first, I will move to Berlin."

48 | *Middle names*

My "poor little mother": actually, she had a pretty good life, and she rarely complained, even though she was saddled with the middle names Gertrud and Hedwig: Renate Gertrud Hedwig! Gertrud after her godmother aunt Gertie, the one who preferred to live with women in her house in Falkenstein near Wiesbaden and who, when she made her will, left something for everybody except her godchild Renate, whom she had totally forgotten. The other middle name, Hedwig, was a tribute to her grandmother in Wiesbaden, of course. My father's middle name was Otto, by the way, because that had been both his father's middle name and his grandfather's first name. I would become Thomas Otto, and I was teased about it not a few times in school. But my brother Michi's fate was worse, much worse. He got the names of both his grandfathers and was christened Michael Albert Alfred. No wonder he had lost most of his hair by his mid-twenties, like his grandfather Alfred. "Bald men make better lovers," Michi likes to say. Doubtless, his grandfather Alfred would have agreed.

49 | *Middle ground*

My mother was not the first-born daughter on whom parents try out their parenting skills for the first time. That was Gerda's fate. Nor was she the pampered last-born daughter who could hardly ever escape her aging father's incessant attention. That in turn was Ursula's fate. Nor, obviously, was she the only son who could never quite live up to his father's expectations. My mother occupied the family's middle ground, so to speak—sometimes taken for granted but other times able to get away with what the others hardly ever could.

By most accounts she was a feisty one. She herself liked telling the story about when her little brother Rolf was in trouble at the schoolyard and she took care of it by beating up a couple of bullies. Her mother's favourite story was the one about when she was punished for being naughty by having to stand in the corner of her room. "As long as she is watching you," her mother said, pointing to her doll in the other corner of the room, "you will remain in that corner." She then left the room for a few minutes. When she returned, she found little Renate happily hopping around her room, playing. "Did I not tell you that you had to stand in the corner while your doll was watching you?" she asked. Renate pointed to the doll, which was now facing the wall, and said: "I turned her around. She could not watch me."

According to another story often told, she used to run up to the staircase landing in the big entrance hall before throwing a tantrum. She had discovered that her yelling was magnified by the acoustics there. Our son Jacob has inherited some of his grandmother's theatrical skills. Barely out of his diapers, we caught him once practising crying grimaces in front of a mirror before bursting into tears in front of us.

We had a patient and understanding mother. But when she had enough, she had enough. On one occasion, my brother and I had a terrible fight (we had many) while she was preparing pancakes for lunch. At some point she got so mad at us that she took the pan off the fire, emphatically dumped the pancakes on the kitchen floor, and trampled on them in her high heels while yelling at us. I have no idea why she was wearing high heels in the kitchen, nor can I remember whether we did or did not get lunch that day (we probably did in the end).

50 | *Skin of our teeth*

She was easily offended and could not hide it. My father said she would pout like her father. My father also said that nothing cheered her up like good food. By a friend, the architect Otto Mayer, he had a picture of a ham painted on a little piece of paper that he carried in his wallet for years. Whenever they had a fight and she started making one of her faces, he would pull out the picture and hold it in front of her. It worked most of the time. Sometimes my brother and I, sensing a tiff, said to him: "Quick, daddy, show her the ham picture." More often than not, she would start laughing before he even had a chance to pull it out.

Like all the Wachendorff children, she was very close to her mother. But she also seems to have had a relationship with her father that was more relaxed than what her siblings endured. Of course, he played his power games with her as well. Time and again he would look at her and say: "You are not really our child. We found you under the bridge." Everybody would giggle. But according to Gerda, this hurt her feelings. In general, it seems that she mostly got along with her father. Maybe she somehow sensed, almost naively, that he could not touch her personality. Maybe I inherited that from her in my own dealings with grandfather.

There was not much that could seriously upset my mother. Quite unlike her husband, she let the past be the past and she did not worry much about the future. Or so everybody thought. Late in 1945, newly wed and pregnant, she went to see a play in Wiesbaden. The German theatres had reopened almost immediately after the war. They now were also free to perform foreign plays. On this occasion it was Thornton Wilder's *The Skin of Our Teeth*. The third act begins with the main characters emerging from a bunker after a nuclear war, and the question is hanging over them whether it is really worth trying to make a new beginning, since human beings never seem to learn from their previous mistakes. My mother had a hysterical fit halfway through that third act and had to be led out of the theatre by her husband.

51 | *War again*

Like her siblings before and after her, my mother went to public school across the street in Hattenheim and then was sent, by train, to the Ursulinen, a private high school run by the Ursuline nuns in neighbouring Geisenheim. She finished and graduated from high school in Wiesbaden, though, for the last year staying at her grandparents' house during the week. The reason was that the Nazis did not allow the Ursuline nuns to administer the graduation exams. One of Renate's teachers in Wiesbaden was Dorothea Wolff, who became a fixture in the extended Wachendorff family—as my grandmother's close intellectual friend rather than as one of Alfred's lady friends. Dorothea at one point got into rather deep trouble when she announced in school, during class, and in more or less unconcealed reference to the ruling Nazi regime: "It is the half-educated I abhor the most."

By the time my mother finished school, the war had already broken out. Under the circumstances, her life unfolded predictably. She first had to do her compulsory half-year of *Arbeitsdienst* (work service). Being a woman, she did not have to cut stone steps into some riverbed like my father. Instead she was assigned to a farming family as farmhand near Colmar in the Alsace.

According to photos taken by her father when the parents visited her, it was a happy time for my mother. She enjoyed the heavy physical work, and she obviously liked the company of these farmers, who soon enough treated her as one of their own. And there was plenty of good, healthy food. A story I have heard in various versions, mostly from her but also from her mother, hints at a harvest romance—perhaps including some rolling in the hay—but I do not really know for sure. In any case, in a country at war and away from home for the first extended time, my mother enjoyed herself in a peaceful rural environment that must have seemed to her far away from it all.

The rural bliss did not last, of course. Next she received training as a physiotherapist and was assigned to a hospital in Heidelberg that specialized in the physical rehabilitation of wounded soldiers. That task included teaching amputees (and double amputees) to use their bodies again to the extent possible. My mother told me she both liked the work and was depressed by it. In the stories she told later on, she tended to leave out all the hardships, focusing instead on the excitement and novelty of the experience.

Those who resent it when people of my parents' generation (the few of them left by now) talk about their youth as if the Nazis had never happened should remember: that generation lived through those dark years while coming of age, going to university, and falling in love for the first time. They must be permitted to remember such things without the baggage of the regime under which it all happened. The alternatives would be lifelong depression or suicide (both of which are common).

After Heidelberg, my mother was conscripted to work in a munitions factory somewhere near Giessen, north of Frankfurt. By then, my father had already appeared on the scene. The family was alarmed—the train ride to Giessen was dangerous. In the dying days of the war, because the munitions factory was adjacent, the railway line was repeatedly bombed. When Renate made her first train journey to her new job, my father managed to reassign his own corporal to accompany her.

As it turned out, the train that time was attacked by British fighter planes. It stopped, and everybody ran for shelter in a nearby forest. For half an hour or so, my mother pressed herself against one side of the first sizable tree she reached, while the planes sprayed the forest with machine gun fire from the other. Then she quickly had to move to the other side of the tree before the planes turned around and began shooting from the opposite direction. Finally, after the fighter pilots got tired of their game and withdrew, everybody boarded the train again and the trip continued.

According to family legend, the corporal had been more frightened than my mother.

The munitions factory was full of young women pressed into service. Many of them were Poles who had been rounded up and brought to Germany as slave labour after their home country had been invaded in 1939. The factory produced grenades as well as the lead cases for storing and transporting grenades. The dangerous handling of explosives was reserved for the Polish women, who, my mother recalled, were treated like cattle. The German women mainly had to weld the cases. Also according to my mother, there was among the German women a feeling of defiance. As often as they thought they could get away with it, they would pretend to trip over something and drop an entire stack of cases, which thus were dented and could not be used any more. This would bring the war to an end more quickly, they hoped.

My mother's first encounter with her future husband had taken place earlier, when she returned to Hattenheim from somewhere else—probably her therapist's job in Heidelberg. She was walking down the cobbled street from the railway station to her parents' house at 33 Hauptstrasse in Hattenheim. She was tired to the point of exhaustion, and she had no idea what the next day would hold. She probably did not care. Of course, she did not have to ring the bell—she had a key. But as she approached the door, it flew open, and there was this funny little man, my father, whom she had never seen before and who looked at her with undisguised curiosity and said: "Da sind Sie ja endlich!" (There you are, finally!)

PART THREE

Renate and Hans

52 | *Presto agitato*

After the first encounter with his future mother-in-law, my father had become a frequent visitor to the Wachendorff house up the street. As my grandmother wrote a few years later, in her essay "Der kleine Doktor" (The Little Doctor) and subtitled *presto agitato*: "It was curious: He had hardly stepped into our house for the first time when we could no longer imagine it without him. Never had we encountered someone who would waste so little time with preliminaries. He began his relationship with us at a point that others reach only after dragging on for weeks with cumbersome politeness."

He played the piano, and he pored over all the pictures and books in the house, "with the uninhibited nonchalance of a well-brought-up boy from a good family," my grandmother noted. He was particularly interested in whatever was cooking in the kitchen.

Of course, my father had to perform his duties at the Heeresentlassungsstelle. But whenever the air-raid sirens blasted, several times a day, my grandmother would hear the quick steps of his hobnailed boots coming up the street. All the doctors from the Heeresentlassungsstelle would in fact come because their assigned bomb shelter was the cavernous basement of the Wachendorff house. Only my father would appear upstairs first. Standing in the entrance hall, he would hold up my grandmother's fur coat (it was cold in the basement) and cheerfully exclaim: "Alarm!" Then he would immediately proceed to the piano or to the nearest bookcase.

He was not the only one who ignored the alarm sirens. One time, those assembled in the basement heard loud banging upstairs and were

The photograph of the "simple country girl" that my father saw before he met his future bride.

afraid that someone had broken into the house or that perhaps the Americans had already arrived from across the Rhine. My father was sent to inquire, and came back reporting that it was Gerda, in the kitchen, pounding a yeast dough. Because she had a small child, she received extra food rations.

Gerda played the piano, and she played four-hand piano with my father. They became quite close friends. So close, in fact, that my grandfather felt compelled to take my father aside one day and tell him he'd best not entertain any hopes for Gerda, who was married after all. Without embarrassment or a moment's hesitation, my father replied that he would never dare to, and that he was in fact looking for a "simple girl from the countryside" as his future bride. "Like *this* one," he added, and he pointed to a framed photograph hanging on the wall, of a young girl with blond braids sitting on a fence in front of a Black Forest farm. "This one is available," my grandfather replied dryly. "She is my second daughter, and she is coming tomorrow."

53 | *Courtship*

My mother was a prickly kind of girl. She did not enter into friendships easily or lightly, and especially not with boys. I can only imagine the indignation on her face when she first saw the young man beaming at her in the doorway of her parents' house, greeting her as if he had known her all his life. His boyish looks made him appear younger than the twenty-nine he had just turned. She was not twenty-one yet. She also was half an inch taller than he.

But her resistance did not last long. "Renate is quite weak and needs fresh air," the little doctor would announce with the serious pathos of a diagnosing physician, and they would take off for long walks along the Rhine. These walks would invariably lead to a wooden bench almost hidden by the enormous branches of an old willow tree, and, only a few steps farther, to a little forest, the Erbacher Wäldchen. Bench and tree are no longer there, and the little forest has been half obliterated by a water-purification plant. But for a long time, whenever we were taken for walks on that upstream path along the Rhine, the grown-ups would inevitably giggle when they saw the bench or reached the little forest. Sometime during the winter months of 1944–45, my parents became engaged, either on that bench or in that little forest.

54 | *The crossing*

Without flinching, my grandfather had approved of his second daughter's engagement to the little doctor. "Hans is very welcome as our son-in-law, and Renate has come back to full blossoming life in the shortest period of time," he wrote in his diary. Perhaps his magnanimity had to do with the fact that Renate was his second daughter and he could not possibly muster the same kind of patriarchal energy as with his first-born daughter Gerda. But surely he also genuinely liked his son-in-law-to-be. And he would always fully trust him as a physician, as would his wife. For the rest of their lives my grandparents would never again enter into any kind of medical treatment before first consulting my father. And often enough, they would come and visit us for a few weeks in Bavaria so that son-in-law Hans could look after their various and mostly age-related ailments.

Who could oppose a little love and romance anyway, at a time when everybody was worried about what might happen next? The Americans had appeared on the other side of the Rhine. Even though it was aimed mostly at the industrial cities farther upstream, the almost constant artillery fire from across the river jarred the nerves. There were relentless clouds of bombers overhead, on their way to Berlin and other cities. Each time they approached, the sirens sounded. There was also the fear that the Americans might choose the Rheingau for the crossing. Because of the island in the river in front of Hattenenheim, it was difficult to see what the "enemy" on the other side was up to. Most nights the Wachendorff family now slept in the hallways of the old house because all the bedrooms faced the river, where the shooting was coming from. More and more often—and more willingly—the family would descend to the basement bomb shelter when the sirens sounded. The basement was large and poorly lit, so at least my father and his bride Renate had a rather good time there.

In 1945, a particular worry was what the German soldiers would do who were still in the area. By early spring, everyone was hoping they would vanish without putting up futile resistance. One morning my grandfather found three soldiers in his lower garden, at the wall facing the river. When he inquired what they were doing, "Well, we are here to prevent the crossing," they told him. My grandfather exclaimed: "What, the three of you all alone?" "No," they replied, "another seven are coming."

Around the same time, a group of four or five soldiers started building a makeshift anti-tank barrier across the narrow cobbled street leading down to the river next to my grandfather's garden. Their reply to the question as to whether this made any sense has become yet another catchphrase in our family. With inevitable giggles, it is invoked whenever something is done that obviously appears futile: "Well, we are putting it up," the soldiers said, "and we'll also take it down again."

These soldiers were mostly local teenagers pressed into military service at the last moment of a war that had been lost quite some time before.

Fearing that their activities might trigger an aggressive response from across the Rhine, my grandfather gently talked them out of proceeding with their plans and into going home.

On 21 March 1945, the Heeresentlassungsstelle was ordered to pack up and leave. There were tears when Renate had to say goodbye to her little doctor. Nobody knew what the future would hold—indeed, whether they would ever see each other again. The final crossing of the Americans was imminent. Several times already, they had engulfed the lower portions of the Rheingau with a yellow chemical fog that gave everybody a bad taste in the mouth. On 23 March the Wachendorffs packed up and left Hattenheim. The plan was to be away from the house during the actual crossing in case there was fighting, and then to return quickly to it before the Americans marched into Hattenheim so that they would not find it abandoned. Some time ago, a wooden shack had been constructed somewhere up in the forested hills, by the crafty Koepp carpenters again, not far from Kloster Eberbach, the beautiful medieval Cistercian monastery that had already survived so many wars and that would also survive this one unscathed.

The monastery became famous during the 1980s when scenes from *The Name of the Rose* were filmed there. One could sometimes spot Sean Connery in one of the better restaurants of Hattenheim. Family gossip had it that Gerda all of a sudden developed a desire to eat at the same restaurant. When I asked her about this during a recent visit, she vigorously denied it.

From my mother's tales, and from those of various other family members, I always thought that the time they all spent in this wooden shack, the *Waldhütte* (forest hut), as they called it, amounted to at least several weeks. But according to my grandfather's diary, which he kept during those trying last moments of the war, they stayed for only six days: they moved up there on 23 March 1945 and were back in Hattenheim on 29 March.

The shack consisted of one room. There was no plumbing. A stove for heating and cooking arrived only on the second day. And the Wachendorffs—my grandparents, my mother, Gerda with her little son Christian, and the youngest daughter, Ursula—were not the only ones there: Herr Enderli, the same who once had pursued my grandmother with his crush, arrived with his wife and their cook. Each family tried to create some domestic space in one corner of the hut. During the first night, Mr. and Mrs. Enderli had such a fight that the next morning, for everybody else's benefit, the cook's bed was pushed in between theirs.

A stream pouring over a rock to form a little waterfall served as the washing station. On the first evening, before the stove had been brought up, the children were fed semolina pudding cooked on the stove of a farm family in the neighbourhood. The grown-ups then walked down to the Eberbach monastery hoping to find some food for themselves there. My grandfather's diary entry is worth quoting: "Life is never without surprises. While a war is going on and everyone is fleeing, it is still business as usual in the Eberbach inn: white tablecloths, a waiter, good food, and wine. We walked back under a full moon and it almost seemed peaceful despite the echo of the distant artillery fire rolling from the hills."

For the children, it must have been like a camping adventure. Aunt Ursula was nine and cousin Christian about three. They slept in bunk beds, with Christian on the bottom because he was not yet quite toilet trained. My grandfather took them for walks. Always the gardener, he showed them all the spring flowers and the puffy patches of moss. Gerda and Renate were sent back down to Hattenheim on bicycles every day to see whether everything was all right in the house and whether there were signs of the Americans. The bicycle ride took only about ten minutes, but higher in the Taunus hills there were several stretches of road that could easily be observed from the other side of the river. Gerda and Renate wore their most colourful clothes so they would not be mistaken for soldiers on the move. The Americans had a habit of shooting at them.

Trips back to Hattenheim were a chance to pick up some wine, which could be exchanged at a farm along the way for a little sack of grain. This grain, wheat or rye, would be ground in a hand-turned coffee mill and then cooked into gruel. Wine had become the Rheingau's substitute currency and would remain so until well after the war. Rolf tells the story of how it was used to get badly needed fuel for the company in Oestrich. Tanker ships regularly steamed up the Rhine to supply the American army headquarters in Frankfurt with gas. Once in a while, one of them would anchor overnight in front of the Oestrich factory. A hose would be attached to it below the water level, leading directly into the factory through the sewer tunnel.

Rolf still gloats when he remembers how the Americans sometimes drove along the riverbank in their jeeps, unaware that valuable gasoline was being pumped across right underneath them. The scheme worked because the Americans were unfamiliar with European weights and measures. The tanker ships were loaded in long tons (1016 kilos), but the load was tallied in metric tons (1000 kilos) at the port of destination. The difference ended up on the black market. The next morning, before lifting anchor, the big crane in front of the factory would gently lower a crate of wine onto the ship's deck.

But back to the Waldhütte: When news spread that the Americans had finally crossed the river and were about to occupy the Rheingau, the family needed to move back quickly. Alas, it had been raining all day, and, overloaded with layers of mattresses tied to the roof, the car got stuck in the mud. A local farmer had to help out with his horse and a chain. By the time my grandfather arrived back in the village, American tanks were rolling down the cobbled village street. Parked on a side street, he had to wait for a gap in what seemed to be an endless military convoy before he could quickly drive into the garage.

55 | *Occupation*

The first American my mother saw was a tall black soldier leaning against the wall of the house below her bedroom window, drinking out of a Riesling bottle. There were constant army convoys going past on the highway between the house and the river. "No wonder the Germans lost that war," my grandfather noted in his diary when he saw what came pouring across the Rhine: endless rows of tanks, trucks, jeeps, and all sorts of supply vehicles. Most of this equipment never went back to the United States, as the Americans would maintain a strong military presence in Germany all the way through the Cold War. For decades to come it would be impossible to drive on the Autobahns without eventually running into one of these American convoys. Actual soldiers were relatively few by comparison. The Americans relied on their material superiority.

Incredible coincidence: a few years ago, my cousin Chris, who lived in Portland, Oregon, for almost thirty years, found on the Internet a photo of three soldiers from Portland posing as liberators in 1945. The photo shows them in front of a pier sticking out into a river. The sign on the pier clearly says Hattenheim.

Almost immediately, the refugees began coming, an endless stream of them, plenty of them with children, some on their own. Some had been driven out of those German territories to the east that had been conquered by the victors. East Prussia was now Russian, Silesia had become Polish, and the Sudeten Germans had been expelled from Czechoslovakia. Others had been displaced by the ravages of war and were simply trying to return home. The Wachendorffs helped where they could, establishing a semi-permanent soup kitchen in the entrance hall, where people could get some rest and some food.

Most came on foot, some pulled little handcarts after them with their few belongings. My mother told me about two little boys coming up the village street with such a handcart. There is an entry about them in my grandparents' guest book: "Paul and Adolf, eight and nine years old, alone and barefoot, on their way home to Cologne from Regensburg, May 16–18, 1945."

Incredible coincidence again: years later, when Gerda and Hans-Erich had been in Portland for ten years, they had a visit from Molly, a Hollywood screenwriter and the daughter of one of their best friends. Molly told them that at a party in New York she had met a man who told her the exact same story about the two little boys knocking on the door in Hattenheim after the war. He had been one of them. My bet is that it was Paul—or, if it was Adolf, he probably had changed his name.

The Wachendorffs were still in their house. It seemed as if the Americans would leave them alone and simply move on. But then, in June, they returned and claimed the house as their local headquarters. The family had twenty-four hours to pack up and leave. Suitcases, trunks, and boxes were hastily filled and carried to a variety of neighbouring houses whose occupants had offered to store them. All was returned eventually, except for one large suitcase that apparently contained silver napkin rings and carnival costumes. And someone had used fluorescent pens to draw naked girls on a large oil painting. "It was an ugly painting, a wedding gift by my ex-brothers-in-law," Gerda remembers. "I had hoped that someone would take it."

The family had to split up. Gerda and Christian moved into a spare room of a neighbouring house up the street. The rest of the family found temporary quarters at the other end of the village. My grandfather had negotiated with the Americans that he would still be allowed to look after his beloved lower garden, which could be entered from a side street. The Americans also conceded further family use of the laundry room, which could be entered from the garage.

One day, my mother was doing some laundry when a couple of American soldiers cornered her there. They were quite friendly but clearly had amorous intentions for the frightened German *Fräulein*. Realizing what was going on, my grandfather, who happened to be in the adjacent garage where his car still was parked, entered the laundry room and intervened, politely, but with fatherly determination. The soldiers apologized and left.

Overall, and considering what they all had been through in the war, the Americans were well disciplined and considerate. They were just big boys away from home. They were rambunctious sometimes, and they drank Riesling. But they did not really mean harm. Some of them were put up in the same house as Gerda. One night, when they came stomping up the wooden staircase, Gerda went out into the hallway and asked them to be quiet because her son was already sleeping. From then on, they always tiptoed up the stairs in their socks.

On another occasion, my grandfather, probably on his way back from the lower garden, noticed a group of soldiers who were obviously partying and who at that particular moment were trying to push the Bechstein piano out a window. When he cautiously intervened again, the soldiers carefully put the instrument back in its place. My grandfather often told me how one of the soldiers patted him on the shoulder and told him, in a broad American drawl: "You're a good chap." When the family was allowed to move back into the house in September (the Americans meanwhile had established their regional headquarters in Wiesbaden), the Bechstein was unharmed and there was very little damage otherwise.

As happened at Ebenhausen, the authorities later placed a number of refugee families in the house as tenants. There was plenty of space. The side buildings were rented out permanently from then on. One family also moved into the main house. I don't know where they were from, or how long they stayed, but they are forever etched into the Wachendorffs' collective memory by the names of their two little scrawny children: Brunhilde-Isolde and Olav-Hagen. The parents obviously had a heroic German future planned for them. Now they were faced with an uncertain future, having to start their lives all over again.

It was not the last time the old house would see the arrival of refugees. During much of the 1990s, a Bosnian family lived in the empty west wing adjacent to the garage. Germany had granted temporary refugee status to Bosnians during the civil war in their homeland, 1992–95. After 1997, however, most of these refugees were made to go back home. The Bosnian family in the Hattenheim house had meanwhile found jobs and friends in the community, and their children had grown up there and spoke German. Rolf unsuccessfully tried to obtain an exemption from deportation for them. We heard once or twice from them after their return to Bosnia, and they seemed to be doing all right. But it was a shame. They would have liked to stay.

56 | *Wings*

For those who had lost neither loved ones nor their property (and, of course, had property to begin with), 1945 and the next few years were a joyous time. The war was over. The Nazis were gone. Nobody had to fill out forms about Aryan blood purity any more. To be sure, there were all kinds of material restrictions on normal upper-middle-class life, but every moment of that life was enjoyed much more intensively than only a few years later, when abundance had been restored. My father never forgot those early postear years. As he put it, luxury had been to see a bowl of buttered peas so full that half of them had to be carried back to the kitchen.

People lived their lives as if they had wings. Some did so more literally than others. Next to the lower garden, beyond the wall with the cherry tree, there was another old villa that had become the temporary residence of an American officer, Alfred L. (Abby) Wolf, and his wife Connie. Abby Wolf was an air force pilot. He had taught his wife how to fly during their honeymoon. Connie Wolf befriended the Wachendorffs, and Gerda in particular. She had her own little airplane in Wiesbaden, and one day she took Gerda (and possibly my mother, though I cannot remember for certain) for a flying excursion. For the first and probably the last time, they saw the Rhine and their house from above. This, one should not forget, happened at a time when most people did not even have gasoline to fuel their cars. "Well, really!" Gerda later recounted, "Connie sat there at the controls in her little costume and high heels."

Connie Wolf went on to become a famous aviator. At one point she was one of only five women in the world who had possessed a valid pilot's licence for more than fifty years. She also developed a passion for balloon flying. It was she who flew the balloon in the 1956 movie *Around the World in Eighty Days*, with David Niven as Phileas Fogg and Shirley MacLaine as an improbable but nevertheless delightful Indian princess. In one scene of the movie, one can see her briefly near the balloon's wicker basket. Connie Wolf also met Gerda and Christian halfway on their journey to Portland, in New York, and helped them get accustomed to the new country.

History books tell us that 1945 for the Germans was year zero. The war had been lost and with it much of German glory and respectability. Millions of soldiers were returning home and looking desperately for work. The occupational forces not only dictated the terms of peace but also determined the contours of the country, including its borders and its new democratic constitution. Yet never was radical change and foreign occupation embraced so readily and optimistically. And never again was America accepted so uncritically as the beacon of democracy and freedom.

One feared the American soldiers even less than the most harmless Nazi bureaucrats. In fact, one did not have to fear them at all. And they had chocolate. American cars and movies dominated the imaginations of children and grown-ups alike. Emigrating to America was a common dream—as it turns out, even for a pair of barefoot little boys wandering alone from one end of the country to the other. Obviously, at least one of them made it.

57 | *Degrees of separation*

Meanwhile, my father had worked his way back to Ebenhausen. The Heeresentlassungsstelle had slowly retreated, moving from town to town, always just one step ahead of the advancing Americans. My father and the other doctors were uniformed soldiers, after all. Before the war was officially over, they could not abandon their duties without fear of getting shot for desertion by some last-minute overzealous Nazi moron. But they also did not want to fall into the hands of the Americans and end up in a prison camp. One day, they were packing up again, and my father was just lifting a bicycle onto a truck when he saw an American tank rolling around the corner. Without even thinking, he took the bike down again and cycled away.

He cycled all the way to Ebenhausen, some 450 kilometres. Along the way, to avoid being accused of desertion, he reported to whatever still-functioning German military detachment he came across. Invariably, he told the officer in charge that he had been separated from his unit, that he was searching for it, and that he had heard it had been moved somewhere to the south. I am not sure that all the officers believed him, but fortunately they did not care anymore. They were probably preoccupied with saving their own skin. Without exception they put the official stamp of approval on my father's papers, thus allowing him to move on.

Ebenhausen was occupied and in disarray. My grandfather Albert had been suspended from his directorship of the sanatorium, and my father was to report to the regional American headquarters in the neighbouring city of Bad Tölz. There was a curfew. But the sanatorium urgently needed an attending physician, both for a number of patients who remained there and for the former Dachau inmates who were already arriving. Somehow my father talked the Americans into exempting him from the curfew and having him officially decommissioned from the army.

The little doctor at his desk in the sanatorium.

He must have produced quite a convincing schmooze. A certificate issued by the Troop Medical Officer of the Allied Command South essentially recounted his entire medical history, from his coughing fits as a young boy in the Swiss mountains (the goat was not mentioned, though), to the various treatments he had received at the hands of the sanatorium's former cardiologist, "Prof. Dr. Edens," to his wounding and pleurisy in Russia. Dated 12 June 1945, the certificate ended with the recommendation that my father be decommissioned from the army because he obviously was no longer fit for duty. He was then given a Military Government Exemption that allowed him "to circulate within an area of 75km of Ebenhausen by any means." The reason given for this exemption from the curfew reads: "Doctor." The document is signed "Allied Expeditionary Force, Military Government Office, 1st Lieutenant D. Toley, 25 June 1945, Detachment No. H2B2."

All the while, my father was separated from his bride and did not know what had taken place in Hattenheim. He desperately wanted to let Renate know he was alive and well. He wrote letters and tried to have them delivered to Hattenheim by anyone he found with plans or intentions of travelling north, towards Wiesbaden and the Rheingau, mostly other decommissioned soldiers trying to get home.

Among my parents' papers I found one of these letters, written on sanatorium stationery and dated 28 June 1945. I have no idea whether it was ever delivered. It is addressed to Fräulein Renate Wachendorff, Hattenheim. It mentions that my father is working as a physician again, treating "serious cases among those released from the concentration camp," and that he cannot leave Ebenhausen because he is needed as a translator for his father. "The weather is so wonderful and I wish you could finally be here," he writes. "Are you all well?" "Can you not write and give the letter to one of those decommissioned soldiers travelling home south?" "Can you not put yourself on to some transport and come yourself?" "I need you. Your Hans."

Not exactly a passionate love letter, but a letter full of confident hope about their future together. Renate did not come—she was fighting off Americans in the family's laundry room. Sometime in August, my father travelled back to Hattenheim. I am not quite sure how, but I remember talk about a car that had been fitted with a wood-burning steam engine. No gasoline was available for civilian purposes.

58 | *Presto agitato again*

It must have been August, because I was born in May the following year. When my father arrived in Hattenheim, the house was occupied by Americans. He was directed to Gerda's quarters. According to Gerda, he appeared at the third-floor door on a hot summer day wearing two coats and a fur cap—probably black-market acquisitions from somewhere *en route* that he thought might come in handy the following winter. His face was so drenched with sweat and anxiety that Gerda immediately yelled across the room: "Renate is alive and well." She still remembers how his face immediately lit up.

What happened next has been subject to considerable secrecy and even controversy in the family. I first heard about it when I was eleven or twelve, in our little house in Tutzing. When my parents had guests or friends over in the evening, I was usually allowed to leave the bedroom door ajar so that I could listen to the conversations before I fell asleep. As my father used to say, I had my ears wrapped half around the doorpost. In this particular instance, however, accompanied by sustained giggles, all I could hear was: "Gerda said that she would not take any responsibility." The next morning, when I asked what the story had been about, there were more giggles and my request for more information was flatly denied.

Later, it transpired that it was the story of my conception. It happened, so goes the story, with Gerda in the room and repeatedly warning them that she would not be held responsible for anything. Without a single spare room available anywhere in the occupied village, Gerda must have offered to put up my father in her room. Renate must have joined him, probably after her parents had gone to bed at the other end of the village.

When I recently asked her, Gerda exclaimed: "Well, really! I don't know anything about that!" But I know it is true because my brother heard it, too. Even my sister Andrea, thirteen years younger, knew about it. Brothers do not talk about things like this to their little sisters. She must have heard it from one of the perpetrators themselves, most likely her mother.

The wedding took place three months later, on 29 October 1945, a shotgun wedding like the one Julia and I celebrated forty-nine years later. The Wachendorffs were back in their own house. The bride and groom were taken to the Protestant church in Oestrich in a horse-drawn carriage, probably as much for lack of gasoline as for style. According to my grandfather, my father forgot the wedding bouquet. Why my father was responsible for it, I don't know. But according to my grandfather again, he had to chase after the carriage in his car (he got gasoline because he was an invalid) and deliver the flowers to the bride and groom halfway between Hattenheim and Oestrich.

It was one of the first occasions for the family to gather again. Everybody had survived. Rolf was back. Besides the family, the wedding party included an assortment of friends, including my mother's former teacher Dorothea Wolff and the painter Raitz von Frentz. He also lived in Hattenheim. He had nearly starved to death by the end of the war, and he was now commissioned to paint the wedding bouquet of red and pink roses (from the lower garden, of course). He painted these twice, once in full bloom, and once a few days later with their heads already bent a little and one of the pink petals already fallen to the ground. This second painting,

My parents on their wedding day, 29 October 1945.

done in tender watercolours, is in our Canadian living room now. My sister has the other one.

From Ebenhausen, apart from the groom, only Mucki was dispatched. The parents of the groom did not make the trip. It is possible that my grandfather Albert was not allowed to leave before his de-Nazification trial was over. He probably also thought that the world and the sanatorium would go under if he left his desk.

How the church ceremony unfolded I do not know. Likely, my parents provided some music themselves. My mother had replaced Gerda as my father's regular chamber music companion. She played the recorder and he had taken to playing the organ in the Hattenheim church. Gerda recalls one instance when my father came storming into the house, went right into the kitchen where my mother was cooking, took her by the hand, and said: "Come, Renate, and take your recorder." The two of them disappeared back across the street into the church with my mother not even having time to take off her apron. The wedding menu has been recorded in detail, in the guest book my parents received as a wedding present. It was all cooked and prepared by Gerda (most of the work) and my grandmother (mainly supervision): clear beef broth, roast chicken with asparagus tips, veal tongue cooked in French (!) red wine, young vegetables, salad and potatoes, peach compote, some sort of cake (I can't read my grandmother's handwriting) with pineapple, Rheingau fruit and nuts, and mocha. There was Riesling from the family vineyard, and *Sekt*.

The celebrations went on for days. There were several house concerts. At one of them, on 5 November, my father played Beethoven and my grandmother recited poetry. At the next one, Gerda played Scarlatti and it was Mucki's turn to provide the poetry. In the guest book there is a photo of her, obviously taken by my grandfather, leaning against the Bechstein piano, open book in hand, all sweet innocence complete with ruffled princess dress.

I discovered this photo only recently and asked Gerda about it. I got quite an earful. Mucki, it turns out, almost immediately advanced to the status of grandfather's lady friend of the moment. Everybody liked her and found her charming. She returned for extended visits at least three times over the next few years. And she took her husband Roger to Hattenheim when she returned from Chile for the first time. Who would have thought!

In October and November 1945, there was still a curfew. The wedding guests from out of town had to stay overnight. The locals had to find their way home through back alleys. My mother remembers it as all very romantic. Raitz von Frentz had to be helped over a garden wall, with my grandfather holding up a heavy silver candelabra.

The grandparents had a pair of these candelabra. Gerda inherited one, Rolf the other. I was always particularly fond of them. They were solid silver, four-armed, and over two feet tall. The grandparents had them on top of a bookcase, and they came down only for special occasions. Gerda has hers in regular use on the dining table. It must have been on my mind one year when I was looking for a birthday present for Julia. This was in the medieval German university town of Marburg. I had given some lectures there, in December, and therefore had missed Julia's actual birthday, which is two weeks before Christmas. She and Jacob were about to join me, and we were going to visit Gerda in Hattenheim and then spend Christmas with my father in Munich. Somewhere in Marburg, I found a silver candelabra, silver-plated only, but four-armed and as tall as

Gerda's. I bought it. Gerda giggled when she saw it. My father's reaction was different: he pulled me aside and said: "One always has to have two of these. I will pay for the second one." He then made me phone the store in Marburg and order another by mail.

So my parents spent their wedding night in Hattenheim. At least they had a room to themselves this time. And there was more privacy in the old house than my mother would encounter after her arrival in Ebenhausen.

I am not entirely sure when and how my parents got back to Ebenhausen. I think that Otto Seeler, the husband of Gerda's cousin Irmela, drove them. Otto had been born in Cuba and therefore had a Cuban passport. Hence he was allowed to buy gasoline. And he had a car. Likely, the main purpose for the long drive south was to find out how aunt Reni and her skiing-instructor husband were doing in the Austrian Alps.

In any case, my parents were back in Ebenhausen by Christmas 1945—their first Christmas as a married couple. Uncle Friedel was there, visiting from Berlin. Trains were running again. In the guest book, he wrote how delighted he was to meet his "new niece." He also mentioned the "hard times" they were are all going through. This must have been on his mind after he had been talking to his brother-in-law. Preoccupied with his court case, with the future of the sanatorium, and more generally with all that was *unanständig* (indecent) around him, my grandfather Albert probably never spent a single thought on how incredible it was that the war was over and that everybody was alive.

I was born on 24 May 1946 in a makeshift maternity ward in downtown Munich. More than half the city's buildings, including most of the hospitals, were in rubble. My mother developed an infection and a high fever. My father ran around the neighbourhood to find ice with which he could cool down his wife. When she felt a little better, she noticed that every evening at the same time, people would come out of a nearby movie theatre whistling a certain melody. She would have liked so much to know what the melody and the movie were about.

For a few days my parents did not know what to name me. One day, however, when my father returned to Ebenhausen on the train, there was a young couple across from him in the compartment. They had a little boy whom my father liked. He was called Thomas. The next day, back in Munich, he suggested to his wife that they name me Thomas as well. My mother did not object. Thomas I was, Thomas I have remained.

59 | *Interlude*

My father was still a general physician when he started at the sanatorium in 1945. The war had prevented him from specializing in his chosen subfield, which was internal medicine and cardiology. To remedy this, he needed to do an internship. He chose the university clinic in Göttingen where Heinrich Martius, his wife's uncle, was still director of gynecology and obstetrics. So in 1949, my father moved to Göttingen for a year, and I moved to Hattenheim with my mother. Göttingen was only a few hours from the Rheingau, and my father could come for weekend visits now and then.

I do not remember much about that year in Hattenheim. I was only three, after all. I remember playing with my cousin Christian on the warm sandstone steps leading to the garden. We shared those steps with little green lizards that after a while stopped running away from us. I remember how Christian and I fought over a certain kind of dessert spoon.

My grandfather had six small silver spoons from his mother, called grandma spoons. They differed from all others because their handles were a bit curled at the end. At the table, however, we were seven: the grandparents, Ursula, Gerda and Christian, and my mother and I. When Else laid the table she did not pay attention to which of us got which spoon for dessert. If it so happened that only one of us got a grandma spoon, the other one was jealous. Grandfather, of course, for educational reasons, did not allow a change in the distribution of spoons once we sat at the table. Only Ursula, then a pouting thirteen-year-old and grandfather's darling, always got a grandma spoon. And of course *he* did.

But what I remember most of all was a trip my mother and I made to see my father in Göttingen. We stayed for a week. I had never been to a real city with streets lined with the same kinds of houses on either side. We all stayed in the one room that my father had rented in one of those houses. It was early summer, and I ate a lot of raw rhubarb growing in the backyard of that house. I remember sharing it with a little girl who lived next door. What my parents probably remember most is the diarrhea the rhubarb gave me. I also vaguely remember my grand-uncle Heinrich, who always wore a white doctor's overall, and his family. We went to their house for meals. I thought that in comparison to our one room, that house was dark and gloomy.

It was exciting that we all slept in that one room. I climbed on top of my father to be able to see out the window, early in the morning, when the garbage truck came by. For some reason, this would be one of the fondest memories my parents retained of their three-year-old son. In later years we would often talk about my childhood, and they would recall how I stood with my naked feet on my father's chest and report to them, blow by blow, how the garbage was being collected outside the window. Come to think, it was perhaps the very first time that the little family was together, in a place of their own, without parents or in-laws in the same building.

Strangely, I do not remember seeing my father play tennis in Göttingen, although there are photos of him on the court, in long white flannels, with me looking on from the sidelines. He was on the provincial tennis team and one of the better German players at the time. He almost always played in long white flannels, even in Monte Carlo, in the middle of summer. Much later he became Bavarian indoors senior champion, and he still beat me when he was in his sixties. Yet he never was very competitive. (I would inherit that trait from him.) When something bothered him, he lost interest and concentration and let the match slip away. Legendary was his exclamation, loudly audible across the entire club grounds, over a lost point, at a tournament somewhere in the Bavarian Alps: "One cannot play tennis in a country where avalanches descend from mountains."

Something else happened after our return to Hattenheim that I do remember vividly: the arrival of my brother Michael. My mother must have been quite pregnant during that visit to Göttingen because Michael was born only a few months later, on 20 September 1949. I was probably told at some point that my mother would have to go to Wiesbaden for a few days and that I would stay with the grandparents. Perhaps my father had already come back from Göttingen by then.

But none of this must have registered in my little head, really, as a momentous change in our lives, because the very first time I became aware of what was going on was when my grandparents told me that my mother would be coming home from Wiesbaden "this afternoon" with "a little brother." So we were all lined up in grandfather's garage again when his Mercedes came around the corner and there, in the back, was my mother with a white bundle on her lap. Later that day, I was allowed to peek into the crib where he lay sleeping. It probably was not until a few years later, when he began to smash my wood-block constructions in the playpen, that I began to realize that life had changed forever.

A few weeks later, my mother, my baby brother, and I took the train back to Munich. At the railway station there, my father was waiting for us and drove us to Ebenhausen in the sanatorium's tiny red Fiat Topolino station wagon. Having been away for a year, I had forgotten Ebenhausen. It was as if I had arrived at an unknown place. To some extent, Hattenheim would always remain my "free homeland."

PART FOUR

Tutzing (1950s)

60 | *Little house on the lake*

What followed after that return from Hattenheim were the Ebenhausen years— growing up in the shadow of the sanatorium, with the shops (and the dentist!) down the hill in Ebenhausen, and the school in neighbouring Hohenschäftlarn. I learned how to ride a bike and to ski, we did our first trip to Italy, and I spoke with such a strong Bavarian accent that my own parents sometimes couldn't understand me. But in *my* mind at least, our family life began for real only after we moved to Tutzing on Lake Starnberg in 1955.

We went house hunting in Tutzing. There was this little house, hardly larger than my grandmother's kitchen in Ebenhausen, standing in a large garden full of apple trees, berry bushes, and a huge old walnut tree that my father noticed immediately. There was a hedge in front of the property, and a wooden gate. Across the garden on the other side, one could see a corner of the lake in the distance.

The only heating was a tile stove in a corner of the living room, with a wooden bench around two sides on which one could sit with one's back against the hot tiles. Other than that, the living room was only big enough to hold the dining table and a small coffee table with two armchairs on either side. A glass door led to a small "boudoir," really only a passage to the terrace overlooking the garden and lake. The room for us two boys would be the largest in the house, but we would have to buy folding beds in order to create some space for playing during the day. The parents' bedroom was so small that when my mother was already in bed, my father had to climb over her to reach his side. As my father sometimes explained jokingly, this is why they eventually had another baby, my sister Andrea.

From the tiny entrance hall, a passage led to the kitchen. It was from that passage that the tile stove in the living room had to be fed with coal, and the coal was in the basement, which was reached through a trap door in the floor. In the basement, potatoes and apples were also stored for the winter. Herr Wallner, who owned the house, said he could supply the coal and the potatoes. The apples in the garden were ours. He would retain the right to harvest the walnut tree, though. It would become my first regular chore to haul up the coal from the basement in a metal bucket twice a day, in the morning before I went to school, and in the evening before I went to bed. Also in the evening, after filling the furnace all the way up with coal, my mother would place two slow-burning briquettes of pressed coal dust wrapped in wet newspaper on top of the coal. That way, there would still be enough embers in the morning to get the fire started again.

The kitchen was hardly bigger than a closet, and behind it was an even smaller bathroom. In that kitchen, my mother learned how to cook regular meals for the first time, for the family and soon also for the many friends and guests whom my parents entertained on a regular basis. The only hot water in the house came from a wood stove that had to be fired up for hot baths, usually on Fridays. The kitchen faucet was equipped with a water heater after we moved in. My brother Michi and I had to take baths together, and we fought over who had to sit on the side with the plug. For a while we alternated, but we still fought over whose turn it was. We also fought over who would get the "flower" on top of the puddings our mother made in a mould. Later, I made a deal with my brother. Being so much older and wiser, I realized that the flower did not taste any different from the rest of the pudding. So I arranged with him that he could always have the pudding flower and I would always get to sit on the "good" side of the bathtub.

This was the smallest house we had ever seen. But to us it seemed like paradise—ours and ours alone. My parents were skeptical about the size and the amenities—rather, the lack thereof. But in the end it was the only house we looked at. I remember my brother and I hopping up and down in front of it, after our initial visit and inspection, on the path leading from the wooden garden gate to the front door, shouting: "We should take it, we should take it." We did. My parents agreed to rent the place for 160 marks a month, and in the spring of 1955 we moved into 1 *Bräuhausstrasse* (Brewery Street) in Tutzing.

61 | *On the town*

For a number of reasons, my parents had not had much of a social life in Ebenhausen. In the 1950s, Ebenhausen was still a town of farmers and craftspeople with whom the Hüglins did not interact much. Their social focus was the sanatorium and its ever-changing clientele. Also, living in three rooms under the grandparents' roof offered few opportunities to entertain.

All of that changed in Tutzing, which was much more urban and diverse. There was a large regional hospital, a small chemical factory that sometimes stank, a textile factory that did not, and an assortment of smaller businesses. Because of its location on the shore of Lake Starnberg, Tutzing also attracted summer guests, who stayed in various hotels and inns. Brahms had been there in the late nineteenth century, composing one of his symphonies. There were several cafés, the Café Hofmayr and its prized orange ice cream among them. To the delight of my father, there even was a delicatessen, Feinkost Peschka, where he went regularly to buy his favourite cured ham.

There was a public beach where we could go swimming all summer, and a pier where the ferries docked that went around the lake. My Hattenheim grandfather would often tease us that these ferries were much smaller than the paddle steamers on the Rhine. And there was a tennis club with two separate courts, both on the Bräuhausstrasse. One of them was next to our house and could be reached by us directly through a hole in the fence rather than by going around to the main entrance like everyone else. This (the court, not the hole) was a particular attraction for my father, of course, who started playing there immediately. I became the regular ball-boy on duty, but I also started playing tennis there myself, with my father's old top-heavy Slazenger racquets.

The club participated in a regional league. Each summer we travelled around to various southern-Bavarian towns for these tournaments. My father would play tennis while we watched the games or went for walks. After the morning singles, there would be a lunch for the players of both teams and their families, in some nearby *Gasthaus*. Naturally, there also was beer. Especially when the tournament outcome was already fairly clear after the morning matches, the doubles matches in the afternoon were not always taken terribly seriously.

Highlights of the year were the annual club tournaments, which my father won several times. His main rival was a young lawyer, Dieter Liphart, who was probably half my father's age. Once, before the final against my

The card Anton Leidl painted and sent us after his encounter with Hattenheim Riesling.

father, Liphart came over to us for a little rest in one of our deckchairs in the garden. My mother gave him something to eat and a cold drink. I thought it was entirely inappropriate for her to lend support to my father's rival. I don't remember who won the final that day.

We soon began to explore the local restaurant scene. One evening during the first winter, we ended up in a typical Bavarian *Gasthaus* where the food is simple and the beer is local. At the next table was a single, middle-aged man with an impressive artist's head drinking wine instead of beer. It took my father about three minutes to strike up a conversation with him and to learn that he was indeed an artist, a painter, that his name was Anton Leidl, and that he lived in his studio down by the lake. My father immediately told him that his wife was from the Rheingau and that the family in Hattenheim cultivated this wonderful Riesling. After our meal, we persuaded him to come up to our new house and try a glass. It became a long evening with at least a bottle if not two. A few days later we received a postcard in the mail on which Leidl had made a little coloured caricature of himself hugging a life-sized bottle of wine. Underneath he had written: "The Hattenheimer has found a new friend."

Anton Leidl was a painter of considerable influence in Munich's prewar art scene. His paintings are in museums all over Germany. In 1943 he had moved to Tutzing when his studio in Munich was destroyed. He became a good friend of my father and, of course, his patient. He sent us many more of these little caricature postcards. He also gave my father a small oil painting, a view of his garden from his studio window. It is the one painting that my brother Michi really wanted when we divvied up the estate after our father's death. Michi turned six the year we moved to

Tutzing, and he first entered school there. He did not have memories of Ebenhausen as strong as I had. Maybe he liked this painting because it came into our lives when his began in a more conscious way.

62 | Boys and girls

The walk to the new school was only ten minutes, and I did not have to go mostly by myself as on the much longer walks from Ebenhausen to Hohenschäftlarn. The school was large and surrounded by an even larger yard. Our grade-three classroom was light and spacious, and we did not have to share it with another grade. We did not have desks but instead little tables with chairs, grouped into pods across the room so that four pupils always faced one another to form a "working group." This was almost revolutionary at the time.

I made my first real friend in Tutzing, Rainer Fiala. I was seated next to him when I joined grade three at the new school. Rainer's father kept a popular restaurant on a nearby hilltop with a magnificent view of the lake and, beyond that, the chain of the Alps behind it. I often walked up to his place after school, about half an hour through meadows and forests. We played cowboys and Indians in the forest. We stole cigarettes and apples from his father's restaurant pantry. After choking on the cigarettes a few times, we just took the apples.

There was a larger circle of friends as well, all boys from the school. They all came when my mother organized a party for my tenth birthday. In the garden we built a series of makeshift booths, like at a fair. At each, there was something to do, like throwing balls at a target or some other small test of skill. At each of these stations there were prizes, nothing more than what you would find in a treat bag nowadays, and my mother made sure there was an even share for everyone. The party was a great success.

I cannot remember a single girl from the Ebenhausen school. For me they simply did not exist. That changed in Tutzing. I fell in love for the first time, in grade four. Her name was Renate Hausmann, and she sat at the other end of the classroom. Sometimes she looked at me from across the room. Unlike my brother, who caused a stir in grade one when he kissed a girl (Gaby Gierke, in the schoolyard), I never dared to even talk to Renate in school, and it was impossible to encounter her alone on the way to or from school because she always was with her best friend, Ulrike Steichele. For a ten-year-old boy, two girls together are an unconquerable fortress. I so much wanted to invite Renate to that birthday party, but I knew that if I ever found the courage to ask her and if for whatever miraculous reason she accepted, none of the boys would have come.

In September of that year, when I entered the *Oberschule* (high school) in Tutzing, Renate Hausmann was gone. During the preceding summer vacation, I had finally made a move. I had visited her at home. While we were sitting in her room chatting away and munching cookies, her mother looked in and told me they were moving away, to Innsbruck in Austria.

I cannot remember how heartbroken I was, but my interest in girls subsided for a while, and most certainly so in public. At the beginning of grade two in the *Oberschule*, when we were assigned our seats, I somehow ended up sitting next to a girl—and it turned out to be Ulrike Steichele. I could hardly contain my outrage and embarrassment. As soon as school was out that day, I ran all the way home up the hill and, bursting into tears, told my mother that I would not enter that school ever again if I had to sit next to a girl. And indeed, I refused to go to school the next day. My mother went and talked to the teacher, Herr Anneser. She came back and reported that the problem had been resolved, and I returned to school the following day. Herr Anneser even apologized to me with a half-embarrassed smile and said he did not know that sitting next to a girl would upset me.

Herr Anneser was the English teacher, and I was his best student. He probably sympathized with my adolescent anxieties. He was a shy man who had a hard time maintaining classroom discipline. His wife, on the other hand, a biology teacher at the same school, was feared by all the students for her strictness. On one occasion, we had Herr Anneser almost in tears. I don't recall the occasion, but we were all out of our seats, surrounding him and yelling. When his wife heard the noise from an adjacent classroom, she charged into our classroom and began flailing the students closest to her husband with an umbrella. (I am not making this up.)

63 | *Catholics and Communists*

We had moved from a mostly rural to a much more urban setting. But we were still in Catholic Bavaria. There was a crucifix hanging in every classroom, of course. At the *Oberschule*, there was religious instruction twice a week for which we split into two groups, Catholic and Lutheran. Strangely, I do not remember any of this from my elementary school years. Our teacher in grades three and four, Herr Kopp, a renowned pedagogue who would continue his career as an instructor at the state teachers' college, told us stories about local history that often had religious overtones. But these stories were meant to stimulate our fantasies and not to instill religious fervour.

I loved those stories. One was about the church in Ambach that we could see across the lake. It sits on a hilltop some fifteen walking minutes from the village. While the locals were cutting the beams to build a new church in the village, so goes the story, they repeatedly cut themselves with their own axes. There was blood on the ground. After a while, they noticed that birds were picking up some of the bloodied wood splinters and flying off with them. Following the birds, they were led to a nearby hilltop, where the birds had dropped the wood splinters. The people concluded that this was where God wanted them to build their church. And so they did.

Another story, also about Ambach, is historically accurate at least in general terms. It is about a brave fisher boy and a marauding band of Pandurs, an eastern-European tribe on horseback. They were ransacking Ambach when they noticed, across the lake, the monastery of Bernried, right next to Tutzing. It was deep winter and the lake was frozen. Anticipating a rich church treasure, the Pandurs resolved to ride straight across the lake to the monastery. Unsure whether the ice would be strong enough to carry them, they demanded to be led across by a local guide. They assumed that they would be safe that way. The fisher boy volunteered but deliberately led them to thin ice, where he drowned with them but saved the monastery.

At the time, I had no idea that Ambach would soon become a second home to us. After we moved to Munich in 1959, my parents missed the lake. Eventually, in 1963, they rented two rooms in Ambach, in an old farmhouse directly on the lake. We kept those rooms for forty years, until a year after my father died in 2002. During the 1960s, when I was a student in Munich, I even had Ambach registered as my primary residence because of the cheaper car insurance rates outside the city. It was then that our landlord, a deeply conservative and devoutly Catholic farmer, Herr Hirn, suspected me of being Communist rather than a Catholic. He told me so himself, years later, and with a good laugh.

The story that transpired was this: since I was registered in Ambach, I was required to vote there in elections. Herr Hirn was not just our landlord—he was also the mayor and chief electoral officer of the village. And whenever he counted the ballots, there was always this one single excruciating vote cast for the Communists, the Kommunistische Partei Deutschlands (Communist Party of Germany) or KPD. He thought it could only be me, the student from Munich with the long hair and the beat-up VW Beetle. Only later did he find out that it had been an elderly widow living alone in a house at the end of the village, who at some point revealed to him that she thought KPD stood for Katholische Partei Deutschlands (Catholic Party of Germany).

My mother voted for the Liberals or, later, the Green Party; my father always voted for the conservatives. He was small-c conservative by nature, and he was entirely in the thrall of the Christian Conservatives' red-scare tactics during the Cold War years. "The socialists will come and take our house away," he often exclaimed when the newspapers reported another political crisis. And he used "communist" interchangeably with "socialist." But my father did not vote conservative because of religion or Catholicism.

Sometime after the war, one of his patients briefly had been Joseph Ratzinger. One day, years later, we were driving back from Ambach to Munich when we saw a black Mercedes limousine gliding stately past us in the opposite direction. My father glanced out the window and exclaimed: "Ha! That's Ratzinger, the asshole." This was when Ratzinger already was Cardinal and Archbishop of Munich and Freising.

It is not that my father objected to religiosity per se. And it wasn't Catholicism in particular that he resented. After the family's experience with the Innere Mission, a Lutheran organization, his scorn was in fact directed more against Protestants, who claimed to be the more enlightened of the two main religions in Germany but then routinely turned out to be even more, in deft Bavarian language, *hinterfotzig* (underhanded). His beef was with the organized institution and power of the church. He had the greatest respect for those simple priests or ministers who devoted their lives to helping others. In Russia, he had often worked shoulder-to-shoulder with them, tending to the wounded and dying, administering physical and spiritual help, respectively. What he couldn't stand was the falseness with which he thought the church exploited the spiritual needs of people for purposes of its own power and wealth. That is what had made his blood boil when he saw Ratzinger glide by in his limousine. But it was also what in the end made him more scornful of Protestants than of Catholics. The latter at least admitted to their power and wealth. Ultimately, in his view, the Catholics allowed more joy of life on earth. You can sin, and then you can repent. You do not have to live your entire life in a state of bad conscience.

Perhaps he had absorbed more of the Bavarian way of life than he was ready to admit. Shortly after moving to Canada, I was asked by one of my sister Andrea's friends, during a visit back in Munich, in the thickest Bavarian accent imaginable: "So, Thomas, you live in Canada now. Tell me, are they puritans over there, or do they have a healthy Catholic double morality?" Sadly, I had to tell him they were puritans, for the most part at least.

Perhaps not so sadly: Canada's is a mild form of Puritanism, and part of it involves a kind of secular discretion that keeps religion out of public life and schools (except, deplorably, in the case of Catholic school boards in Ontario). On the one hand, this has prevented the unholy alliance of Christian fundamentalism and neoliberalism from poisoning civil society as it has south of the border over the past thirty years. Yet on the other hand, I sometimes regret that my son will never learn all the biblical stories that fuelled my fantasies as a child and that are part of the Judeo-Christian tradition we belong to.

When I move back and forth between the Old World and the New, this cultural difference is sometimes driven home in awkward albeit comical ways. On one of our visits to Germany, when Jacob still was in a stroller, we visited the place where King Ludwig II of Bavaria drowned in Lake Starnberg after he had been declared insane and confined to one of his summer residences near Berg, also on the Ambach side of the lake. The spot where he drowned is marked by a simple wooden cross a few metres from shore. On the shore a monument has been erected in his honour that consists mainly of a huge crucifix. With all kinds of people milling around the place, little Jacob pointed up at the crucifix and asked loudly: "Who's that guy hanging up there?" Julia and I could not help feeling embarrassed, and we were hoping (in vain, of course) that nobody understood English.

64 | *The hotel*

We moved to Tutzing because of the Hotel Kaiserin Elisabeth in neighbouring Feldafing. It was in this hotel that my father began his second career as a physician after he had been forced out of the sanatorium in Ebenhausen. I believe he first encountered that hotel at the end of the war, at a time when it had briefly been transformed into a makeshift field hospital and his sister Mucki worked there as a physiotherapist. He must have remembered that when he was looking for a venue where he could continue to practise what was now his specialty: treating in-patients who did not require full hospitalization in a sanatorium-like environment of comfort and care.

The arrangement seemed mutually beneficial. The hotel was a golf hotel with one of the most beautiful golf courses in Germany sloping gently down to the lake in front of it. In 1955, only a few people had the time or money to indulge in golf. The hotel was half empty and in dire need of renovations and general upgrading. So the owners welcomed an arrangement that promised a more stable income from patient-guests, who of course were expected to stay much longer than just the occasional golfing weekend. The arrival of Vera Kalman with her Cadillac and entourage was a promising beginning indeed.

A number of rooms were reserved for my father's patients. Also, two rooms on the first floor were converted into a practice. The hotel kitchen accommodated his patients' dietary needs. A new brochure noted that the hotel now contained what effectively was my father's private clinic. My father's patients mingled indistinguishably with the other hotel guests. At first it seemed a bit odd, perhaps, that my father and the one nurse he brought with him from Ebenhausen walked around the hotel premises in white smocks, but soon enough that became a normal sight and people stopped noticing.

The hotel owners were two sisters, Frau Borchard and Fräulein Kraft. Frau Borchard had lost her husband in the war. She had two daughters, Erika and Issy, and she drove a VW Beetle. Her sister Fräulein Kraft was a fiercely single woman who drove a Porsche. She was generally known to us as Tante (aunt) Mädi because that's what the Borchards called her.

My father and the rest of us befriended Frau Borchard and the girls. Our two families almost became inseparable. We went to concerts and the opera together. We went swimming together at the hotel boathouse. We went on Sunday excursions in the Bavarian countryside. We regularly ate supper together, not in the hotel's formal dining room but in the more informal pub, where the menu was simpler and draught beer was available.

The next time my parents went to Bayreuth, my brother and I were put up in one of the hotel rooms and the Borchards looked after us. On one occasion I accompanied Frau Borchard and her daughters to Verdun, that old battlefield of two world wars where the girls' father had perished in 1943 and where they went every year to place flowers at the one simple white cross, among thousands, that bore his name.

It was an experience I never forgot. We visited the Fort Douaumont Ossuary, where one can see the bones of some 130,000 French and German soldiers, peacefully united at last. I also saw the infamous Bayonet Trench, where a dozen French infantrymen were buried alive by a German shell in the First World War. Fifty years later, their rifle bayonets were still sticking out of the ground. Right there and then I formed the opinion that soldiers are not heroes, at least not by choice, but rather victims of political folly.

Tante Mädi was the older sister and for that reason called most of the shots at the hotel. She controlled the hotel's finances, and she also controlled Herr Stöcklein, who was in charge of accounting and supplies. Gossip had it that Herr Stöcklein also provided other services for Tante Mädi, but I think it can be assumed more safely (at least so my mother did) that she was not interested in men. She could be prickly, and everybody seemed a bit afraid of her—except me. I played Ping-Pong with her, I had long conversations with her, and I thought she was "cool." Maybe it was the Porsche.

My father never really took to Tante Mädi. Right there lies the reason why the arrangement between him and the hotel did not work out in the end. We moved to Munich in 1959, where he began his third medical career by opening an outpatient practice. Frau Borchard was a kind woman with a big heart, but she did not play a central role in the management of the hotel, and she was also a bit spacey. Because he neglected his relationship with Tante Mädi, my father remained outside the inner loop of decision-making authority.

I am not entirely sure what led to my father's break with the hotel. I suspect there was always some tension, because Frau Borchard would say yes to something or other and Tante Mädi would then renege on it—possibly for entirely sound reasons from the hotel's perspective. Perhaps Tante Mädi sensed, towards the end of the 1950s, that the hotel no longer needed a clinical ward. She was an avid golfer, and perhaps she simply got tired of seeing my father and his nurse in their white smocks among an increasingly trendy golfing crowd from Munich and elsewhere.

But for five years, the Kaiserin Elisabeth was the centre of our social life. The hotel was named after Elizabeth ("Sisi"), the last Empress of Austria. She was a Bavarian princess from Possenhofen right next to Feldafing, and a cousin of King Ludwig. After her move to Vienna she would stay at the hotel during her regular family visits. Her favourite dessert was ice cream made from violets. It is still served at the hotel, with frozen violet petals on top. She was a fearless equestrian, which is why stables were added to the hotel. Except for one, in which Frau Borchard kept two horses for her daughters, these stables were later converted into garages, and it was in one of those that the pageboy crashed Vera Kalman's Cadillac against a concrete pillar.

Sisi was in Feldafing when King Ludwig drowned on 13 June 1886. She hurried to Berg and is said to have collapsed inconsolably at the sight of her dead cousin. The circumstances of the drowning were never cleared up. Officially, his death was declared a suicide. The king was on a walk in the castle park with his psychiatrist-physician, a Doctor von Gudden, when he suddenly dashed for the lake. Von Gudden caught up with him, and they engaged in a struggle, in the course of which von Gudden was either killed or drowned. The king then swam farther out into the lake and drowned himself.

Even at the time, few believed all this. The water where the king was found was barely a metre deep. Ludwig was known to be an excellent swimmer and would have sought deeper water if his intention had been to kill himself. And he could easily have escaped the twenty-years-older von Gudden by running or swimming away from him. The suspicion has never been put to rest that the king was murdered for reasons of state. He had been dethroned—so goes the story—not because he was insane but because his excessive spending had driven the Bavarian state into bankruptcy. Ultimate irony: Ludwig spent most of that money on all the castles he built throughout southern Bavaria. Visited by thousands of tourists from all over the world each year, these castles are now a major source of income for Bavaria and its inhabitants.

The prevailing story around the lake is a different one yet: the king and Sisi were lovers. He intended to swim across the lake, where Sisi was waiting for him. Sisi was said to be unhappy in her marriage to the Austrian emperor. They wanted to flee together and begin a happier life—an unlikely story. Even so, to this day the simple cross by the lake near where the king died has remained a favourite destination for lovers.

There was an obvious reason why my father went to Feldafing after being forced out of Ebenhausen. All his life, except during the war, he had lived in the vicinity of large luxurious hotels, and his years as sanatorium doctor had more or less amounted to a continuation of that life. Not since they had been wine growers in the Kaiserstuhl had the Hüglins lived so frugally as we did in our little house in Tutzing. The hotel in Feldafing provided an athmosphere allowing my father to think that nothing much had changed.

By the time we arrived at the hotel, its glory had faded, but it was still a fabulous place. There were still pageboys in red uniforms and caps at the doors and in the elevator; there was still the head porter, Herr Lumpert, always formally attired in white tie and tails; there was still the formal dining hall with its white linen; and the headwaiter, Herr Lavont, complete with French accent, also in formal attire, a white serviette hung over one sleeve; and there was the hotel food, brought to the tables on platters covered by shiny metal lids.

It was in this atmosphere that my father felt at home. He could continue to treat and interact with celebrities. Vera Kalman was only the first of them. Peter Ustinov came a little later. He, my parents, and Frau Borchard regularly descended to the bowling alley in the hotel's basement. They played as two teams, and Ustinov always insisted on teaming up with my mother. I was in charge of putting the pins back in place at the other end and of rolling the balls back to the players.

Another regular was Benvenuto Hauptmann, son of the dramatist Gerhard Hauptmann and of Margarete, who had been my father's patient in Ebenhausen. Benvenuto's wife Barbara had been a renowned theatre actress before her marriage and she was the one my father was really interested in (like many sons of famous fathers, Benvenuto was kind of a bore). Their daughter Anja became one of the first female television anchors in Germany—and my father's godchild when, as an adult, she decided to be christened.

Benvenuto drank too much—usually an entire bottle of Moselle with dinner—and my father said that the sugar that was added to that wine would one day kill him. Dedicated aficionados of Rheingau Riesling had only contempt for wines from the neighbouring Moselle Valley. My father even claimed that there was an underground sucrose pipeline from the Ruhr industrial zone to the Moselle. I still remember Benvenuto, very tall but also rather overweight in a white dinner jacket, sitting at his regular table in the hotel dining hall, a bottle of Moselle in front of him.

Years later, when we were in Munich, Benvenuto did almost die, in Switzerland, where he lived most of the year. As we heard later, he was already delirious; a phalanx of doctors from a nearby university hospital had just about given up on him when he came to momentarily and demanded to see "the doctor Hüglin." My father received a telegram from Barbara and the very same evening boarded a small propellor plane for Lugano. There was a storm that night and the plane had to circle for several hours before it could land. After the landing, it was still a couple of hours by taxi. When my father finally arrived in the wee hours, Benvenuto was alive but unconscious. My father realized that the heavy man was being killed by his excessively high blood pressure. He decided to bleed him. He looked for some sort of receptacle. All he could find was a teapot. So my father cut a vein in Benvenuto's arm and bled him into the teapot. A few hours later, when the local doctors arrived with skeptical professorial faces, they found Benvenuto sitting up in bed and happily chatting away with my father.

The hotel became my favourite playground. I roamed the extensive park that belonged to it, with the white marble monument to Sisi at the end, right next to the tennis court. I inspected all the fancy cars in the garages. I spent hours in the bar, which was in the basement and had a dance floor where I played all the dance music on the record player while nobody was there during the day. My favourite record was *Delicado* by the Percy Faith Orchestra, the only recording with a harpsichord that ever made the pop charts. And I milled around with the hotel guests and staff, always eager to strike a conversation.

The hotel became an important new focus of our family life. We went to the elegant dining hall for birthday dinners, we had tea with the Borchards on the terrace, and we played tennis in the park. Then there were the New Year's Eve parties we attended, big formal dinners that were followed by all kinds of entertainment, including sketches performed by Herr Lumpert, who had a great sense of humour even though he was Swiss. Herr Lumpert was my good friend. I was allowed to call him Lumpi. He let me ride the elevator and operate the switchboard. During one of these New Year's Eve parties, however, unbeknownst to everyone, I came down with mumps. On New Year's Day I developed cheeks like a hamster, and I infected my friend Lumpi. Having to stay home and in bed for a week, I was afraid that Lumpi would be cross with me (he was unable to work for a week as well). But he never held it against me.

65 | Erika

Everybody had a crush on Erika Borchard, the younger daughter, a lively and pretty teenager about four years older than I and therefore about fourteen when we first met. My father had a crush on her, I did, my little brother did a little later, and most certainly my grandfather Alfred in Hattenheim did. Whenever the grandparents came visiting, often twice a year, they now stayed in the hotel—another reason I spent so much time there. Erika almost instantly advanced to the status of favourite female companion, obviously an entirely innocent affair of mutual affection. Erika visited Hattenheim repeatedly in later years. She accompanied the grandparents on several trips to Italy and became grandfather's latest victim in front of his camera. There is a particularly lovely picture of her lying on the hotel lawn, alas with my little brother next to her rather than me, while she taught him how to whistle on a blade of grass.

Erika and my brother Michi on the hotel lawn.

Erika taught me how to swim. Later, we played tennis in the park. Later again, when we had already moved to Munich and I had been to dancing school, we danced together during afternoon teas on the hotel terrace. We practised downstairs in the empty bar. We also went skiing. Erika was a very accomplished skier; I was better at tennis. It was a wonderful friendship for years. We were buddies. Of course she had no idea that I was also in love with her.

My grandfather perhaps harboured a fleeting thought that his favourite grandson and his favourite object of doting attention might become a romantic item. This happened much later, when I was already at university. Erika wanted to visit friends at an Adriatic resort, and my grandfather, in Feldafing at the time, persuaded me to go with her so that she would not have to do the long drive alone. He even gave me the money for the trip. And off we went, in Erika's VW Beetle, following the same route my grandparents had taken so often, over the Grossglockner Pass in the Austrian Alps and down to the Adriatic.

Disaster (almost) struck: Erika had forgotten to take with her the exact address of the place where her friend was staying. Our destination, the resort town of Bibbione, halfway between Venice and Trieste, turned out to be one of those mass-tourism places where dozens of streets and hundreds of houses look exactly alike. Attempts at phoning the hotel back home and recovering the address proved fruitless. So after a long and dusty road trip, we first jumped into the water to freshen up and then began to search for the place. All we had was a letter that Erika had received from her friend, which described the walking distance to the shore and a little park or wooded area in the vicinity. I must admit it was Erika who insisted we would succeed; I thought we were looking for the proverbial needle in a haystack. But succeed we did. About midnight that day, after endlessly driving up and down all those streets and precariously close to getting into a serious fight, we found the place.

The friend was the baroness Maltzahn, who had once been the lover of our joint piano teacher, count Gessler (more about that later). She had a young son, and he was how we finally found them: once we were in an area roughly resembling the description in the letter, we started going from house to house asking whether anybody had seen a single mother and child. The houses were mostly occupied by larger families.

The baroness was not a single mother. Her husband, the baron Maltzahn, arrived a few days after us. He had been delayed—how could it be otherwise?—by a hunting trip somewhere in northern Germany. He was still wearing his hunting gear, and when he took off his boots an alarming amount of blood came gushing out of one of them. He had partied the evening before his departure and—still quite drunk in the morning, just before driving over a thousand kilometres from northern Germany to Italy—when he went to put on his boots, he could not find a shoehorn. Using his hunting knife instead, he had almost sliced off half his heel. He hadn't even noticed. Such were the anaesthetic qualities of alcohol. All those Western movies where the hero takes a swig of whisky before having a bullet cut out with a bowie knife suddenly rang truer.

Although we had hardly seen each other for a few years, Erika and I rekindled our friendship quickly and had a grand time in Bibbione. Misjudging our joint arrival, the baroness insisted that we were, or should be, a romantic item. So we goofed around pretending to be one, walking arm-in-arm and holding hands. In fact I would by no means have been opposed to a belated little summer affair had the occasion arisen. And who knows what might have become of it. My father certainly would not have minded seeing his first-born continue the Hüglin tradition of involvement in the hotel business. He later told me as much. Nothing happened in the end, not even a kiss. My advances were so cautious that Erika probably did not even notice. She certainly did nothing to encourage them.

After that, our friendship faded away. I continued university in Switzerland, and Erika got more and more involved in the management of the hotel. She never married. Her mother, Frau Borchard, died a couple of years ago, in 2008, at the ripe age of 101. I still visit Erika from time to time when I am in Europe. We still joke about the old times. But we are far apart now.

66 | Piano lessons

My father had to buy a piano. The Blüthner stayed in Ebenhausen, of course, and a grand piano would not have fit into the little house in any case. Indeed, the upright we bought barely did. It was a Schimmel, and it was installed in the tiny boudoir, which also held my mother's desk, the piano bench, and a chair. With all of that, one could hardly get through to the terrace door.

The piano came with piano lessons. My teacher's full name was Friedrich Karl Graf von Gessler. If the name sounds familiar, it should not come entirely as a surprise. Gessler is the Hapsburg governor of Switzerland who makes Wilhelm Tell shoot an arrow through the apple on his son's head in Friedrich Schiller's drama. Wilhelm Tell is fiction; Gessler, though, was a historical figure, and my piano teacher was a direct descendant. He wore a family ring with the same crest as can be found in a memorial chapel on the shores of Vierwaldstätter Lake near Lucerne, where the Tell saga is said to have taken place. The crest in the chapel has an axe stuck in it. Count Gessler always joked that there were places he still could not travel because there had been a warrant out for his family since the Middle Ages.

Count Gessler came from an old Prussian family of professional officers. He was born in the Silesian town of Breslau, which is now in Poland and called Wroclaw. He was the only musician in the family. The Gesslers were landowners and could afford one of their sons indulging in a musical career. Friedrich Karl was sent to study piano with the renowned pedagogue Robert Teichmüller at the Leipzig Conservatory. Teichmüller is known today mainly for his editions and arrangements of classical piano music. In particular, he added fingerings and rearranged the orchestral parts of piano concertos for a second piano. Wherever and whenever in the world a graduating piano student has to play a concerto for a final exam accompanied not by an orchestra but by a second piano, the likelihood is that she or he owes that accompaniment to one of Teichmüller's arrangements.

Teichmüller trained a slew of pianists who played mainly in the eastern-European part of the musical world. Count Gessler was one of them. Before the war, he toured regularly in the Baltic and other eastern-European states. But he remained rather unknown in the west. The war destroyed his career, and his family lost all its possessions. Gessler became one of thousands of destitute refugees pouring into West Germany from the east. For some time he tried to survive as a night watchman in Munich. Then he moved to Possenhofen on Lake Starnberg, rented a tiny room near the castle where Sisi had been raised, and tried to make it as a piano teacher.

My father probably met him through the Borchards. He was the piano teacher of both Borchard girls. For my lessons, my father would pick him up in Possenhofen, five or six kilometres from Tutzing. The count and I would then squeeze into the boudoir for the lesson. Count Gessler smoked incessantly and usually had his hand with a burning cigarette on the edge of my mother's desk. A few times he singed the hair on the back of my head. The first real pieces of music I learned to play was one of Mendelssohn's *Songs Without Words*. The first time I played it through successfully, count Gessler gave me a small chocolate bar he had been keeping in his pocket. It was a huge gesture. I knew he did not have any money.

Some time later came Mozart's *Sonata Facile*, which is everything but "facile." Alone at home and practising one day, I threw a major tantrum when I could not get those damned runs in the first movement to sound even. Just then my father came back from Feldafing and told me that he too had thrown such tantrums as a child, that he had once thrown his music across the salon, and that he then had to carefully put the pages back together again so his parents wouldn't notice.

Count Gessler usually stayed for supper before my father drove him back to Possenhofen. He was an emaciated little man with an expressive face, a large, aristocratic nose, and even larger hands with long, spidery fingers. He craved those meals, which came with animated conversations about music, about how everything had been so much better in the past, about how Karajan would never have had a significant career as a conductor had Furtwängler still been alive, and about how the whole world was going down the tubes. Then we would listen to Furtwängler's 1953 recording of Schumann's Fourth Symphony, made a year before the conductor died and, according to both Gessler and my father, one of the few Furtwängler recordings true to the way they had experienced the maestro in concert. We also played other records, of course, but this one we must have listened to a hundred times. I even once tried to fool the two of them by secretly placing on the turntable a different recording of the Schumann symphony—by Georg Solti, I think. Gessler noticed from the opening bars. "Are you the ultimate prey of madness?" he exclaimed on that occasion and many others.

I loved those evening meals, too. Instead of sandwiches and a glass of milk, or the flower pudding, there would be a series of elaborate dishes—meat and gravy with rice or noodles, followed by dessert. My mother liked cooking for count Gessler, who was grateful for anything put in front of him and who ceremoniously kissed my mother's hand when he left. And of course I loved the conversations, about music, about the war, and about the various princesses, countesses, and baronesses Gessler mentioned in passing when he told us about his other connections and activities around the lake. While my father drove him home, mother and I would clean up, giggling about the number of noble lady friends he seemed to have. He never mentioned anyone male.

For reasons that now escape me, the location of the weekly piano lessons shifted from Tutzing to Feldafing after a year or two. I took the train or went on my bicycle. It probably was a matter of convenience. Erika was having her weekly lesson in the villa behind the hotel, and it was arranged that I would have my own lesson directly afterwards. Depending on the train schedule, or on how soon I left on my bike, I could sometimes sit through all or part of Erika's lesson. She was much more advanced.

One day at the Borchard villa in Feldafing, Count Gessler showed us his most prized possession, the only thing he had been able to rescue at the end of the war, carrying it lovingly under his coat on the long trek to the west: a copy of what is sometimes called Robert Schumann's second piano concerto, the *Introduktion und Allegro Appassionato*, Op. 92. That copy contained fingerings and interpretative comments written in longhand by Clara Schumann, Robert's wife.

Some years later, he actually got to perform that piece, in Freiburg, with the local symphony orchestra. He was so nervous in the weeks before the concert that he did not tell us until after the fact. For good reason, he feared that we would all show up in my father's hometown for the event. When he did tell us, he brought along a tape of the concert and we all listened to it. He had done very well, it seemed.

Especially when we had not practised, Erika and I would try to get him to tell stories. For the most part he gladly obliged. Only once, after a particularly frustrating lesson (I had not worked on my scales at all), did he take me aside and threaten to quit teaching me if I did not come better prepared. He was not a very good piano teacher. I had a very good ear, and after struggling through a particular piece a few times was usually able to play and practise from memory. So I never did learn how to read music properly. He either did not notice or did not care.

But I owe much of my general musical education to him. One afternoon the three of us—Gessler, Erika, and I—sat in front of the record player and listened to Wagner's *Tristan and Isolde* with him while he explained orchestration and harmonic structure from the open score in front of us. I was maybe twelve. I sat through my first live performance of *Tristan* when I was not quite fourteen, at the Prinzregententheater in Munich. Hans Knappertsbusch conducted; Martha Mödl and Ramon Vinay sang. I sat between my father and count Gessler. Whenever there was a particularly important or beautiful moment, I got elbowed from both sides. There were many such important and wonderful moments, so my ribs were quite bruised by the end of the evening. During one intermission, we ran into the widow of Wilhelm Furtwängler. Of course my father knew her. It was their first encounter since the conductor died. She hugged my father with tears running down her cheeks.

The lessons continued after we moved to Munich. For Gessler, this was a long trip by train and tramway for just one lesson. He probably came mainly for the food and the company. Around that time, he went on his only other concert trip, for a recital in Montreal. It had been arranged by one of his noble lady friends who had a Canadian connection. I cannot remember why and how (I think she had been Mrs. Boothby in a first marriage), but she was the one who would later become the baroness Maltzahn, whom Erika and I visited on that memorable trip to Bibbione. Count Gessler told me all about his voyage across the Atlantic and how he had avoided seasickness by standing at the ship's bow and watching the waves.

Twenty years later, shortly after arriving in Canada, I befriended Harald von Rieckhoff, a professor of political science at Carleton University in Ottawa, and his wife, who was the descendant of a Baltic noble family. We talked more about music than about political science and at some point I mentioned my former piano teacher's trip to Montreal. The von Rieckhoffs remembered well the count's name; indeed, they had been at his recital.

The lessons in Munich did not last much longer. Count Gessler became afflicted with some back problem and checked into the hospital in Tutzing. When we visited him there, we found him chasing nurses in a silk bathrobe. He was in his early sixties by then. After being released from hospital, he was invited to recuperate in the company of some aristocratic friends in a castle somewhere in Bavaria. During one of his first afternoons there, he fell asleep in a deckchair on the castle's terrace in the blazing sun. He never woke up. He had died from sunstroke.

Erika and I went to the funeral. Around the open grave were gathered half a dozen or so weeping women, all princesses, countesses, and baronesses. Their tears and jewellery were not the only items that shone in the afternoon sun. There also was a kind of steely glitter of incredulity in the eyes of all these dames. Each had obviously thought that she was the only one. When I told my mother later that day, she remarked drily: "That's probably why he never put on any weight." But she didn't giggle that time. She had liked the count. And he had only been after her food.

67 | *Music, caviar, and space*

My father got back into the habit of organizing concerts, both in our house in Tutzing and at the hotel. The house concerts in Tutzing mostly were piano recitals, owing to the lack of space; the hotel provided more options. Count Gessler and the cellist Hermann von Beckerath played a recital there, and I particularly remember a performance of the Brahms Cello Sonata in F, Op. 99, which has remained one of my favourite works. Beckerath was a professor at the Munich Academy and the son of Willy von Beckerath, a painter known for his portrait of Brahms seated at the piano with a cigar in his mouth. Hermann von Beckerath sweated profusely when he played and always had a huge white handkerchief in his breast pocket with which he wiped not only his forehead but also the steady trickle of sweat running down his cello and disappearing into one of the F-holes.

Also at the hotel, count Gessler once accompanied a singer in a recital of *Lieder* by Herr Thomsen, a regular guest there and, naturally, also my father's patient. Herr Thomsen owned the Lysell fish cannery in Hamburg. The songs were somewhat esoteric but well received. My brother and I liked Herr Thomsen mainly because every Christmas he sent us a two-pound piece of Lübeck marzipan shaped after the famous bunny picture by Albrecht Dürer. With the marzipan would come an entire box full of canned fish products.

Herr Thomsen liked to talk about his time in the war. Like my father, he had served in Russia. He had ended up on the Crimean Peninsula, which was the Russian centre for caviar production. Since he was expert in preserving and canning fish, he was placed in charge of caviar production there during the German occupation. Herr Thomsen, a gentle and soft-spoken soul, told us he felt guilty that only the officers indulged in as much caviar as they could get their hands on. So one day he decided to include small portions of it in the rations of the soldiers stationed in the area. After a few days he received a written complaint. The soldiers were tired of always having to eat this "salty jam." I guess caviar washes down best with champagne, and I do not suppose these soldiers were given that in their rations as well.

The Keller String Quartet often performed in Feldafing. Erich Keller was concertmaster of the Bavarian Radio Symphony Orchestra. His wife Elisabeth Schwarz was a highly accomplished pianist and chamber musician who often joined her husband's quartet for the performance of various piano quintets. The Kellers were good friends of my parents. After their Feldafing performances, the entire quartet usually ended up at the house in Tutzing. On one occasion, the viola player, Franz Schessl, had a terrible cold and was banished to the boudoir with a big glass of brandy. Right next to the entries of the Keller Quartet members in the guest book is another one, by the *Heldentenor* Hans Hopf, who wrote: "The salami and the champagne—I will come more often!"

Sometime in the late 1950s, we went to Munich for one of the Keller Quartet's outdoor concerts, in the courtyard of the castle residence of the Bavarian kings. It was a warm summer night, but during the first part of the concert it suddenly started to drizzle. Some of us had wisely brought umbrellas. We stepped forward and joined the musicians on stage, holding our umbrellas over them. They did not miss a beat. The skies cleared for the second part of the concert and the Kellers were in the middle of a slow movement when all of a sudden, one after another, the heads of the audience turned skyward. This was when we all saw for the first time one of the Russian *Sputnik* satellites on its lonely path around the world.

That was the first time that music had intersected with space in my life, but it was not the last. On 20 July 1969, Apollo 11 was preparing to land on the moon. My father had bought tickets for that day for a performance at the Bavarian State Opera's summer festival. It was *Tristan* again. I had to go with my parents. Erika came along as well. I was so incensed that I took a little transistor radio with me, pressing it to my ear during the performance. But there was no reception inside the opera house. During the first intermission, I raced down to the steps outside the grand entrance and listened to what was taking place somewhere up there in the sky. The lunar module with Neil Armstrong and Buzz Aldrin had successfully separated from Michael Collins's command module.

Quite a few distinguished operagoers in their tuxedos and evening gowns gathered around me to hear the latest developments. During the second intermission, I heard the famous words: "The *Eagle* has landed." Back in my seat at the last moment, with the large central chandelier already rising, I hissed into Erika's ear next to me: "They are down." Then the curtain rose and we were back to the shepherd playing his sad melody on the English horn and the mortally wounded Tristan hallucinating about Isolde floating towards him on King Marke's ship. Later we stayed up all night to watch the fuzzy black-and-white image of Neil Armstrong climbing down the ladder to the lunar surface. Some hundred kilometres away in Ehrwald, of course, aunt Reni thought it was all a hoax.

Not all the musical events around Lake Starnberg were organized by my father. Remember Elly Ney, who lived in Tutzing and whom my father had visited as an aspiring piano student during the 1930s? Tutzing owed its own annual music festival to her. She played piano concertos with a local pickup orchestra conducted by her husband, Willem van Hoogstraten. It was said that the two of them were actually divorced but were now living together again in their old age.

Their musical presence in the community was a mixed blessing. Both were in their eighties, and while she had colossal memory lapses, he routinely fell asleep with the baton in his hand. When he dozed off, she would yell at him from the piano. (I am not making this up!) Once, when she got hopelessly lost, everything came to a grinding halt while someone fetched the sheet music from her apartment. Strange coincidence: Hoogstraten had been the principal conductor of the symphony orchestra in Portland, Oregon, from 1925 to 1937, and Gerda heard him there later when he returned for occasional performances as emeritus guest conductor. She giggled when she found out that it was our turn now to be exposed to his baton. She did not think highly of his conducting abilities.

Going to hear Elly Ney play in Tutzing was like going on a historical music pilgrimage. During her best moments, she was still a formidable performer. I was reminded of how deeply she has remained anchored in Germany's collective musical psyche when I saw Maurizio Kagel's 1970 movie *Ludwig van*. It had been commissioned for the Vienna Music Festival for the two hundredth anniversary of Beethoven's birth that year. It caused a major scandal. People were throwing chairs. Kagel had made a biting satire about the music business and its Beethoven cult. In one of the central scenes, a mummified Elly Ney is playing Beethoven's *Waldstein* Sonata, Op. 53. During the throbbing opening chords, the camera slowly moves from the end of the piano to the front, eventually revealing that the Elly Ney character is wearing mittens and playing on the keyboard's closed lid. The chords are alienated by an underlying rhythm borrowed from Stravinsky's *Sacre du Printemps*.

The Elly Ney character was played by Klaus Lindemann, the film's cinematographer and the director of many prized music films in Germany at the time. I got to know Lindemann shortly after he had filmed *Ludwig van*. He was part of the musical circle around the German piano virtuoso Ludwig Hoffmann, my first wife's piano teacher at the Music Academy in Munich. We all had a few good laughs when he told us how he had filmed himself in that scene.

Neither Austrians nor Germans take their music lightly. That I learned from another concert experience during the Tutzing years. The Munich Philharmonic often performed youth concerts. Always on the day before one of their main subscription concerts, there would be a performance of the same program for schoolchildren at practically no cost. These youth concerts were available to schoolchildren not only in Munich but all over upper Bavaria. From Tutzing, we would board a chartered bus that would take us to the concert hall in Munich and back.

One of these concerts is etched in memory. On the program were Claude Debussy's three orchestral nocturnes. To be appreciated, these subtle works require a rather well-trained ear. The juvenile audience was unruly. There was a lot of coughing. At some point during the first piece, the conductor, Rudolf Kempe, stopped the performance, turned around, and gravely addressed his audience: "These are very delicate pieces. In order to enjoy them, you must be quiet." He then started all over again. We were stunned. You could have heard a pin drop in the large hall for the rest of the evening.

Then there was the concert my father gave for the Lions Club. Gerda in distant Portland giggled when she heard that her brother-in-law had joined it (and that her brother Rolf was active in the Rotary Club). It seems that service clubs were by then passé among her circles in America—not least because at the time they were for men only. The Lake Starnberg Lions Club held its monthly meetings in the Hotel Kaiserin Elisabeth, over hotel food and wine, and its purpose was to raise money for all kinds of good works in the area. My father was for some years assigned to provide food and medical attention to the last living *Fahnenträger* (flag-bearer) of Ludwig II, who lived in a little house at the end of the lake, in poverty and nearly hundred years old.

Among the club members was Herbert Pschorr, heir to one of the big breweries in Munich and related to the composer Richard Strauss, whose mother had been the daughter of the brewery's founder. Probably occasioned by my father's endless tales about music, Pschorr persuaded him to play a recital for the club and to combine it with a short lecture on music.

My father practised for nearly a year. The concert-lecture was a tremendous success. With some hotel guests and the Borchards added to the Lions Club audience, my father talked eloquently (and not nearly so endlessly as his family had feared) about the biographical and musical connections among some of his favourite nineteenth-century Romantic composers: Schubert, Mendelssohn, Schumann, Chopin, and Liszt. In between, he played a few pieces by each. I remember the first of Mendelssohn's *Songs Without Words*, one of the brief Consolations by Liszt, and Chopin's first prelude. After the concert, Pschorr gave him a nicely framed copy of an unpublished one-page piano composition by Richard Strauss.

I had my own run-in with the Lions Club. Its members were a rather conservative bunch. When Willy Brandt became Chancellor of West Germany after the 1969 federal election, my father was not the only one fearful that the socialists would come and take away his house and possessions. I got into a heated discussion with some club members about social democracy in the course of which they challenged me to give a speech to them at one of the next club meetings. I did. After all, I was at university by then and knew everything better anyway. And Willy Brandt, who had replaced the ex–Nazi Party member Kurt-Georg Kiesinger as federal chancellor, was at least for now the undisputed hero of the '68 student generation.

So I went to Feldafing and for about an hour waxed about the need for more social equality. Socialism—leave alone social democracy—did not mean that private homes would be taken away, but it *would* mean limits to private accumulation. So I declared. There was a lively discussion afterwards and I was generally commended for having taken my lefty views right to the Lions' den, so to speak.

Frau von Ehrlich, the wife of a very wealthy factory owner and blessed with a rather extrovert nature, repeatedly and ostentatiously clapped at various points during my speech and afterwards launched a lengthy tirade about socialism really being the ultimate salvation for humanity. She was shut up by Herr Gierke, also very wealthy, a film producer and the father of the girl my brother had kissed in grade one. He was a Berliner and had the wickedly dry sense of humour attributed to the inhabitants of that city. He waited until Frau von Ehrlich took a breath, then leaned forward and asked her, sweetly and innocently, but audible from across the room: "My goodness, your ladyship, how much is it actually that you have socialized already?"

68 | Star-struck

Another no-nonsense Berliner who affected our lives quite substantively was Ilse Kubaschewski. She owned Germany's second-largest film-production and -distribution company, Gloria Filmverleih. To see a movie in the company's downtown Munich theatre, the Gloria Filmpalast, was almost as exciting and glamorous as going to the opera. The main attraction apart from the films themselves was a so-called water organ. For about ten minutes before the film started, someone played schmaltzy music on a Hammond organ synchronized with a wall of multicoloured water jets rhythmically rising and falling from a basin in front of the screen.

Frau Kubaschewski, "the Kuba," as she was generally referred to in the media as well as by her friends, lived in a villa-bungalow outside Starnberg. Its most talked-about feature was a ballroom in which she held enormous parties. At the push of a button, the hardwood floor would disappear and give way to a swimming pool underneath. Rumour had it that this button was sometimes pushed when the dance floor was full of film starlets in skimpy outfits, but that was just that—a rumour. On top of the villa-bungalow was a large roof terrace, also suitable for parties. It was on that terrace that Herr Kubaschewski once tried to kiss my mother. Of course, my mother giggled when she told me. That was the only time that Herr Kubaschewski was ever mentioned. He played no role in his wife's professional and public life. He also died rather young, soon after which the Kuba surrounded herself with a series of lovers mostly half her age. It is not entirely out of the question that my father briefly might have been one of them. She possessed enormous charm and usually got what she wanted.

The films produced or distributed by the Kuba were for the most part terrible. *Die Trapp-Familie* (that aforementioned German precursor to the equally terrible *The Sound of Music*) was one of them. In a newspaper interview, the Kuba revealed what had been her principles of film-script selection: only nice characters in leading roles; no flashbacks; always a happy ending; lavish images of local scenery; as much music as possible; and always something to laugh about. You easily get the picture of why the postwar German film industry did not exactly enjoy an international reputation. But the Kuba did have an uncanny sense for what German audiences wanted to see, and she did not shy away from more highbrow projects when she thought they would sell. She distributed Fellini's *La dolce vita* in Germany, for example, and she produced the legendary film version of Goethe's *Faust* with Gustav Gründgens in the title role.

Ilse Kubaschewski was born in 1907 in Berlin. Her mother operated a small movie theatre and accompanied the silent movies by playing the piano below the screen. When little Ilse was seven, she was made to learn the violin and soon found herself playing along with the movies and her mother. During the 1930s, she married Hans Kubaschewski, who at the time was a producer at UFA Studios in Berlin. After the war, she started her own film business.

I do not remember how my father met the Kuba. But she became a faithful patient for many years, first when we lived in Tutzing and later in Munich as well. He always went to see her at her villa-bungalow in Starnberg, making house calls at least once a week. Often, on the way back from a Sunday family excursion, he would announce: "I just have to make a quick visit to Frau Kubaschewski." He would park the car in front of the high wall surrounding her property, take his medical bag with the stethoscope, the syringes, and whatever else he carried with him, and disappear behind the huge gate. The "quick visit" often lasted more than an hour, during which we had to mope in the car. My mother was often quite annoyed, to put it mildly.

It was Frau Kubaschewski who persuaded my father to quit the increasingly unpleasant hotel scene in Feldafing and open a practice in Munich. There, she told him, she could supply him with a whole slew of new patients from the film business (and she did). She owned the apartment block into which we moved in 1959, with the practice across the hallway. She also told my father that he charged far too little, so she routinely doubled the amount on the semi-annual bills he presented her. Every Christmas, she gave him a gift coupon for a new suit to be made to measure by Max Dietl, the best and most expensive tailor in Munich. Obviously, she thought that his usual outfits were not good enough for the clientele she wanted to introduce him to.

My mother did not like very much the idea of her husband being turned into a kind of kept doctor. I don't think she ever suspected him of having an affair with Frau Kubaschewski. That idea occurred to my brother and me only much later and in hindsight. But the entire setup violated her sense of pride and independence. My father, on the other hand, never harboured such thoughts. Having grown up in his father's grand hotels, he had always moved in the circles of the rich and famous as if he naturally belonged in them. So he accepted expensive gifts as easily and freely as he spent his own money. We never had much money during those years, and whatever we did have, my father for the most part left in expensive restaurants. So my mother put up with it. There was nothing wrong with her husband finally having a few decent suits.

Living in the shadow of the Kuba had its compensations. My parents attended the gala premieres of all the *Gloria* films in Munich; they were also invited regularly to the legendary annual *Gloria* film balls, for which my mother had to have a new evening gown every year while my father kept wearing his old tux. I have no idea why the Kuba never gave him a gift coupon for a new one of those.

The hype surrounding the annual *Gloria* film balls of the 1950s and 1960s easily matched that associated with the Academy Awards in Hollywood. They were must-be-seen-there events for Germany's high society. Every established or aspiring film star had to attend. There is a nice photo of my parents on the dance floor floating past Romy Schneider, the legendary German actress who rose to fame with a series of "Sissi" movies about the princess from Possenhofen (the name misspelled, to the chagrin of the Borchards). And there are dozens of little black-and-white photos of all kinds of stars and starlets that my father took with a miniature Minox camera that Frau Kubaschewski had given him as a present.

The glittering connections to the world of film did not by any means interest only my father. My mother almost swooned when she told me about all the leading men she had been introduced to. There was a moment when she found herself in the back of a taxi next to the great Italian-American-tenor-turned-movie-actor Mario Lanza, loudly singing into her ear. Lanza had come to Munich for one of his *Gloria*-produced films, and they were on their way from a reception to the film's premiere. Of course my mother never really swooned. But she giggled a lot.

69 | *Beaulieu-sur-Mer*

To the Kuba we owed two long summer vacations on the French Côte d'Azur. She had a house there, in Beaulieu-sur-Mer, halfway between Monte Carlo and Nice. She told us that the house usually stood empty and that we could use it for a month before she arrived at the end of the summer. This was in 1958. The summer turned into a grand tour of Europe. It would cost my parents three thousand marks, an enormous sum of money at the time, almost the equivalent of two years' rent for the little house in Tutzing. My mother had fits about it. She had to scrape for every household penny during those lean years. There were no banking machines back then, and my father had obviously never heard of traveller's cheques. He kept all his money in one ever-diminishing wad in one of his Dietl jacket breast pockets. My mother had fits about that, too.

He would carry cash like that till the end of his life, even after bank machines had asserted their presence everywhere. After my mother died, he had a Polish cleaning lady come twice a week, a young and pretty woman who commanded much of his attention during his lonely last years. "Ah," he would exclaim, looking at the date on his watch, "tomorrow my little Polish girl is coming." By then, my sister Andrea would go to the bank for him and supply him with cash. At some point she noticed that the money was disappearing far more rapidly than made sense, considering that my father hardly went out anymore. Checking up on him, she realized that whenever the "little Polish girl" was leaving, he would pull out his wallet, open it in front of her with the entire wad of money sticking out, and say: "Take whatever you need." My sister did not stop him. The "little Polish girl" was the last joy of his life. By my sister's account, she had enough sense not to exploit his generosity too far.

The trip to Beaulieu and back has been well documented in a journal that our mother had my brother and me make as a Christmas present for our father at the end of that year. We had to write little essays about our various adventures during that trip. We then had to type them on the Brother typewriters we each had been given the previous Christmas. My mother added to these stories and arranged them in a binder with lots of photos, postcards, museum tickets, and other mementos.

The first entry is about a long day of driving, from Tutzing all the way through Austria and Switzerland, past St. Moritz and down the Maloya Pass to Chiavenna, the first big town in Italy. I had been looking forward to the Maloya Pass with great anticipation, because it played a central role in one of my favourite children's books, Johanna Spyri's *Heimatlos* (Homeless). Spyri is much better known as the author of *Heidi*, but in our family (I suspect, going back to a choice my grandmother in Hattenheim had made for her children) the more cherished book was *Heimatlos*.

It is the story about an Italian boy, Rico, and his little Swiss girlfriend Stineli. Rico's father is a widower who has left his hometown of Peschiera on Lake Garda in Italy, in grief over the loss of his wife. When the story begins, they are all living in Sils-Maria, a mountain village near St. Moritz. Sometimes in the evening, after a hard day's work in the mountains, Stineli can hear the father play his violin and sing, together with Rico, a song full of longing for the lost homeland: *Una sera, in Peschiera* (One Evening in Peschiera). When Rico's father dies suddenly, the orphaned boy decides to go home to Italy, which he knows lies somewhere beyond the Maloya Pass at the end of the valley. So one day he says goodbye to Stineli and boards the mail coach, earning his passage by playing the fiddle he has inherited from his father. I have forgotten much of what else happens in that book, but in the end Rico brings Stineli home to Peschiera, where they get married. I completely agree with the Kuba: happy endings are important and good for the soul.

70 | *Disaster*

Just as I am writing this last sentence in the revised version of my family memoir, disaster strikes: my wife and partner of twenty-one years, Julia Roberts, *my* Julia Roberts, the *real* Julia Roberts, is leaving me. Ironically, having read parts of this memoir may have contributed to her decision. The brilliant professor of history has concluded that all the historical baggage of family, music, and name dropping has become too much for her to find her own way in life. No more giggles: Jacob and I have to go on living alone in this big, empty house, so full of memories, and now, shockingly, already part of history itself. How did Jacob put it so incomparably: "There should be a part of the book that people cry over." This will now be the part for me to cry over.

71 | *A few months later, back to the memoir*

What else can I do? According to my journal entry of that first day of travel, the Maloya Pass was disappointing, full of car traffic and not a single mail coach anywhere in sight. But things quickly improved after that. A few days later, having seen the cathedral in Milan and the ships in the port of Genoa, we found ourselves in San Remo on the Italian Riviera, stopping for lunch at one of the former gems in the Hüglin collection of spas, the Grand Hotel Albergo Bellevue Excelsior. It had been expropriated without compensation at the end of the Second World War after the Italians got rid of Mussolini at the last minute and started pretending they had been on the side of the victors. My mother tried in vain to prevent us from going there. She was embarrassed and feared that the reception would be hostile. My father as usual had no qualms about barging right into the place, announcing to all that his family had once owned it. As it turned out, we were welcomed by the new owners and treated to a fabulous lunch in the elegant dining hall. My father was greeted especially warmly by the old chief porter, who still remembered him from way back when he had been a boy.

Later that day, we arrived at the Italian–French border town of Mentone or Menton. Strolling through the old town, we learned that who should be playing a piano recital in the evening but my father's old friend Wilhelm Kempff? We decided to stay overnight. The recital took place in the open, on one of the squares overlooking the Mediterranean. I do not remember a single piece Kempff played, but it was a memorable warm summer evening. The next day we finally arrived at La Sevillana, Kubachewski's house in Beaulieu.

We stayed for a month. La Sevillana was a spacious Spanish-style bungalow atop a cliff right above the sea. It was surrounded by a garden full of exotic plants and palm trees. It had its own private beach. My brother and I had our own apartment in the chauffeur's quarters, complete with its own entrance at the back of the house. I spent quite some time in that apartment—whenever I managed to get away from my brother, that is, because under the mattress of my bed I found a stack of French porn magazines. As far as I can remember, they were quite harmless compared to what is freely available on the Internet these days.

We went to the local tennis club almost every day, and my father played with a Russian prince, le prince de Bariadinski, who always had a huge ring of keys rattling in his pocket and who regularly farted when he played a backhand. Strangely, his forehands did not produce the same effect. Once, after one of the little summer tournaments my father participated in, there was a party at the club with free champagne. My brother and I got quite tipsy sipping away while nobody paid attention to us.

There was another occasion when I got drunk. I got stung by a *meduse*, one of those nasty pink Mediterranean jellyfish. I managed to get dirt into what was really just a little wound, and in the evening my father noticed that the veins on my inner arm were turning red, a sign of blood poisoning. My father thought the arm needed cooling down with alcohol, but it was Sunday and the pharmacies were closed. So he took a bed sheet, soaked it with the better part of a bottle of whisky from Frau Kubaschewski's well-stocked liquor cabinet, and wrapped it around my arm. I probably slept well that night just from sniffing the fumes. But the makeshift remedy worked. The next morning, the redness had disappeared.

To my father's delight, we were surrounded by celebrity yet again. We saw Charlie Chaplin water-skiing. His place was just a couple of houses over. And a few bends farther down the winding coastal road was the secluded villa of Greta Garbo. From the road one could see only a small portion of her terrace. Of course, my father stopped the car repeatedly in order to stare down there, and he claimed that he saw her on one occasion, or, rather, that he saw someone with huge sunglasses.

We made excursions: to Monte Carlo and St. Tropez and to some of the picturesque mountain villages nearby—Eze-sur-Mer, St-Paul-en-Vence, and Grasse, where my mother got some local perfume and a necklace of little round pieces of blue and green ceramic, said to have been based on a design by Picasso. In St. Tropez we waited in vain for a sighting of Brigitte Bardot. In Monte Carlo, Grace Kelly had become Her Serene Highness the Princess of Monaco just the previous year, but we never caught a glimpse of her either. Instead we admired Aristotle Onassis's enormous white yacht *Christina* in the harbour. My father immediately proceeded to go aboard because, as he told us, our painter friend in Tutzing, Anton Leidl, had done some of the decorations on the ship. This time my mother managed to stop him.

We ate our way through the region's restaurants. Among our favourites were the upscale La Chèvre d'Or in Eze, with its breathtaking view of the entire coast, and Les Hirondelles, at the end of Cap Ferrat, a far more modest place but with a young and pretty waitress who shamelessly flirted with my father, which doubtless had a enormously positive impact on the tips he gave her. At Les Hirondelles, we usually had *petites fritures*, a plate of tiny deep-fried fish eaten in their entirety, head, tail, and all. In one of the open-air restaurants in Villefranche, right on the Promenade des Marinières, we ate *langouste*, the Mediterranean version of lobster.

Apart from the lobster, the main attraction of eating at the Villefranche *promenade* was that we could watch the busy harbour. A huge American aircraft carrier was anchored in the bay, and launches full of sailors in impeccable white uniforms came and went all evening. Also anchored there was the three-masted sailing ship of Stavros Niarchos. There were parties on that ship every evening we ate at the harbour of Villefranche—which was often. Clusters of elegantly dressed guests were picked up by fast little motorboats. Onassis and Niarchos were fierce rivals in the Greek shipping business, and the story was that Niarchos had turned the old sailing ship into a state-of-the-art yacht in order to outdo Onassis's *Christina* in the harbours of the Mediterranean. Later, he would do more than that by running away with Onassis's wife Christina, after whom the yacht had been named. I am convinced that Onassis later married Jackie Kennedy mainly as one last act of upmanship over his rival.

After the lobster, we would stroll along the harbour and my father would buy strawberry ice cream for all of us, from a shop next to the fishermen's chapel, the interior of which had been decorated by one of Villefranche's many famous residents, Jean Cocteau. For years, whenever we had ice cream anywhere else, my mother, my brother, and I would look at each other and say: "*Quatre fois fraises.*" My father spoke excellent and almost accent-free French.

That excellent French would serve him well on one other occasion, in a small provincial town on the way home. We arrived on the evening of 25 August. There was some festival going on, and the entire town was out in the streets. Over dinner, my father struck up a conversation with various people sitting at tables around us. When he asked what everyone was celebrating, he was told that it was the liberation of Paris from the Germans in 1944. Without missing a beat, my father raised his glass with the locals in celebration of that event.

The only one not entirely happy during that trip was my mother. She did not take well to the Mediterranean summer heat, and she felt uncomfortable with what she thought was playing housekeeper for Frau Kubaschewski. That sentiment was reinforced by the Kuba's request, before our departure from Tutzing, that my mother look for a ring she had forgotten in Beaulieu during her last visit there. The ring had a sapphire the size of a hazelnut, and my poor mother felt obliged to wear it during our various excursions so that it would not be left in the house unattended.

But when the Kuba finally arrived with her entourage one late afternoon, we were not at all dismissed like housekeepers. Frau Kubaschewski was a very friendly woman with a warm personality (which is not what they said about her in the film business), and she treated us like old friends. Since it was late afternoon when she arrived, she even asked us to stay for another night. My mother later told me that she felt guilty about what she had been thinking about her. Nevertheless, we left that same evening and drove northward into the night. A year later, when we returned to Beaulieu for a second summer, my mother felt far more at ease.

72 | *Geneva*

It would be almost two weeks before we returned to Tutzing. That first night, after an endlessly winding drive through the French Sea Alps, and after seeing a bright comet in the sky, we ended up in a hotel in Digne. It was past midnight, and despite its name it was not a grand hotel. We had hardly gone to bed when our parents heard us yelling and had to come running to our room. My brother and I discovered that it was full of spiders. It took some time to get rid of them all, and our sleep for the rest of the night was short. Then we stopped in Aix-les-Bains (because of all the famous people who had stayed there, including Queen Victoria and Woodrow Wilson), and in Annecy (because of the Hotel L'Impérial Palace, where we stayed for two nights and spent almost as much money as on the entire rest of the trip). Then we finally reached Geneva, the last major stop on our long journey, where we visited our Swiss relatives, whom we had never met. This is when I first met uncle Aloys, the music critic.

His son, Alexandre, the radio technician, lived with his family in an old villa on the outskirts of Geneva, in Chambésy, near the airport where I would later land on the occasion of my first flight. His wife Olly, a German-Swiss from Zurich, not only made the best French fries in the world but also treated us to *Kulebiaka*, a pastry dish filled with curly kale, chopped-up hard-boiled eggs, and lots of butter—an obvious tribute to the Moosers' former connection to Russia and the conservatory in St. Petersburg. The two girls, Elisabeth and Denise, were only mildly interested in their younger German cousins.

That would change four years later, when Elisabeth appeared in Ambach, where she stayed with us for a few summer weeks. She had grown up a beautiful young woman and turned heads on the village street. She certainly had *my* attention. I was barely sixteen and she was eighteen going on twenty-five. All kinds of young men all of a sudden began milling around at the *pension* where we stayed. One of them introduced himself and invited her on a boat ride across the lake. She accepted, but the young man was quite disappointed when he showed up with his boat the next morning and Elisabeth insisted that I come along, too.

We took her to the opera in Munich for a performance of Wagner's *Lohengrin*. I will never forget how, just as the titular hero finally tells his leading lady, Elsa von Brabant, his real identity—"Lohengrin, son of Parsifal"—my father turned to Elisabeth and hissed a translation in her ear, so "discreetly" that the entire house could hear it: "Lohengrin, son fils, c'est moi." Of course, Lohengrin must then depart from his beloved, the same way he came, on his swan (again, I am not making this up), because he had earlier told Elsa that under no circumstances can she ask him about his origins. It is all very tragic and very romantic.

She did not mind going out on the lake in a boat alone with me. We did so one evening when everyone else had gathered on the shore around a bonfire. After dark, cousin Elisabeth mercilessly seduced me in that boat (she was a very distant cousin). When she left a few days later, there was a tearful goodbye at the railway station in Munich with my father discreetly looking away. Shortly afterwards, I received a little package from her in the mail, containing a record by a popular French pop singer at the time,

Richard Antony. The title of the main song: "J'entends siffler le train." It was all very tragic and very romantic.

It was because of Elisabeth, of course, that I flew to Geneva the following Easter. But as it turned out, she had a boyfriend with a car by then, so no chance for me to compete. Instead, her younger sister Denise took me under her wing, but after a few days of romantic entanglement, first in a downtown movie theatre where we went to see *Les Vacances de Monsieur Hulot*, and then on the outside platform of the suburban train back to Chambésy, we settled for a friendship that would last for many years. The song had changed as well. Instead of "J'entends siffler le train," we listened to Jacques Brel's "Le plat pays." During this visit Olly made one of her famous and alcohol-laden cheese fondues. At the end of the evening, my two cousins practically had to carry me upstairs to my room. It was still all quite romantic but no longer tragic.

I strongly recommend *Les Vacances de Monsieur Hulot* as a most suitable movie for bilingual dates, by the way. It is a 1953 classic by the French actor-comedian Jacques Tati. It is highly entertaining, yet it contains practically no dialogue: hence no need to understand French (mine was close to nonexistent) and no need to concentrate on subtitles (in Geneva, of course, there weren't any to begin with).

Years later, I visited my two cousins with a friend from school and university, Nicki, whose claim to fame was a little red sports car. We had been in Paris for Easter and had seriously run out of money. So I suggested we drive to Geneva to visit Elisabeth and Denise. Both were married by then. We not only got the lavish meals we had hoped for but also got to borrow their husbands' skiing equipment. And off we went, across the border into France, for a glorious day of spring skiing. When we were crossing that border and the guard asked what the purpose of our trip was, Elisabeth leaned out the window, smiled at him, and said: "On va bronzer à Megève." My French was good enough to understand that much. I have never forgotten it because it gave me a feeling of belonging to the jet set, driving into the mountains with two beautiful women for a day of sun tanning. We did do a lot of skiing that day, though.

I saw Denise only one more time, a few years later, while I was passing through Geneva on my way to Spain. She was a young mother by then, pushing a stroller with her first-born daughter. I had just arrived when she told me, all excited, that she had to show me something and I had to come with her immediately. The three of us—Denise, her daughter in the stroller, and I—ended up at the end of Geneva airport's runway, not the end almost falling into the lake, of course—the other end! Soon enough, we saw the first SwissAir jumbo jet descend from the sky. It looked so big it almost seemed to stand still in the air.

I also saw Elisabeth only one more time, when she came to Ambach for a second visit. This time, I was the one pushing a stroller. We went for a long walk along the lake while little Jacob took an afternoon nap in the fresh air. Alexandre had died years earlier. Olly passed away only a few years ago. I have not been in Geneva in more than twenty years.

73 | *On the radio*

Apart from our occasional forays into the world of luxury and glamour, the years in Tutzing were simple years. For my parents, life in the little house on the lake was not as carefree as it appeared to us children. For my father, the move to Tutzing had been the result of a serious existential crisis. With his hotel clinic never working out as well as he had hoped, he constantly worried about the future. But despite his angst (not to mention his dread of Russians and socialists), he had an infectious capacity to enjoy and celebrate whenever there was something to enjoy and celebrate—and it did not have to be something grand or expensive.

There were two books in the house in Tutzing that my father especially liked (otherwise he mostly read celebrities' memoirs). One was a German version of Dale Carnegie's 1948 bestseller *How to Stop Worrying and Start Living*. The other was *Leberecht Hühnchen* by Heinrich Seidel. This essentially was the story of a family living modestly in a small house on the outskirts of Berlin during the 1880s and enjoying the pleasures of a simple life in which even the slightest improvement called for a celebration. The story rang true for all of us, and we all read and enjoyed it. Years later, when I was living in Canada, my father asked me whether I had taken the book with me, because he could no longer find it. I had not, but one day some time later again, to my great surprise, I found a copy of it at a sale of old books at Wilfrid Laurier University, of all places. Perhaps not so much of a surprise: Kitchener-Waterloo has a large German-Canadian population, and the book must have come across the Atlantic with some immigrant family. I bought it for a few dollars and took it back to Germany during my next visit, only to find that not only my father but also my brother had meanwhile bought a copy again.

My mother also had worries. She, too, had been thrown out of a sheltered bourgeois upbringing and into a life of uncertainty. In some ways, she may have been more traumatized by the war than my father. Perhaps it was because my father at least had been given something to do that kept him going, despite the winters on the Russian Front, and despite having been seriously wounded. My mother was much more a passive victim of it all.

More than anything else, my mother feared another war. The 1950s were a time of political tension. The Cold War had quickly ended all hopes for a better and more peaceful world. My mother did not care about Russians, socialists, Americans, or whomever. She worried about war, period.

News about the rest of the world came to us through the radio. We listened to it constantly, at home and in the car. Not all was bad. I remember how my mother and I glued ourselves to the radio during the Stockholm Equestrian Olympics in June 1956. It was the year of the Melbourne Summer Olympics, which would be held later, in November. Because the Australians insisted that all the horses for the equestrian events had to be quarantined for six months, the decision had been made to separate the "Olympiad of Horses" from the rest of the games that year.

All of Germany was listening in on the last day, when the show jumping event was decided. The leader of the German team, Hans-Günter Winkler, and his horse Halla were the favourites. They had already won two consecutive world championships prior to the Olympics. Then devastating news came over the airwaves: During the first round, Winkler had ruptured a groin muscle. In excruciating pain, he had barely been able to stay in the saddle for the last two jumps. A withdrawal from the second and deciding round would mean personal defeat for him and would also deprive the German team of any chance at a team medal.

Winkler decided to ride. The hectic voice of the radio announcer fell completely silent. Instead, we could hear Winkler crying out in pain every time Halla landed after a jump. When it was over, the stadium erupted in deafening cheers. My mother and I jumped up and yelled in triumph—rider and horse had completed the course without a single mistake. They had won the individual gold medal, and they had secured the gold medal for their team. Winkler later said that he had barely been conscious and that Halla had done it all by herself. Winkler would go on to win medals at five more Olympics, including another team gold, with Halla—now dubbed the "miracle horse"—at the Rome Olympics in 1960. Thus Winkler would become the only rider in Olympic history to win medals at six different games, and Halla the only horse with three gold medals.

But the German triumph at Stockholm was just about the only good news on the radio that year. On 23 October 1956, the Hungarian Uprising began with a mass demonstration against the Soviets in Budapest. A few days later, my father came storming into the house saying that something terrible must have happened because the American radio station (American Forces Network, AFN) had begun to play sombre music nonstop during one of its broadcasts. We all sat there in front of the radio again, anxiously waiting for the announcer to give an explanation. When it came, it was sad but hardly earth-shattering: the French-German pianist Walter Gieseking had just died in London.

A few days later, however, when I came home from school, on 29 October 1956, the news was not so harmless. I found my mother in front of the radio, crying. Britain, France, and Israel had begun to bomb Egypt over President Nasser's annexation of the Suez Canal, which had been under British control. The Soviet Union had announced that it would back the Egyptians. My mother was certain the Third World War was about to start.

The Hungarian Uprising was crushed by Soviet tanks, and the Suez Crisis was brought to an end by a UN resolution that for the first time established a peacekeeping force—a solution that earned its proponent, the Canadian Foreign Minister Lester B. Pearson, the Nobel Prize for Peace. By the time the 1950s drew to a close, we thought we had learned to live with the volatilities of the Cold War and of post-colonialism.

But then, of course, came the Berlin Wall, on 13 August 1961, and the Cuban Missile Crisis, in October 1962, when we heard Kennedy, this time on television, begin his famous speech: "Unmistakable evidence has established the fact ..." That crisis eventually passed as well, and the Wall became part of political normalcy in Germany. Nobody thought it would ever disappear. What was unmistakable, however, was our realization, gradually and reluctantly, that two world wars had not really gotten us any closer to a solution of the "riddle of history," as Marx once had put it, or to the "end of history," as the neo-liberals would put it later. But before I began thinking about any of this, I first had to explore teenage life in the city. Sometime early in 1959 we moved to Munich. If Tutzing was the 1950s, Munich definitely became the 1960s.

PART FIVE

Munich

74 | *Esmeralda*

I cannot remember the move at all. The first thing I do remember about Munich was my mother and me getting out of the tram at the stop almost in front of our new apartment, and some guy pushing my mother because he thought she was too slow. It was summer and my mother was very pregnant. I yelled at that guy. I was very protective of my pregnant mother. Later that summer my brother and I were sent to Hattenheim, where we awaited the arrival of our sister Andrea. Before she was born, our name for her was Esmeralda. After she was born, on 13 August 1959, our grandfather forbade us to refer to her as Esmeralda. It took us some time to get Esmeralda out of our systems.

When we returned to Munich, there she was, a tiny little bundle. My mother became very sick soon afterwards, and I had to learn how to change diapers in a hurry. My grandmother came from Hattenheim a few days after my mother had been hospitalized. Nobody knew what was wrong with her. She could not keep down any food. The physicians at the hospital had practically given up on her when my father insisted on exploratory surgery. They found that a large benign tumour was blocking her colon. It had not shown up on X-rays. My mother soon recovered and came home. We were a family of five now.

75 | *The apartment*

We now lived in a brand-new apartment building. There were four such buildings, some not quite finished, and grouped around a large inner courtyard. Each was three or four stories high and contained about nine apartments. There were no elevators. Our apartment was on the second floor. My father's practice was on the same floor across the hallway. We were in the building closest to a large street that ran south out of Munich in the direction of Lake Starnberg. It was the first building ready, and Frau Kubaschewski thought it would be the best one for opening a practice. Compared to Tutzing and Ebenhausen, the neighbourhood was loud. There was a constant flow of traffic. The loudest noise came from the trams, which screeched around a slight curve in the street and slowed down for the next stop, which was ours.

There was a living room that contained the dining table, my mother's desk, and the piano; a small bedroom for the parents out front next to the living room; a larger room with two windows towards the courtyard, which my brother and I shared; and a small kitchen and bathroom. There was an electric boiler that supplied hot water day and night—that was a big improvement. So was central heating: no more carrying coal up from the basement.

Michi and I liked the new place immediately. We did not mind that the floors were linoleum now rather than hardwood, or that the terrace and garden had been replaced with a narrow balcony that could hardly be used because of the traffic noise and the dirt that came with it. It was all different, unlike anything we had ever seen before. It was new.

My parents made the best of it. They were quite shocked, initially, at how small it all was again. We needed thick curtains to block out the streetlights at night, and of course all the windows had to have sheers as well for privacy. My mother liked the "modern living" aspect after all the old houses she had been in. She wanted new furniture but had to fight for quite some time before my father relented and we got a set of teak furniture with a kidney-shaped coffee table. When my father brought along friends or dragged patients over from the practice, he would say: "This is our little city apartment." He liked it, too, but in the back of his head was always the villa in Solln that he would move back to one day. No need to buy new furniture: there would be an overabundance of old furniture there.

The apartment really was too small. My brother and I had to share a room again, which I began to resent, being thirteen years of age and all. My parents had a tiny bedroom, again, which now also contained Andrea's crib as well as the changing table. The practice across the hallway also was rather small: a consulting room that held my father's desk, as well as a couch with a portable ECG machine on one side and an X-ray machine on the other; a waiting room with two chairs and a sofa grouped around a round table, and with a large table at the other end where Fräulein Wehe did the lab work, doubled as receptionist, and did the books; a bathroom; and the kitchen, which had been converted into the living quarters for Fräulein Wehe.

Fräulein Wehe was a nurse who had already followed my father from Ebenhausen to Feldafing. The daughter of a well-to-do family, she had been trained in nursing during the war without ever imagining that her livelihood would depend on it some day. She was a refugee from Silesia like count Gessler, and my grandfather had hired her because she was from a "good family." But she was not a very good nurse. My father kept her mainly because he could not bring himself to let her go. He knew she would never find a job elsewhere. Once, when she was ill, my father had to bring in a temporary replacement from a professional agency. We were all speechless at the degree of efficiency that had taken hold of the practice all of a sudden.

A year after moving to Munich, we found Fräulein Wehe a small apartment in the neighbourhood, and I moved into the spare room in my father's practice. Brother Michi got my parents' small bedroom to himself, and my parents with baby Andrea moved into our old room. And when I left five years later, in 1965, after high school graduation and about to begin military service, my brother moved into the practice and Andrea, then six years old, moved into his room. So it all worked out, though I was quite miffed at first that I now had to sleep on the living-room couch when I came back from military service on weekends or for holidays. Two years later again, in 1967, when I entered university in Munich, I got to rent a room up the street.

It was because of this room in the practice that I sometimes found one of my father's prominent patients lying on my bed when I returned from school. The main advantage of living in my father's practice, however—an unimaginable piece of luck for a teenager, really—was the separate entrance. When I came home late from a night on the town, I did not have to sneak past my parents' bedroom. On a few occasions, it was so late that I barely had time to crawl under the covers and pretend to be asleep before my mother came over to wake me for school. My brother later told me that he sometimes did not even have enough time to get out of his clothes before he slipped under the covers.

At least initially, I did not adjust to the city streets nearly as well. Shortly after the move, when I took my bike out to explore the neighbourhood, I promptly went through a red traffic light with cars coming to a screeching halt all around me. Nothing happened, but I was quite shaken. I probably had never before crossed an intersection with traffic lights by myself.

A year later, the scare was considerably bigger, even if only in hindsight. I had been downtown with my bike on a Saturday morning—17 December 1960, it turned out to be. When I came home, the radio was on, the television was on, and my mother was all worried about where I had been. A small American plane had developed engine trouble after its takeoff from the Munich airport. Engulfed in thick fog and disoriented, the pilot had clipped the steeple of St. Paul's church in downtown Munich and then crashed the plane into a busy city street. All thirteen passengers and seven crew members on the plane died, and all thirty-two passengers burned to death in a tram car that had been struck by one of the plane's full fuel tanks. On the evening news, we watched the charred hull of the car being pulled away slowly through the city streets, still on its tracks, in a ghostly procession. I had biked across the intersection where it happened only a few hours earlier.

76 | *The Doctor*

So the Hüglins had descended from the lofty heights of bourgeois splendour at the beginning of the century, with hotels, villas, parks, servants, and horse-drawn carriages, to the pedestrian lows of apartment life on a busy suburban street by the 1960s. One might almost be compelled to invoke the Buddenbrooks dynamic. Following the narrative of Thomas Mann's famous novel, it suggests a certain inevitability in the rise and fall of bourgeois families over several generations: the first generation seeks economic success, the second wants power and prestige, and the third indulges in culture and the arts. But the metaphor does not really work in the case of the Hüglins (nor in that of the Wachendorffs). None of them were interested in power. None of them ever became politically involved. Of course one had a certain status in society, but one did not brag about it.

And as far as indulging in culture and the arts is concerned, it was the middle generation of my grandparents that could afford the madonnas in Ebenhausen and the garden in Hattenheim. My father did not gamble away any family fortunes. Those were lost in two world wars, to a changing world that no longer needed sanatoriums or, for that matter, small, family-owned chemical factories. Towards the end of his life, my father sold most of the madonnas in order to survive financially.

The question is a different one: How is it that my father was just about the only physician in all of West Germany who did not become rich during the postwar boom? Every other physician we knew drove a Mercedes, lived in a big house, and had another house somewhere in Italy. There are a number of possible explanations.

One is that my father was really bad with money. If he had it, he spent it. If he ran out of it, he panicked. I am the same. I actually got an ulcer after we bought our house in New Dundee and mortgage rates began to skyrocket. Julia took over the family finances all on her own. She still does all the bills, even though she has bought a house and moved away. Apart from Jacob, that is the only connection between us now.

Another reason is, as the Kuba kept telling my father, that his bills were ridiculously low. He had some red book with lists of basic rates provided by the German Medical Association, and he never padded those rates. Fräulein Wehe was so incompetent that my mother and I were convinced that quite a few of his temporary patients never received their bills. Such was the case with the movie actor Dirk Bogarde, for example, whom my father briefly treated on a film set near Munich. It is not that Bogarde did not mean to pay, of course. But he left Munich and neither my father nor Fräulein Wehe did anything about getting the bill to him. Maybe this was part of the lost-bourgeois-splendour syndrome: one did not haggle about money. There were no longer any staff around to do it—that is, competent staff.

There was one time, however, when my father did haggle over a bill, and he would tell this story many times. A patient of his for several months had been an ex-president of Lebanon, who resided with his large family in a suite in Munich's most expensive hotel, the Vierjahreszeiten. I cannot remember the name of that ex-president, but I vaguely remember seeing a picture. Judging from that memory, and from a quick Web search, it must have been Bechara El Khoury. In any case, my father went to the hotel at least once a week until one day he was told that the family would be departing soon and that he should bring the bill at the time of what would be his next and last visit. So my father had it all added up according to the red book, by Fräulein Wehe. Then he headed to the hotel with the bill. He was a bit apprehensive about it, because the grand total even under the basic rates had grown to some three thousand marks.

At the hotel, my father as usual went to the reception desk and asked the chief porter to ring the suite and inform the ex-president of his arrival. The chief porter, however, instead of doing so, took my father aside and asked him: "This is about the bill, isn't it?" Before my father could ask him how this might be any of his business, the good man explained that the ex-president would insist on haggling, and that if my father wanted to receive in the end what was his due, he would first have to double everything.

With some trepidation, my father took the advice. He went to the hotel salon and rewrote the bill, by hand, on hotel stationery, doubling each item. The chief porter then phoned the suite and my father proceeded to the elevator.

When he arrived at the suite, the ex-president was seated in an armchair with his entire family around him. "Did you bring the bill?" he asked my father. My father said yes and handed it to him. As the ex-president started to read, the room fell silent. When he was finished, he almost seemed to have collapsed in his chair. With a dramatic gesture, he handed the bill to his wife, who took one glance at it and burst into tears. In no time the entire family was wailing loudly about the outrageous amount my father had demanded and how it would surely spell the ruin of the entire family. It took my father a moment to grasp the situation and remember what the chief porter had told him. So he stepped forward, grabbed the bill from the shaking hands of the ex-president's wife, pulled out his pen with a dramatic gesture, crossed out the new sum of six thousand marks, wrote the old sum of three thousand marks underneath, and handed the bill back to the ex-president. Instantly, the wailing and the tears stopped, there was laughter, and the bill was paid in cash. After hugs from every single family member, my father departed.

But the main reason my father never got rich from his practice was that he liked his patients too much and spent far too much time on them and with them. Also, he preferred making house calls to seeing patients at the practice. This was an old-fashioned way of practising medicine for which the red book did not list any rates. At a time when family practices were taking on the characteristics of production lines, my father continued to spend his time on a fraction of the number of patients that other physicians would see. The rich and famous among his patients appreciated this lavish individual attention but did not compensate him for the enormous amount of time he gave them—they were not asked or expected to do so.

All the while, my father was an excellent physician. He carefully listened to his patients. He encouraged them to make written lists of what they wanted to ask him so that they would not forget. He did not distinguish in the least between, say, the famous baritone Dietrich Fischer-Dieskau and the penniless old woman who came to his practice from the nearby retirement home (well, except that only Fischer-Dieskau would get to lie on my bed). And if the penniless old woman could not afford the drugs my father thought would be best for her, he gave them to her anyway and charged her only for the cheaper ones, the ones her public insurance would pay for.

His specialization was internal medicine and cardiology. His passion was treating his patients with intravenous injections of this, that, or the other. If someone was afraid of injections, he had a trick for that. On the wall behind the examining couch he had hung a little framed picture of a man in a meadow painting on an easel, with a cow behind him, watching what he was doing over his shoulder. My father asked his fearful patients to turn their faces to the wall and look at that picture. Given how sure and steady his hands were, many of these patients did not even notice the injection.

There was one other reason why my father did not become rich. He firmly believed in teamwork. His specialization was cardiology, but before he even examined a patient's heart thoroughly he always made certain that its problems were not caused by an infection somewhere else in the patient's body. So he sent his patients first to a dentist, to an ear, nose, and throat specialist, and, if they were women, to a gynecologist. He believed that teeth, tonsils, and uterus were the main loci for infections affecting the heart.

He had proof of this in his own family. When my sister Andrea developed a heart arrhythmia and was plagued with fatigue, my father sent her to a series of doctors and cardiologists, because he never treated his own family. When they came up with nothing, he took her to a dentist, who found an infected root. A few days after the root had been treated, all her heart problems were gone.

His friend, the dentist Günter Hossfeld in Ebenhausen, became rich, and so did his doctor friend in Starnberg, the ear, nose, and throat specialist Doctor Zimmermann. Women were sent to the university clinic in Munich, where Gerhard Martius—one of Heinrich's sons and the second smallest in the infamous photo with Hitler—had become chief gynecologist.

These friends and colleagues surely were not wealthy merely because of the patients my father sent them so often. But it must be said that they rarely sent patients back to him. And sometimes they betrayed him. The Hüglins always seem to be betrayed in the end, with selfishness getting the better of friendship. We may be loud-mouthed, opinionated, arrogant at times (mainly towards our superiors), and overbearing in our expressions of past accomplishments, but we have never had it in us to manipulate, cheat, or deceive. And human nature being what it is, we regularly seem to end up hurt. My father once asked one of his patients in Starnberg why she had not returned for her multivitamin shots for quite some time. She happily reported that Dr. Zimmermann was now administering them to her. She had gone to see him—at my father's recommendation, of course—for a throat infection, and when she mentioned that she was on her way to Munich for her vitamin shot, Zimmermann suggested that she did not have to drive all the way into Munich for them—he was quite willing to do them himself.

My father may have been an old-fashioned doctor, but he always remained up to date. The latest medical journals were always on the desk in his practice, and he read them regularly and carefully. In one of those journals he found a notice that somewhere someone had voiced concerns about the possible side effects of thalidomide. This was in 1959, when my mother was pregnant with Andrea and suffering from morning sickness. Thalidomide was sold under the name Contergan in Germany, and my father had received samples from a pharmaceutical sales rep. He had just passed the samples on to my mother. I can still remember how he stormed across the corridor from his practice into our apartment, slamming doors and telling my mother to throw out those pills immediately. She hadn't taken any yet.

Because he never compromised on what he thought was the best treatment, my father lost a few patients as a result of arguments with them. One of them was Fischer-Dieskau, who had some chest problem and who never returned to the practice after my father told him he should quit smoking and change his breathing technique. (Hello? You tell the world's most famous baritone that his breathing technique is wrong?) The decades-old relationship with Frau Kubaschewski also came to an end. My father treated her sister, and after he insisted that he would stop seeing her unless she made certain lifestyle changes, both women abandoned him. The main casualty was my father's wardrobe: towards the end of his life, the old Dietl jackets had become rather threadbare.

At least once, my father lost a patient over an argument that had nothing to do with medical issues. One of his newer patients in Munich was the widow of the Russian composer Alexander Glazunov. She was a very old lady by then, having survived her husband by some thirty years. Quite often, my father would come running over from his practice, throw the apartment door open, and announce: "The widow Glazunov is here." My mother then had to prepare some tea and, no matter what we might have been doing at the moment, we all had to endure Mrs. Glazunov's tales about how the world still had not sufficiently recognized her husband for the genius he was. One day, though, she stormed off in a fit, never to return, after she once again complained that the world preferred Rachmaninov to her husband and my father replied that Rachmaninov was simply a better composer. Perhaps it's that same opinionatedness that drove Julia from me in the end.

77 | *The piano*

The upright Schimmel piano had moved with us to Munich. After count Gessler died, Hans Krey became our new teacher. He was another impoverished pianist-turned-piano-teacher. He could not even afford his own instrument and therefore practised after hours on a beat-up old grand piano in a bookshop below his tiny apartment in Munich. He was the very opposite of Gessler: a pedantic pedagogue who inspired little enthusiasm for the music he had me play. After a few years, I packed it in for good. The piano itself, however, enjoyed quite a career, with several unforeseen twists and turns, almost like the "red violin" in the Canadian film of that same title.

Its career had begun in Tutzing, where I had struggled with Mozart's *Sonata Facile* and where my father had practised for his Lions Club recital. A young Chinese pianist, Gi-in Wang, whom my father had met God knows where, played a house concert on it, leaving a delicate little Chinese note in my parents' guest book that nobody could read. And when my aunt Ursula came with her violin for a visit when she was an art-history student in Munich, my father played violin sonatas with her.

In Munich, various musician-patients played on it. The Czech-American composer Rudolf Friml played his famous *Donkey Serenade* for us. His guest-book entry says: "For my wonderful doctor in kind remembrance." Underneath, Friml scribbled a few measures from one of his other famous melodies, "Indian Love Call." A few years later, it was Alexander Tcherepnin's turn. He played some of his own compositions as well, and my father recorded them on my tape recorder, erasing some of the music I had recorded previously. I was deeply annoyed, because I did not like Tcherepnin's music at the time. Unfortunately, we lost that tape. The famous Russian-American composer came to see my father a number of times, always accompanied by his wife, who was an accomplished musician in her own right. Her entry in the guest book is also in Chinese. His, underneath, is a line of music again, without caption, and a brief thank-you note in flawless German.

Sometimes I had to play for various patients my father dragged over from his practice across the hall. One of these was the cellist Hermann von Beckerath. I was practising a little Brahms Intermezzo at the time, probably the technically most advanced piece of music I was ever able to master. Krey may have been pedantic, but he did improve my technique. After I finished the piece, Beckerath remarked that I had made a descending harmonic sequence in the left hand sound like a cello. I guess that was a compliment. I also had to play for "the widow Glazunov," of course.

The piano then moved to the villa in Solln with my parents, where it remained unused in the basement for a few years. After all, there were not one but two grand pianos upstairs. The piano's silent sojourn in the basement ended rather dramatically in 1977 when my first wife Suzanne Bradbury and I moved to Italy, where I spent three years at the European University Institute in Fiesole. Suzanne's Steinway grand came with us, of course. But as we wanted to get to know my beloved Tuscany, and because Suzanne had to practise all the time, we bought an old van, converted it into a camper, and put the piano in the back as a camping piano.

The piano travelled with us all over Tuscany and much of the rest of Italy as well. It also travelled to Spain and Mallorca a number of times. And it crossed the Alps repeatedly, with our cat usually sitting on top of it and staring out the rear window at the stream of cars passing us. With the heavy piano in the back, fitting perfectly between rear-wheel cases, we rarely reached eighty kilometres per hour, and certainly not on the Brenner Pass itself, which we had to creep up almost entirely in second gear.

Miraculously, the piano stayed in tune very well. The main problem was finding level ground whenever we stopped or parked for the night so that the keyboard did not slant in whichever direction. Certain pieces of piano music associated with particular landscapes and vistas are still indelibly etched in my memory: Alban Berg's Piano Sonata under a pine tree with the silhouette of San Gimignano in the distance; Chopin's four ballads at the foot the Serra de Tramuntana in Mallorca; and even the Alpini song "Il Testamento del Capitano," which Suzanne practised in the van before playing it in Rome at the wedding of a friend, who had done his military service with the famous Italian mountain infantry unit.

The camping piano had a number of illustrious visitors. There was the piano tuner Herr Reinhart, who normally tuned the pianos at Munich's concert halls and at the Bavarian Broadcasting Corporation, where Suzanne made many of her recordings. Herr Reinhart was quite surprised when we led him into the van for the first time.

Then there was Stefan Askenase, the legendary Polish Chopin specialist whom Suzanne occasionally visited for private lessons at his home in Bonn. He played the piano in a parking lot in front of his hotel in Garmisch, where he was vacationing. In Spain, Suzanne's blind teacher José Ortiga played on it. He was more excited about exploring the van's interior with his hands. Suzanne's teacher in Munich, Ludwig Hoffmann, tried it out in front of his summer villa south of Rome. And in Positano, it was inspected by Wilhelm Kempff—although I cannot remember whether he actually played it.

This was a couple of years after Suzanne attended the Beethoven master course at Casa Orfeo, Kempff's summer domicile in Positano, on the Amalfi Coast south of Naples. It was the year of Kempff's eightieth birthday. German television came to film one of the lessons, and Suzanne was chosen to play the *Les Adieux* Sonata, Op. 81a. I was allowed to attend the lessons. It was an unforgettable experience. Kempff invited no more than eight students each year. They had to play two sonatas each from the early, middle, and late periods, as well as two of the five piano concertos. Kempff played *all* the concertos as well as *all* thirty-two sonatas—except for the monumental *Hammerklaviersonate*, Op. 106, that is, which none of the students had chosen. When the students played the concertos, Kempff accompanied them from memory at the second piano. He also went swimming every day at the beach six hundred steps below his house. Not bad for eighty years old.

Two years later, we had moved to Italy. We had the van, we decided to visit Kempff and his assistant, Annette von Bodecker, whom we had befriended. We parked the van at a scenic spot directly below his house, and that is when he came to inspect the piano. He perhaps did not play it, but he loved the van. We took him and Annette on several excursions into neighbouring towns, inevitably ending the day with a memorable dinner. For some reason having to do with his failing eyesight, he did not like to look ahead in cars. In the van, he could sit sideways on the camping bed, explaining the scenery to us, legs elegantly crossed.

I chauffeured Kempff on one other occasion. We were still living in an old Tuscan farmhouse in the hills above Fiesole when he came to play a Beethoven concerto with the Florence Symphony Orchestra. Annette phoned and asked whether I could drive him from the hotel to the concert hall and back. What a sight: here I was, pulling up to the main entrance of the Mediterraneo Grand Hotel in my old rust bucket of a van; here the famous pianist coming out the door in his tails, bow tie, and patent-leather shoes, and climbing into the van through the sliding side door, and off we went for another memorable evening of music. Afterwards, over food and wine, even Kempff, a rather restrained Prussian character, giggled when we remembered the startled faces of the hotel's elegant clientele.

Piano and van moved with us to Konstanz in southwestern Germany for another three years while I completed my postdoctoral degree at the university there. Both served us well for a number of trips. One of these was to the South Tyrolean Alps, where I taught a summer course. It was quite an experience, because the students were mostly mountain climbers who persuaded me to join them on a two-day hike in the Dolomites, promising there would be no rock climbing. On the second day, however, we arrived at the top of a three-hundred-foot cliff, the plan being to descend on iron hooks driven into its face. I categorically refused to do it. Some of the students who were familiar with the area took pity on me and walked me back a different way, around the cliff—a detour of some five hours. The next day there was a farewell dinner and dance at the local gym. There was also a live band in need of a piano. The band members had mistakenly assumed that the gym would have one. So I backed the van through one of the gym's double doors. We grouped the musicians around it, opened the van's back door and, *voilà*, we had a complete band.

When I moved to Canada, I sold the van to a student who planned to drive it around the Mediterranean. The piano returned to the basement in Solln, where my sister Andrea restored the varnish, which had suffered from years of exposure to sun and wind. There it stood in peace and quiet for almost twenty years. Then, when Julia and I decided that Jacob should have piano lessons, we had it shipped across the Atlantic, where it found its new place in our kitchen, across from the table where Jacob does his homework, underneath the portrait of Beethoven by my great-grand-uncle Maurice Baud. Jacob is still taking lessons, and I have improved considerably my music-reading ability by supervising his practice. Jacob, now a fifteen-year-old teenager and a certified Canadian snowboarding instructor, plays quite nicely once he has forgotten how opposed he is to the whole idea of piano lessons and playing in principle.

78 | *Dallas*

The Munich years saw a general escalation of musical activities for the family. Opera and concert halls were now only a tram ride away. Truth be told, we never took the tram. My father always drove into town. Family anecdote has it that he used public transportation only once in his adult life, when his car had broken down. On that occasion, he stared at all the people around him and announced, quite loudly, according to my sister: "I do like to mingle with common people every once in a while." If true, he did not say this out of arrogance. He meant it quite literally. Unlike his father, he got along with farmers, plumbers, and shopkeepers just as well as with princesses, film stars, and opera singers.

We went to concerts at least every other week. Strangely, I do not remember what we did with Andrea when she was still too little to come along. There must have been babysitters or neighbours looking after her. We mostly went to symphony concerts and piano recitals. To my mother's chagrin, my father did not much care for string quartets. Perhaps that is why I particularly like chamber music now.

These days, I often attend concerts by the Penderecki String Quartet, whose members have been artists in residence at Wilfrid Laurier University for more than fifteen years. Two of them, Jerzy Kaplanek (violin) and Christine Vlajk (viola), have become close friends. Immersed in their circle of friends and musicians, I get the warm and fuzzy feeling that my Canadian life can continue, with the same love of good food, wine, music, and art celebrated in the pages of this family memoir.

In Munich, we heard Leonard Bernstein conduct the New York Philharmonic during his first European tour. We were there when a very young Dietrich Fischer-Dieskau sang Schubert's *Winterreise* for the first time in Munich (this was an exception to the symphony/piano-recital rule: a patient, Mara Pringsheim, voice teacher at the Music Academy and sister-in-law of Thomas Mann's wife Katia, had told my father not to miss this concert). We also sat through an entire Bruckner symphony cycle with Eugen Jochum and the Bavarian Radio Orchestra (I sometimes fell asleep during slow movements). And we listened to a whole new generation of up-and-coming pianists (not to mention the old ones), from Van Cliburn (after he won the Tchaikovsky Prize in Moscow) and Martha Argerich (after she won the Chopin Prize in Warsaw) to Alfred Brendel (a somewhat late bloomer with no major prizes) and Maurizio Pollini (Warsaw again).

After each concert, my father would have one of two reactions: either "This was wonderful—I now have to have something good to eat," or "This was awful—I now have to have something good to eat." Either way, we ended up in an expensive restaurant. It is possible that my brother and I did not mind these endless concert outings because we knew that the food was coming afterwards. Often we did not get to bed until after midnight and were quite tired in school the next day.

Then there was opera. Mainly, we worked ourselves through the local specialities—Mozart, Strauss, and Wagner. Since most operas lasted too long for a restaurant visit afterwards, our reward was vanilla ice cream with hot raspberry sauce during intermission. Sometimes we did go out afterwards to meet up with some of the singers my father knew. I remember only one—Martha Mödl, who had triumphed as Kundry under Hans Knappertsbusch in Wagner's *Parsifal* during Bayreuth's legendary reopening season in 1951. She lived in Munich and was a friend of the Borchards in Feldafing. I had already heard her as Isolde in Wagner's *Tristan*, the night I was elbowed by my father and count Gessler. On one occasion, she sang the role of Leonore in Beethoven's *Fidelio*. After the performance, we waited for her, with the Borchards, at the artists' exit and then proceeded to her apartment. There was food and animated conversation as usual, but all I can remember is how stunned I was by Mödl's transformation. Less than an hour earlier, she had been on stage, a glamorous diva receiving ovations, and now here she was, looking like a rather ordinary middle-aged woman serving refreshments to her guests.

At the time, opera performances took place in the old Prinzregententheater on the far side of the Isar River. The Bavarian State Opera downtown had been levelled by bombs in 1943, and it would not reopen until twenty years later, in 1963. For years, in order to raise money for its reconstruction, there was an annual lottery in Munich. We bought tickets for that every year, but all I ever won was a jar of rosehip jam. My father was a founding member of Freunde des Nationaltheaters (Friends of the National Theatre), which organized the lottery and more generally lobbied for the reconstruction of the opera house in its original classicist form. As a member of the Freunde, my father could buy tickets for the annual opera festival prior to the general sale, and he could attend the gala that followed the festival's opening night. There was an exquisite buffet on those occasions, and one could mingle with all kinds of musicians, celebrities, and politicians. My parents usually attended together, of course, but sometimes my mother could not or did not want to go, and I got to go instead.

Most certainly, my parents attended the opera's reopening festivities. On 21 November 1963, there was an opening ceremony solely for the political brass, invited guests of honour, and members of the association. Hans Knappertsbusch conducted Beethoven's *Weihe des Hauses* (Consecration of the House) Overture, Op. 124. Among my parents' papers, I found a signed photograph of "Kna" (as he was popularly called). It shows him conducting the orchestra with one of his typically sparse gestures. Behind him, in the first row of seats, one can see the bland faces of Bavaria's politicians at the time. According to the date my mother scribbled on the back, the photo was taken on the day of the consecration.

The first public performance, two days later, on 23 November, was to be Wagner's *Die Meistersinger von Nürnberg* under the direction of Josef Keilberth. Kennedy had been shot the previous day. Two of the principal singers, Claire Watson (Eva) and Jess Thomas (Stolzing), were American. Only a few hours before the scheduled performance, still nobody knew whether it would take place or would be cancelled. There was the question of whether Watson and Thomas were willing or able to sing under the circumstances, or what instructions they might receive from the U.S. Embassy in Bonn. There also was the question of what the German authorities might decide in order not to offend American sensibilities. At the time, pre-Vietnam America was still Germany's best and most admired friend and ally. Only five months earlier, Kennedy had been in the divided city of Berlin and had spoken his famous words to an adoring crowd of 120,000: "All free men, wherever they may live, are citizens of Berlin, and therefore, as a free man, I take pride in the words *Ich bin ein Berliner*." I will never forget his nasal voice and accent when he said that. School had been cancelled that day while all of Germany sat in front of the television.

Watson and Thomas were not my father's patients. But like almost all opera singers who lived in or visited Munich during those years, they were regular patients of Dr. Zimmermann in Starnberg. It was from him that we heard what happened that day. It was November and flu season. The morning before the performance, Claire Watson had gone to Starnberg, half an hour from Munich, to have her vocal chords checked by Dr. Zimmerman one last time. She then simply hung out there, at his practice, for most of the day until she found out what would happen.

What did happen was that someone finally decided that the performance would go ahead. So my parents got into their fancy clothes (my father's tux was quite old and worn even then, but it still fit) and left for the opera while I remained at home glued to the television and the continuous news coverage from Dallas and Washington. When they came back, my mother told me that at the beginning the audience had been asked to stand. Under Keilberth's baton, the opera orchestra thundered the American national anthem through the darkened house, transposed into C for the occasion. Then, after a moment of silence, the orchestra followed suit with the equally thundering first bars of the *Meistersinger* overture, also in C, of course.

79 | *School again*

Life in Munich was not all concert halls, operas, and fancy restaurants. These things were only if regular interruptions to a teenager's daily life in school and with his friends. And at least initially, the big-city school proved to be a formidable challenge to a hapless country boy.

To begin with, the new school, Klenze Oberrealschule, was not a ten-minute stroll away; instead, it required a half-hour ride on a usually crowded tram. Also, the school schedule alternated between mornings and afternoons: 1 p.m. to 6 p.m. Mondays to Wednesdays, and 8 a.m. to 1 p.m. Thursdays to Saturdays. This was because fourteen years after the war the bombed-out school building had still not been rebuilt; thus we had to alternate morning and afternoon schooldays with another school, the Theresiengymnasium, which incidentally had been my father's school and which was playing host to the Klenze Oberrealschule for the time being. There was still school on Saturdays back then, but since it was considered unreasonable for students (and parents) to have school on Saturday afternoons, the alternating scheme meant we had school only every other Saturday morning.

All of this required considerable adjustment to the weekly routines of children and families. On Wednesdays, for instance, I came home at suppertime in the evening and then had to be back in school Thursday morning. During the long winter months, I did not see daylight in between those two schooldays. Afternoon school also meant that I had to have lunch before leaving for school when my brother had not even returned from his. At the time, he was still attending a neighbourhood elementary school. On the other hand, I could sleep in Monday mornings.

I actually loved those evening tram rides back home in the dark, with my friends, jammed in between all the people returning from work or shopping, with the city lights all around us. It made me feel grown up. Often, the tram was so crowded that the conductor never reached us to collect the fare. I quickly learned to check where the conductor was before entering and then to stand as far away from him or her as possible. If the conductor did not make it through the crowd, I had pocket money for an extra snack at the school cafeteria the next day. Sometimes, if the conductor was getting too close, I got off a stop early and walked the rest of the way.

The relations with my teachers changed at the new school. That had less to do with the school itself than with my growing up and developing a rebellious teenage personality. I no longer saw teachers as beyond questioning and developed a tendency to talk back. My first run-in was with a math teacher, Frau Professor Blumenthal (for some reason, we had to address all teachers as "professor"). She liked to tease her students, and once, after we had argued about some piece of homework, while I was leaving at the end of class, already wearing the Bavarian hat I was sporting at the time, she yelled after me: "Hüglin, don't think you can impress me with that hat." Without thinking, I yelled back: "That would be the last thing on my mind."

The next day she handed me a formal reprimand "for an inappropriate remark," which had to be signed by a parent. When I explained to my father what had happened, he went to see her, demanding that she withdraw the reprimand because he thought my remark had been provoked. She did. This was one of the two or three times my father ever stepped into one of my schools. Parents back then were not as involved in their children's school lives as they are now, and my parents were less so than most others. Professor Blumenthal and I learned to get along with each other, and over several years we even developed a grudging mutual respect.

Then there was the English teacher, Herr Professor Aschenbrenner, who unexpectedly entered my school life when the previous teacher had to retire suddenly due to illness. English was my favourite subject and I usually was among the best in class. Professor Aschenbrenner was a deeply insecure little man who resented my assertiveness. All of a sudden my grades plummeted. Aschenbrenner marked my written exams in the harshest possible way, and when he hauled me to the front for in-class oral tests, he chose deliberately difficult words so that I could not answer his questions.

This happened in grade twelve, in the new school building we had moved into several years earlier. My response to this difficult and undeserved challenge was twofold: during the summer vacation I went to a summer school in England, where my English improved so dramatically that Aschenbrenner could no longer trick me with his questions. (This was the trip to London when I met my weird uncle Wolf Eicke and almost got run over by Prince Philip's horse.) And I successfully appealed to the school principal to have all my written exams marked again by another English teacher throughout grade thirteen. In the end, when I graduated, my marks were back to normal.

Ah, and then there was Herr Professor Eggerer, the homeroom teacher during those last two high school years. He taught German and world literature and stifled the entire class with his boring renditions of the classics. We read Homer's *Odyssey*. When we came to the part about the beach encounter between the naked hero and the princess Nausicaa,

Eggerer's interpretation was that the two met with royal restraint and due modesty. True enough, a close reading of Homer supports that interpretation. Even so, my romantic soul saw sparks flying between them. When I wrote that in an essay, I received a C-.

Eggerer obviously was a prude. By the time I submitted my Odysseus–Nausicaa essay to him, he had disapproved of my behaviour for quite a while. To get from the tram stop to our new school, one had to go down a flight of concrete steps. At some point, my friends and I had met a girl there, who passed that same spot on her way to work every day. It became a habit that we stopped every morning for a chat with her while almost the entire school, teachers and students, walked past us. It was an entirely harmless encounter, yet Eggerer repeatedly scolded us in class: we were setting a bad example for the younger boys. One day, I was late for school, and when I entered his class with whatever excuse and apology, he burst out that I probably stayed back deliberately so that I could talk to that girl alone.

Eggerer probably also knew and disapproved of the fact that we hung out at a nearby ice-cream parlour after school, where we listened to music on the jukebox (we all groaned along with "I wanna go home," the opening line of "Detroit City" by Bobby Bare) and where Emma, the Italian waitress, always put an extra maraschino cherry on top of my ice cream. My mother disapproved of those visits, too, because they meant I would be late for lunch.

When I finally graduated from high school—astonishingly, with one of the better grade averages that year—I drove to Italy with my first car and my American girlfriend Susan Donahue. From Rome, I sent Eggerer a postcard, quoting from *Buddenbrooks*, in which Thomas Mann characterizes one of the dynasty's younger members in words something something like these: "He passed through high school without making any particular effort, but, because he somehow understood that such an effort was not necessary, we cannot call him mediocre." I thought I would needle Eggerer one last time.

Years later, I met someone who had attended the Klenze Oberrealschule a few student generations after I did. When I told him about the postcard with the quote, he exclaimed: "That was you!" He then told me that Eggerer had pulled out that postcard and read it to the class as a shining example of how much better and more original students had been in the past. I was almost moved. I met Herr Eggerer one more time. He came to our twenty-fifth class reunion in 1990. He was very friendly but also very old and could not remember any of it.

80 | *The group*

The school in Munich was my first boys-only school. I soon had a new circle of friends. The most important of these was Jürgen Gerlach. We went through these last high school years together, and although our friendship was interrupted by my two years of military service, we remained close almost all the way through university after that.

It was from Jürgen that I learned how to manoeuvre through the unfamiliar life of the city. In fact, for several years, whatever Jürgen did or had, I had to do or have. When he appeared for the new school year with a new kind of sweater, I persuaded my mother to buy me the same kind. When he showed up with a new bike, I sold my electric railway and bought the same bike from the proceeds. During a camping trip we did together over Easter, I started to smoke a pipe because he did. And I began to read newspapers and discuss politics because he talked about politics. For a while at least, I felt almost embarrassed about opera and concerts because he listened only to pop music.

Only much later and in hindsight did I catch on that Jürgen's obsession with consumer goods and politics had to do with his working-class background. He lived with his working mother in a very small apartment, and he was the first one in his family with a high school education and aspirations to go to university. I came from an upper-middle-class background, which meant that quality clothes and expensive bicycles were not something we paid particular attention to, because naturally we *had* them. For Jürgen and his family, the direction that West German welfare-state politics might take was existentially important. At the time, I had only been regurgitating the conservative prattle I heard at home.

Jürgen and I were part of a close-knit group of friends. The others were Nicki, Butz, and Hartmut. Nicki was one year younger than the rest of us and a grade behind us in school. His mother provided us with the group's home base. She was a pediatrician with a busy practice and a small house in the neighbourhood. We met in her living room at least twice a week, and we routinely raided her pantry for snacks and drinks—lemonade at first and beer later. She did not mind and even encouraged us to use her home this way because she thought we might have a positive influence on her son, who was growing up without a father. Once some of us had driver's licences, she let us borrow her car for day trips into the countryside. Nicki drank far too much beer far too young. When he turned eighteen, his mother bought him the little red sports car with which we later embarked on the trip from Paris to my two cousins in Geneva.

Butz was a couple of years older and one grade ahead of us. His idols were James Dean and Django Reinhardt. He always wore an old American army coat to school. He was terrible in school and already had failed one grade, which meant he had to repeat the entire year. But at an age when we hardly dared speak to girls, he was already all about them. He blew up condoms and hung them up overnight in his room to test their reliability.

Hartmut played the guitar, and he had a band, The Starlights. During the last years of high school they played on weekends in a café on the outskirts of Munich, Saturday evenings and Sunday afternoons. I dragged my parents there one Sunday afternoon. My father thought of course that rock music spelled the twilight of Western civilization, and a single afternoon did not persuade him otherwise. But he appreciated the skill of Hartmut and his colleagues. For him, they even played a rock version of Mozart's *Sonata Facile*, and Hartmut's runs on the guitar were cleaner than mine had ever been on the piano. Other than that, The Starlights played a lot of the new Beatles songs that were flooding out of Liverpool at the time. Long before the Internet, I spent hours in front of a tape recorder trying to figure out the lyrics for Hartmut and his band.

So Nicki provided the home base, Hartmut the music, and Jürgen the lifestyle advice. I am not quite sure what my contribution was, except friendship and loyalty. We went to school together, we hung out together, and when we were older we went to parties and clubs together. I once organized one of those parties at my father's practice. By then we were already in university. The parents and my siblings must have been away that weekend. We emptied out the waiting room and stored everything in my father's consulting room. Then we threw mattresses on the floor and added candles in old bottles. With the consulting room locked for good measure, we had enough space for about twenty-five people: the waiting room, my room, the corridor, and the bathroom. At the time, one of Willy Brandt's sons had made the news by posing in a photograph wearing only a bathing suit, to which he had attached a Second World War bravery medal. The whole republic was incensed at this lack of respect for veterans. So I got the idea to greet my guests lying in the bathtub filled with water and with my father's war medal attached to my bathing suit.

The party was a great success. I had taped hours of the latest music from the radio. Since my room was a converted kitchen, it contained the stove on which Fräulein Wehe had cooked her meals when she lived there. Butz used it to make mulled wine. The party went on until the wee hours of the morning. Then we carefully cleaned up and put everything back into place. The parents never knew.

Eventually the group drifted apart. I moved to Switzerland, where I continued university in St. Gallen. Nicki never finished university and became involved in the film business. Apparently he never stopped drinking, because I heard just recently that he died from liver cirrhosis. Hartmut never went to university and remained in the music business as a bandleader and music arranger. Butz bombed in his final exams in architecture and embarked on a successful career as a travel agent. When I last met him he was director of operations for one of Germany's leading travel agencies in Mallorca. This was after I had fallen off a horse, ruptured my liver because the horse then landed on me, and spent three weeks in intensive care. Butz invited me to recover in his villa overlooking the Mediterranean. That was the summer I met my first wife, Suzanne, who lived in an artists' colony on the other side of the island.

I wish I could say I was still friends with Jürgen Gerlach. We had resumed our friendship when I returned from two years of military service and we both studied in Munich. Of course he was two years ahead of me now. None of the group members except me had done military service. Once again, Jürgen became my guide for a new life. I studied business and economics, which at the time just about everyone studied who did not have any concrete career plans. Jürgen studied law.

Business was boring. Economics was full of formulaic certitudes that I did not believe even at the time. Jürgen began dragging me into public or state law lectures. The star professor was Peter Lerche, who was also an adviser to the Bavarian government in matters of constitutional law and federalism. Lerche was an engaging speaker who brought to life even the driest legal matters. During afternoon lectures he sometimes appeared in coattails, and we knew what would happen then. Some time before the end of the lecture, the door to the hall would open and a university clerk would appear, Lerche's overcoat over his arm, and announce: "*Herr professor*, the government limousine is waiting." It was at least partly because of Lerche's lectures that after two years I left business and economics, and Munich, in order to study politics in Switzerland, with federalism soon becoming my primary research interest.

During that second year at the university in Munich, Jürgen became more and more reclusive, and he began talking about East German agents being after him. Then he disappeared altogether. It took us weeks to discover that he suffered from schizophrenia and had been institutionalized. His mother had tried to keep this secret because she was embarrassed that her son was mentally ill. We were shocked when we visited him at what struck us as a nightmarish lunatic asylum. He was unhappy, confused, and surrounded by all kinds of much more serious mental cases. This is why I could never watch movies like *One Flew Over the Cuckoo's Nest*.

When he was released, nobody had told him that the electroshock treatments would wipe out much of his memory. Four years of university studies were gone. He became depressed and repeatedly tried to commit suicide. Then, after another round of institutionalization, he reappeared all drugged up and artificially hyper. Soon afterwards, I moved to Switzerland.

I saw Jürgen a few times more. He eventually became a fairly successful businessman in the computer industry. When he got married and had two sons, we all wondered whether he had told his wife about his condition. It turned out that he had not. When his illness returned, and he refused treatment, his wife left him. By then he had lost his last job, and he ended up as a homeless vagabond. The last I heard, he has been incarcerated repeatedly for violating a court order to stay away from the Munich airport, where he liked to loiter.

I know this from our last remaining mutual friend, Renée Bischoff. Jürgen had brought her to the party where I greeted everyone from the bathtub. That must have impressed her, because she became my girlfriend a few years later. We are still in touch, mostly via e-mail now, and Jürgen sometimes calls her from public phones. She once bailed him out of jail. She also is in touch with his family. They all want to help him, but without his cooperation nothing can be done.

81 | *Girls*

There was something monastic about our group. I cannot remember girls ever being present during our meetings in Nicki's living room. Of course we talked about them. But Nicki's living room—rather, his mother's—was our refuge from a threatening world of conquest and defeat. During most of the teenage years, girls are so much more life-savvy than boys.

Fortunately, there were organized encounters with the female kind that took from us the burden of having to make the first step. Every year, Munich's various dancing schools sent their flyers to all grade-ten high school classes advertising their services. We chose Thea Sämmer, one of the oldest establishments of its kind. Its studio was on top of Munich's Deutsches Theater, where balls and dancing championships were held along with musicals and other shows such as those of the magician Kalanag I had attended as a child. Thea Sämmer was an old lady and a legendary German dance instructor. My father and perhaps even my grandfather had already danced under her tutelage, and it was my father who urged us to choose her school over the others.

This was about ballroom dancing: Viennese waltz, foxtrot, slow waltz, boogie-woogie, and the newest craze at the time, the cha-cha. All of the above required physical contact. We had to hold hands with one outstretched arm, with the other arm around the dance partner's waist. We knew this would be required: the habit of dancing in front of one's partner without touching had not really developed yet. (While I was writing this down, my son Jacob appeared in my study. I asked him whether he might be interested in taking ballroom dance lessons. He rolled his eyes.)

We needed suits, ties, black leather shoes, and courage. Thea Sämmer took care of everything else. The girls sat in a row of chairs along one side of the ballroom, the boys on the other side. When Thea Sämmer or one of her assistants told us to choose a partner, the boys had to cross the dance floor and ask one of the girls for the next dance. The rather reluctant collective move across the floor the first few times soon enough turned into a kind of race for the most popular girls. After a few weeks, most of us ended up with a regular partner. Mine was Christa Kohlenberger. She was one of the best dancers. I wasn't so bad either, and because of that, she chose me rather than the other way round.

The dancing classes were on a weekday evening, but we often went for practice dances on Sundays as well. For the final ball, we had to pick up our lady partners at home, a pink carnation in hand. Christa and I were selected to showcase the boogie-woogie. The music was the number-one hit at the time, "Tintarella di Luna" by the Italian pop star Mina. My parents were there, too, and witnessed one of their son's more memorable performances.

Over the course of a year, Christa and I took several more courses in advanced dancing, one dedicated entirely to rumba (I think I knew twenty-one different steps by the end, all of which I have forgotten). We became good friends. At the private parties we went to, there were even a few kisses. One Sunday afternoon, however, Christa invited me to her home in downtown Munich. We had coffee and cake with the parents, and then she started opening all kinds of cupboards and drawers to show me her dowry: linen, towels, silverware. I fled when she looked at me meaningfully and announced what has become a standard saying in my family: "And next year my father is going to buy me the bedroom furniture." We say that and giggle whenever we think someone appears a bit too eager about something.

By then, Christa and I had already danced the last dance at Thea Sämmer's, at the end of the final rumba lesson. It was the end of an era in more than one sense. The instructor slid a new record from its cover and told us there was a new dance we might be interested in. What we then got to hear for the first time was Chubby Checker's "Let's Twist Again." The instructor showed us how to do it: twisting movements in front of one another, no more touching.

Christa Kohlenberger was not the first girl I kissed. That was Katrin Stübbe, a neighbourhood girl I met when we had just moved to Munich. We played hide-and-seek in an unfinished apartment building across the street from ours, after hours, when the workers were gone. We were thirteen. When Katrin was seventeen, she became involved with a man twice her age. It was a bit of a scandal. He was American, he lived in the neighbourhood, and he drove a humongous American jalopy of a car. That alone had been a sensation in our kind of neighbourhood. The two of them eloped to the United States, got married, and lived somewhere in Florida. I saw Katrin only one more time, decades later, when she visited her parents in Munich. By then she was divorced and had remarried, to a dentist in Massachusetts, I think. Her hair now was platinum blond; otherwise, she still had the boyish looks that had first lured me into that half-finished apartment building.

Then there was Daniela Moll, whom I met the following year on Lake Garda in upper Italy. Actually, my father met her first. In 1960, the year after our second (and last) vacation at Frau Kubaschwewski's villa on the Côte d'Azur, we were invited by another rich female patient-friend of his, Frau Schicht, to spend the summer in one of her two houses in Malcesine. Frau Schicht was possibly even wealthier than Frau Kubaschewski, because she owned a large chunk of Unilever shares. In any case, my father came back from one of his strolls along the beach one day and announced that he had met "this mother" and "her two lovely daughters," and that we should come and meet them. So we did.

One of the daughters was Daniela, with whom I soon began to walk hand in hand, with whom I swam daily to a little wooded island out in the lake where we usually were alone, and for whom I performed a thirteen-metre dive from a rock near the town's castle-fortress because her older sister had a boyfriend who could do it (I did it once and never again). Although we were never quite able to rekindle the magic of that summer's innocent romance, we visited each other for the next few years. The Molls lived in Wiesbaden, only a short distance from Hattenheim. In fact, Daniela became an art teacher at the same Ursuline high school that my mother and Gerda had attended, and several of my cousins' children were her students.

And finally, there was Jane (pronounced Yah-nee) Linde, whom I never kissed even though she is the one whom family lore has firmly established as my first steady girlfriend. I met her at the tennis club. One early summer Sunday morning in 1961, with school not quite over, I stood at the gate of the club with a few tennis friends. Among them was a blond girl in a blue summer dress whom I had never seen before. She must have just come from church because she was carrying a hymn book. We were talking about the summer and what we would be doing. I complained that I had to go to a boring village, Ambach, on the eastern shore of Lake Starnberg. The blond girl looked at me with cool blue eyes and said calmly: "Ambach is not boring. I'll be there." That was Jane.

Her real name was Christiane Linde. Her great-grandfather, Carl von Linde, had invented the refrigerator, and her father was the director of the Linde company in Munich. I was his oldest daughter's first boyfriend, and he did not like me. Once, when he came back from work and found me still there at the Linde mansion, he was so angry that he turned on his heel and left again. "You should leave now," his wife told me. Jane's mother liked me. She liked to talk a lot, and so did I. All that Jane and I ever did was play tennis and listen to classical music.

Jane later married the son of one of her father's business partners in Paris. At the wedding, as we were lining up for the buffet, Herr Linde suddenly put his arm around me and sighed: "Ah, Thomas, did it have to be a Frenchman?" It was not his son-in-law's nationality that he deplored so much as the distance between Munich and Paris that would now separate him from his favourite daughter. Jane's father and I were friends then. He was an excellent amateur violinist. Later again, after I had married Suzanne, he sometimes asked her to play violin sonatas with him.

My parents had to adjust to their oldest son's growing interest in girls as well. My mother did not comment much. Sometimes she admonished me to behave properly, by which she meant to treat girls with courtesy and respect. I think I did. My father offered no advice at all, but he did impose a curfew of ten o'clock, no matter what the occasion. It is funny how parents always think that the bad stuff happens after ten and not at nine or eight. Even Jane was allowed to stay out until eleven, and it was simply embarrassing to have to leave parties an hour earlier.

This really happened only once, when I was fifteen and Jane had turned sixteen. It was the annual end-of-season party at the tennis club. Prizes were being handed out, and there was a live band. We lived at least half an hour from the club, which meant that to make it home by ten I would have to leave at nine-thirty, when things were barely getting into full swing. There were other boys at the club who had their eyes on the pretty blond with the blue eyes. I stayed until about ten to ten and then raced home on my bicycle. My father was waiting for me at the open door of our apartment, furious. It was almost ten-thirty. But when I explained the situation to him, he felt so badly for me that he offered to drive me back for an hour. I told him there was no point, because by the time we arrived again, Jane would have left. But I went to bed telling myself that I had a nice father after all.

As their children grow up, parents learn to adjust and relent. When my sister Andrea (thirteen years my junior) wanted to introduce her first boyfriend to her parents, it was arranged for us to meet at a particular restaurant in downtown Munich. I had left home long before, of course, but I must have been visiting. Dinner went well. Afterwards, however, as we were walking back to my father's car, my sister all of a sudden turned around, hopped onto the back of her boyfriend's motorbike, and calmly announced: "See you tomorrow, then." My father did not say a word. My mother and I got into the car and waited for his outburst. But halfway back to the house, he turned to his wife and just as calmly said: "Well, if she gets pregnant we can raise the child."

82 | *Ambach*

That first summer in Ambach was all about Jane. The village stretches along the lakeshore for almost a mile. My parents had rented two rooms in a *pension* at one end; Jane lived in her family's summer house at the other end. The daily barefoot walks from one end to the other became that summer's most important routine. There were no street lights. At night when I walked her home in the dark, we would count the steps until our feet landed in a cow patty. Then we would move our toes to see whether it was fresh or whether it was old with a crust on top. Such was romance in rural Bavaria.

There was more to it, though. Halfway between our *pension* and Jane's house lived an Australian pianist, Bruce Hungerford. We never got to see him, but he had a student with him that summer, David, a handsome young man with a long black artist's mane, who lived in a wooden shed with an upright piano. He played Chopin for us sometimes, with the shed lit by a few candles. Jane had eyes only for the pianist, and I for only her.

My family's favourite photo of me during our first summer in Ambach.

There were others who gathered at the shed on those occasions. Jane had lots of friends in Ambach. "Are you part of Jane's comet's tail of friends?" her aunt Marga asked me when she met me for the first time. Marga lived permanently in Ambach. The other Lindes came only for the summer. So did most of Jane's comet's tail. There were Giga and Atsche, Jane's best friends. Against the combined girl power of those three, boys did not stand a chance. Atsche had an older brother, Anatol, who could play Mussorgsky's *Pictures at an Exhibition* on his guitar. Giga's parents had an old farmhouse with a library where we hung out on rainy days. There was also Bernd, who came out from Munich a few times, who had his eyes on Giga, and who read to us from the short story he was writing. And there was Hans, who had a sailboat, who clearly was interested in Jane as well, and who sometimes managed to take her out on the lake without me. But then again, Hans would leave at the end of summer. My courtship would continue back in Munich.

The big event that first year in Ambach was Jane's sixteenth birthday, on 14 August. I am sure there was a party and that I had a carefully chosen present for her. But all I can remember—all that anybody *would* remember—was that the Berlin Wall had gone up the previous day, 13 August 1961. Someone had heard he news on the radio. We probably did not give it much thought on that warm, sunny summer day that was Jane's birthday. We did not know yet how the Wall would affect our lives for the next twenty-eight years. Ironically, it made us better citizens and democrats. We became the 1968 student generation.

We all had been born after the war. We all had parents who accepted uncritically the liberal-capitalist restoration of the West German state under Konrad Adenauer and his conservative Christian Democrats. Voting for the Social Democratic opposition, our parents thought, would have been synonymous with selling out to communism and, ultimately, to the Soviet Union. For the most part, we parroted our parents' political values. But the sharp and visible separation between East and West created by the Berlin Wall brought with it a general thrust of politicization that made us take a more critical look at our own system.

Perhaps it was because we were just then entering the rebellious years of growing up. None of us became particularly active members of the student movement that was beginning to take shape. But we were nevertheless part of a new generation of Germans who were learning—perhaps for the first time in German history—that democracy requires a vigilant civil society rather than stolid obedience. Nine years after East German communism had shown its ugliest face with the construction of what it deemed to be an "anti-fascist protective wall," West Germans elected Willy Brandt as their first Social Democratic chancellor.

All of this happened long after that first summer in Ambach was over and we had returned home to school and to city life. And while the Berlin Wall, along with communism, turned out to be but a fleeting moment in the *longue durée* of history—even our own history—Ambach endured. We returned to the *pension* for a second summer. That year my father found the two rooms we would rent as our country refuge for the next forty years.

The rooms were simple. One contained a table and chairs, a wood stove, and two beds for the parents. The other held three beds for the children, a cupboard, and a small cooking stove. Across the hallway was an unheated bathroom with cold water only. On the far side of that was the village post office. We were regularly woken up in the morning by the post lady stamping the outgoing mail. But we had a little garden in front of the old farmhouse, a private beach, and a view from our windows that stretched across the lake all the way to the distant Alps. Right across the lake was the Bernried Monastery, the one that the brave fisher boy had saved from being ransacked by the Pandurs.

For our parents, Ambach became much more than the lakeside retreat they had missed since we had moved away from Tutzing. The Tutzing years had given us our own living space in the little house, but they were overshadowed by financial insecurity and Cold War angst. My father continued to worry about all kinds of things in Munich. My mother did not really like living on the noisy street in the big city. In Ambach, where we now went almost every weekend, rain, shine, or snow, they both found the inner peace that had eluded them for so long. Not even the Berlin Wall could change that.

We had no radio and no telephone. We read books and played cards. Of course we explored all the inns and beer gardens in the vicinity. When it was summer and warm, the parents often simply sat on the wooden bench in front of the house and chatted with whomever came by. For my mother, Ambach became the place where she could be herself, the simple country girl my father had fallen in love with so many years earlier. For my father, who was not a simple country boy, Ambach was a place where he could be completely at ease. All the angst and nervousness fell from him. Ambach was where we giggled as a family.

In Ambach I learned to love long walks, along the lake, up the hills overlooking the lake, and into the forest. I also developed the habit of swimming far out into the lake, with my mother, so far that we could look around the next bend and all the way down to Starnberg some twenty kilometres away at the lake's end. I still swim far out at the public beach in Grand Bend on the shore of Lake Huron, where Julia and I bought a cottage a few years ago. I have to do this before noon or after six in the evening, though; otherwise the lifeguards on duty whistle me back. Jacob is one training course shy of becoming a lifeguard now, and his plan is to land a summer job in Grand Bend so that *he* can whistle me back.

We bought that cottage with my share of the money my siblings and I inherited from my father. He had owned three properties left over from his father's and grandfather's business activities. Unbeknownst to him or to us, they were worth a small fortune. When we took possession of the cottage, Julia declared that this was the best thing we ever did. Right by the door I hung a picture of my father, taken in Ambach a year before he died. Julia had been to Ambach many times. The dream cottage on the lake was to become our New World Ambach. Then she was gone. Among the few Old World treasures that went with her were my Hattenheim grandfather's two floral prints, those with the Kunst Schäfer label on the back. When I told Gerda, we could not help giggling. I spend a lot of time alone with Jacob at the cottage now. Most of the revisions for this book were done there. It is still a dream cottage on the lake. I hope it will be filled with giggles again sometime.

Books in the Life Writing Series
Published by Wilfrid Laurier University Press

Haven't Any News: Ruby's Letters from the Fifties edited by Edna Staebler with an Afterword by Marlene Kadar • 1995 / x + 165 pp. / ISBN 0-88920-248-6

"I Want to Join Your Club": Letters from Rural Children, 1900–1920 edited by Norah L. Lewis with a Preface by Neil Sutherland • 1996 / xii + 250 pp. (30 b&w photos) / ISBN 0-88920-260-5

And Peace Never Came by Elisabeth M. Raab with Historical Notes by Marlene Kadar • 1996 / x + 196 pp. (12 b&w photos, map) / ISBN 0-88920-281-8

Dear Editor and Friends: Letters from Rural Women of the North-West, 1900–1920 edited by Norah L. Lewis • 1998 / xvi + 166 pp. (20 b&w photos) / ISBN 0-88920-287-7

The Surprise of My Life: An Autobiography by Claire Drainie Taylor with a Foreword by Marlene Kadar • 1998 / xii + 268 pp. (8 colour photos and 92 b&w photos) / ISBN 0-88920-302-4

Memoirs from Away: A New Found Land Girlhood by Helen M. Buss / Margaret Clarke • 1998 / xvi + 153 pp. / ISBN 0-88920-350-4

The Life and Letters of Annie Leake Tuttle: Working for the Best by Marilyn Färdig Whiteley • 1999 / xviii + 150 pp. / ISBN 0-88920-330-x

Marian Engel's Notebooks: "Ah, mon cahier, écoute" edited by Christl Verduyn • 1999 / viii + 576 pp. / ISBN 0-88920-333-4 cloth / ISBN 0-88920-349-0 paper

Be Good Sweet Maid: The Trials of Dorothy Joudrie by Audrey Andrews • 1999 / vi + 276 pp. / ISBN 0-88920-334-2

Working in Women's Archives: Researching Women's Private Literature and Archival Documents edited by Helen M. Buss and Marlene Kadar • 2001 / vi + 120 pp. / ISBN 0-88920-341-5

Repossessing the World: Reading Memoirs by Contemporary Women by Helen M. Buss • 2002 / xxvi + 206 pp. / ISBN 0-88920-408-x cloth / ISBN 0-88920-410-1 paper

Chasing the Comet: A Scottish-Canadian Life by Patricia Koretchuk • 2002 / xx + 244 pp. / ISBN 0-88920-407-1

The Queen of Peace Room by Magie Dominic • 2002 / xii + 115 pp. / ISBN 0-88920-417-9

China Diary: The Life of Mary Austin Endicott by Shirley Jane Endicott • 2002 / xvi + 251 pp. / ISBN 0-88920-412-8

The Curtain: Witness and Memory in Wartime Holland by Henry G. Schogt • 2003 / xii + 132 pp. / ISBN 0-88920-396-2

Teaching Places by Audrey J. Whitson • 2003 / xiii + 178 pp. / ISBN 0-88920-425-x

Through the Hitler Line by Laurence F. Wilmot, M.C. • 2003 / xvi + 152 pp. / ISBN 0-88920-448-9

Where I Come From by Vijay Agnew • 2003 / xiv + 298 pp. / ISBN 0-88920-414-4

The Water Lily Pond by Han Z. Li • 2004 / x + 254 pp. / ISBN 0-88920-431-4

The Life Writings of Mary Baker McQuesten: Victorian Matriarch edited by Mary J. Anderson • 2004 / xxii + 338 pp. / ISBN 0-88920-437-3

Seven Eggs Today: The Diaries of Mary Armstrong, 1859 and 1869 edited by Jackson W. Armstrong • 2004 / xvi + 228 pp. / ISBN 0-88920-440-3

Love and War in London: A Woman's Diary 1939–1942 by Olivia Cockett; edited by Robert W. Malcolmson • 2005 / xvi + 208 pp. / ISBN 0-88920-458-6

Incorrigible by Velma Demerson • 2004 / vi + 178 pp. / ISBN 0-88920-444-6

Auto/biography in Canada: Critical Directions edited by Julie Rak • 2005 / viii + 264 pp. / ISBN 0-88920-478-0

Tracing the Autobiographical edited by Marlene Kadar, Linda Warley, Jeanne Perreault, and Susanna Egan • 2005 / viii + 280 pp. / ISBN 0-88920-476-4

Must Write: Edna Staebler's Diaries edited by Christl Verduyn • 2005 / viii + 304 pp. / ISBN 0-88920-481-0

Food That Really Schmecks by Edna Staebler • 2007 / xxiv + 334 pp. / ISBN 978-0-88920-521-5

163256: A Memoir of Resistance by Michael Englishman • 2007 / xvi + 112 pp. (14 b&w photos) / ISBN 978-1-55458-009-5

The Wartime Letters of Leslie and Cecil Frost, 1915–1919 edited by R.B. Fleming • 2007 / xxxvi + 384 pp. (49 b&w photos, 5 maps) / ISBN 978-1-55458-000-2

Johanna Krause Twice Persecuted: Surviving in Nazi Germany and Communist East Germany by Carolyn Gammon and Christiane Hemker • 2007 / x + 170 pp. (58 b&w photos, 2 maps) / ISBN 978-1-55458-006-4

Watermelon Syrup: A Novel by Annie Jacobsen with Jane Finlay-Young and Di Brandt • 2007 / x + 268 pp. / ISBN 978-1-55458-005-7

Broad Is the Way: Stories from Mayerthorpe by Margaret Norquay • 2008 / x + 106 pp. (6 b&w photos) / ISBN 978-1-55458-020-0

Becoming My Mother's Daughter: A Story of Survival and Renewal by Erika Gottlieb • 2008 / x + 178 pp. (36 b&w illus., 17 colour) / ISBN 978-1-55458-030-9

Leaving Fundamentalism: Personal Stories edited by G. Elijah Dann • 2008 / xii + 234 pp. / ISBN 978-1-55458-026-2

Bearing Witness: Living with Ovarian Cancer edited by Kathryn Carter and Lauri Elit • 2009 / viii + 94 pp. / ISBN 978-1-55458-055-2

Dead Woman Pickney: A Memoir of Childhood in Jamaica by Yvonne Shorter Brown • 2010 / viii + 202 pp. / ISBN 978-1-55458-189-4

I Have a Story to Tell You by Seemah C. Berson • 2010 / xx + 288 pp. + 10 pp. (24 b&w photos) / ISBN 978-1-55458-219-8

We All Giggled: A Bourgeois Family Memoir by Thomas O. Hueglin • 2010 / xiv + 232 pp. (20 b&w photos) / ISBN 978-1-55458-262-4

www.ingramcontent.com/pod-product-compliance
Lightning Source LLC
Chambersburg PA
CBHW052020070526
44584CB00016B/1833